Black Feminist Politics from Kennedy to Trump

Duchess Harris

Black Feminist Politics from Kennedy to Trump

Duchess Harris

palgrave
macmillan

Duchess Harris
Macalester College
Saint Paul, MN, USA

ISBN 978-3-319-95455-4   ISBN 978-3-319-95456-1   (eBook)
https://doi.org/10.1007/978-3-319-95456-1

Library of Congress Control Number: 2018948202

Cover credit: GlobalStock/Getty Images
Cover design by Tjaša Krivec

This Palgrave Macmillan imprint is published by the registered company Springer Nature Switzerland AG
The registered company address is: Gewerbestrasse 11, 6330 Cham, Switzerland

This book is lovingly dedicated to Jon V. Thomas, M.D., M.B.A.

We met on October 10, 1993. It was a crisp autumn Sunday. We went for brunch and to the Minneapolis Institute of Art. On the day that we met, I told you that I'd write a book about Black women. You talked about your belief in the harmony of athletic, intellectual, and artistic pursuits. Most women would have been impressed, but I was a myopic 24-year-old Ph.D. student who had never dated anyone who didn't love poetry. You sensed my hesitation, and later that day, you gave me a collection of Toni Morrison's essays and a Maya Angelou poem.

I reflect back on the twenty-five years of our relationship and marvel at how I almost ignored the guy who didn't love poetry. At the time, I considered myself a premier student. What I didn't know was that a poetry lesson could be learned from a scientist. It wasn't until I saw you running in marathons, in your garden, at the piano, in the operating room, and playing with our children that I actually knew what poetry was. It's quite simple: You are poetry in motion.
Jon, Austin, Avi, Zach, and Duch. Together we are JAAZD.

FOREWORD

Isabella Baumfree was born a slave in Ulster County, New York, in 1797. After having been sold several times and her last owner was quite cruel, Isabella escaped in 1826. Friends later bought her freedom. In 1843, Isabelle Baumfree changed her name to Sojourner Truth, in recognition of her religious and abolitionist activities. Sojourner Truth was among a small group of free, Black, feminist-abolitionists in the North in the early nineteenth century (McClain and Tauber 2017: 174). This group also included Maria Stewart (1803–1879), born a free Black but at some point became an indentured servant until she was sixteen and later became an abolitionist and lecturer, and Frances E. Watkins Harper (1825–1911), a free Black abolitionist, suffragist, author, and poet (McClain and Tauber 2017: 174). Truth began to connect the issue of the abolition of slavery with women's rights during the nineteenth century. Truth was probably the first to highlight the complexities of the Black women's race and gender identities.

In 1851, the Women's Rights Convention was held in Akron, Ohio, and Sojourner Truth addressed the audience. She emphasized the important difference between white women and Black women in terms of their relationships to white men in her legendary "Ain't I a Woman" speech. Part of her speech specifically addresses the differences in how white women and treated relative to Black women—

That man over there says that women need to be helped into carriages, and lifted over ditches, and to have the best place everywhere. Nobody ever helps me into carriages, or over mud-puddles, or gives me any best place! And ain't I a woman? Look at me! Look at my arm! I have ploughed and planted, and gathered into barns, and no man could head me! And ain't I a woman? I could work as much and eat as much as a man - when I could get it - and bear the lash as well! And ain't I a woman? I have borne thirteen children, and seen most all sold off to slavery, and when I cried out with my mother's grief, none but Jesus heard me! And ain't I a woman?

In 1989, 138 years after Truth's speech, Kimberlé Crenshaw, a Law Professor at Columbia University Law School, put a name to the complexity of Black women's lives that Sojourner Truth identified in the nineteenth century. She coined the term "intersectionality" in a paper, "Demarginalizing the Intersection of Race and Sex: A Black Feminist Critique of Antidiscrimination Doctrine, Feminist Theory and Antiracist Politics," published in the *University of Chicago Legal Forum* (Vol. 1989: Iss. 1, Article 8) as a way to help explain the oppression of African-American women.

Professor Harris reminds us that the ideas articulated by Truth were an early form of Black Feminism, and that the issues she identified in the lives of Black women still need to be addressed. Just as white Elizabeth Cady Stanton and Lucretia Mott did not understand or care about the plight of Black women, Harris identifies that white feminist for the most part still do not recognize or, in some instances, care about the issues of importance to Black women or how the lives of white women and Black women diverge in experiences. For those not familiar with many of the Black feminist writers, Harris introduces readers to the work of Michelle Wallace, whose book *Black Macho and the Myth of the Superwoman*, that I enjoyed reading in 1979 when it was published; the poet Ntozake Shange, whose play *When Colored Girls Consider Suicide When the Rainbow is Enuf*, which was turned into a Broadway play; Alice Walker author of *The Color Purple*, also made into a movie and a Broadway play; Anita Hill's accusations of sexual harassment against Clarence Thomas that pushed the issue into the public debate; the Combahee River Collective; and, among many others, the women who founded the Black Lives Matters Movement. She situates these writers within the US presidents that were in office at the time and discusses the political environment in which these women wrote and were politically active.

Harris' historical and current view of the power of Black women and the distinctiveness of Black Feminism demonstrates that contrary to popular myth, Black women to not shy from feminism, but they embrace their own particular form of feminism—Black Feminism. This is a significant update on a very important book, one that has stood the test of time.

Durham, NC, USA   Paula D. McClain
                                                         Duke University

Reference

McClain, Paula D., and Steven C. Tauber. 2017. *American Government in Black and White: Diversity and Democracy*, 3rd ed. New York: Oxford University Press.

ACKNOWLEDGEMENTS

The word collective was used often throughout this book. The effort that went into this intellectual journey was indeed a collaboration. I'd like to begin by thanking the Mellon Minority Undergraduate Fellowship Program at the University of Pennsylvania, especially Dr. Valarie Swain Cade-McCollum, Dr. Herman Beavers, and Patricia Ravenell. This work was also funded by the Committee on Institutional Cooperation, the Helen Hinton International Alumni Fund of the University of Minnesota, the Rockefeller Foundation at the Womanist Studies Consortium at the University of Georgia, the Career Enhancement Fellowship for Junior Faculty sponsored by the New Jersey based Woodrow Wilson National Fellowship, the G. Theodore Mitau Junior Faculty Sabbatical grant at Macalester College, and the Bush Leadership Fellowship.

The scholars who helped shape my work (in alphabetical order): Lisa Albrecht, Sharon Austin, Susannah Bartlow, Bruce D. Baum, Shanna Greene Benjamin, Michel Tracy Berger, Mary Frances Berry, Rose Brewer, Jennifer Devere Brody, Lisa Gail Collins, Maria Damon, Angela Dillard, Erica Dunbar, Natanya Duncan, Nikol Alexander-Floyd, DoVeanna Fulton, Alexis Pauline Gumbs, Janet Hart, Tiffany Willoughby Herard, Michelle Scott Hillman, the late Endesha Ida Mae Holland, Leola Johnson, Peniel Joseph, Heidi Lewis, the late Manning Marable, M. J. Maynes, Carol Miller, Mark Anthony Neale, Anthony B. Pinn, the late Guillermo Rojas, Benita Roth, Evelyn Simien, Kimberly Springer, Dennis Valdes, Cally Waite, and Julia Jordan Zachery.

xii ACKNOWLEDGEMENTS

I would also like to thank every student that I have taught at Macalester between 1994 and 2018. My "crew" at Macalester has been invaluable: Lizeth Gutierrez, Cárol Mejía, Sedric McClure, Linda Sturtz, and Nate Tittman.

I am sincerely grateful to Yolanda Cabral who has been an "other-mother" to my children.

This book would not exist without the innovative and precise editing of Julie Schwietert Collazo, who has lived with this project for more than a decade.

Finally, my life changed in 2015 when I found Red Line Editorial and Abdo Publishing. Thank you, Bob Temple, Paul Abdo, Monte Kuehl, and Dorothy Toth, for introducing me to the world of Librarians. I am forever changed.

CONTENTS

Introduction: The Departure of Michelle Obama from the White House and the Need for Black Feminism

2017 was a monumental year for Black women in America due to two important events: First Lady Michelle Obama left the White House, and it was the 40th anniversary of the Combahee River Collective Statement.

When I first published *Black Feminist Politics* in 2009 and 2011, the cover art was Faith Ringgold's "The Purple Quilt." In "The Purple Quilt," panels of text from Alice Walker's *The Color Purple* reinforce portraits of characters found in the novel. In hindsight, I would have chosen Ringgold's "The Flag is Bleeding." Ringgold has long used her art to voice her opinions on racism and gender inequality. In 1967, she created a series of paintings, "The American People," focused on racial conflict and discrimination. "The Flag is Bleeding," number 18 in the series, depicts an African-American man standing next to a white couple. Although the three seem united, the African-American man's wound indicates otherwise. I love this work of art because its significance is not solely about who is represented in the flag. When I share "The Flag is Bleeding" in the classroom, I often ask students, "Who do you think is missing, and what do you think Ringgold is trying to say about America?"

Many Americans are missing, but my principal concern is the absence of the Black woman. I think Ringgold is trying to say that Black women are often invisible in America's political narrative, despite the fact that we are integral to its very fabric.

In the wee hours of the morning on Wednesday, November 9, 2016, we found out that the next president of the United States A would be Donald J. Trump. As a demographic, Black women supported him less than any

© The Author(s) 2019
D. Harris, *Black Feminist Politics from Kennedy to Trump*,
https://doi.org/10.1007/978-3-319-95456-1_1

1

other group at a mere four percent. The inverse of this equation is that Black women voted for Democratic presidential nominee and former Secretary of State Hillary Clinton at a whopping 94%. Notice I said "voted for." I didn't say that we were #WithHer, because many of us weren't. The main reason? Feminism—that is to say, *white* feminism—has historically taken credit for Black women's ideas and achievements while at the same time writing them out of narratives, failing to welcome them at the metaphorical (and often literal) table. In this way, Hillary Clinton was no different from most white feminists. For many Black women voters, she simply was the lesser of two evils.

In *Black Feminist Politics from Kennedy to Clinton*, I noted that Vijay Prashad wrote that once Bill Clinton was sworn into office in 1993, "The braying of the right was so abhorrent and hypocritical that Bill Clinton gained some measure of forgiveness from those who were otherwise livid with him. It was in this context that Toni Morrison said that he was being treated like a Black man: given no quarter, shown no mercy, but treated as guilty as charged without any consideration or process." Prashad explained how things changed between 1998 and 2008, when Hillary Clinton first ran for president:

> But now, finally Bill Clinton has given us some honesty. He has opened his heart during this primary season, joining Hillary Clinton in pandering to the Old South, the hard core racist bloc that was never reconciled to Civil Rights, that continues to blame Blacks for the vivisections of their economic fortunes. It is this bloc that handed Hillary Clinton the primaries of Pennsylvania, Indiana, West Virginia, and Kentucky. After her loss in the South Carolina primary, where the Democratic electorate is substantially Black, Hillary Clinton's husband, Bill, told the press, "Jesse Jackson won South Carolina in 1984 and 1988. Jackson ran a good campaign and Obama ran a good campaign here."[1]

It was after these remarks were made that I predicted that Toni Morrison would take back Bill Clinton's invitation into the Black family, and indeed she did. Some say that it's unfair to entangle Hillary with the actions of her husband, but elite white feminism teaches us that marrying a president is the best way for a woman to become a presidential candidate.

---

[1] Prashad, Vijay. (2008). "The Revelation of Bill Clinton." Zcommentaries. https://zcomm.org/zcommentary/the-revelation-of-bill-clinton-by-vijay-prashad/.

Hillary's pandering to the Old South in 2008 might have been for-given by some once the Obamas campaigned for her, but an early colos-sal mistake—one underscoring that her feminism was largely for white women—was treating the women from #BlackLivesMatter with dismiss-ive condescension in 2016. When Ashley Williams confronted Clinton during a fund-raiser in February of that year—a fund-raiser for which she had paid the $500 ticket—to ask why, in 1996, Clinton had defended her husband's crime bill by denigrating Black communities by refer-ring to some kids within them as "super-predators." The super-predator image and Clinton's crime bill are largely considered to be the precursors to the current and escalating epidemic of the mass incarceration of Black people, and Williams demanded during the fund-raiser that Clinton explain herself and apologize. Clinton's response? "Well, can I talk? And then maybe you can listen to what I say."[2]

By August 2016, the tensions between the Clinton campaign and Black Lives Matter activists had escalated. Many BLM activists and people of color generally were deeply dissatisfied when Clinton spoke publicly in response to the July shooting in Dallas, in which five police officers were killed and nine were wounded. Following the shooting, she met with police chiefs from around the country and went on record as saying that the Dallas officers "represent officers who get up every day, put on their uniforms, kiss their families goodbye and risk their lives on behalf of our communities."[3] Meanwhile, BLM activists were urging her to be clear about her positions regarding aggressive policing and mass incarceration. Clinton, speaking to the General Conference of the African Methodist Episcopal Church, seemed to be keenly aware that she was on a tightrope, one that would leave nearly everyone dissatisfied. "I'm talking about criminal justice reform the day after a horrific attack on police officers," she said. "I'm talking about courageous honorable police officers just a few days after officer-involved killings in Louisiana and Minnesota…. I know that just by saying all these things together, I may upset some people."

[2] Scott, Eugene. (2016, February 25). "Black Lives Matter Protestors Confront Clinton at Fundraiser." CNN. https://www.cnn.com/2016/02/25/politics/hillary-clinton-black-lives-matter-whichhillary/index.html.

[3] McCammon, Sarah. (2016, August 19). "Between Police and Black Lives Matter, Hillary Clinton Walking a Fine Line." NPR. https://www.npr.org/2016/08/19/490622277/between-police-and-black-lives-matter-hillary-clinton-walking-a-fine-line.

Within weeks, the BLM-Clinton relationship would simmer into a boil.

When activists were not allowed into a campaign event in New Hampshire (the campaign said the local fire marshal prevented them from allowing more people into the venue), Clinton scheduled a meeting to discuss concerns with the activists, who included Daunasia Yancey, founder of Boston's Black Lives Matter chapter. Far from assuming a posture of listening, Clinton instead assumed the posture so familiar to white feminist leaders: The white woman knows best. CNN's Dan Merica described Clinton's attitude in the encounter as follows:

> Throughout the 15-minute conversation, Clinton disagreed with the three activists from Black Lives Matter who had planned to publicly press the 2016 candidate on issues on [sic] mass incarceration.... The 2016 candidate even gave suggestions to the activists, telling them that without a concrete plan their movement will get nothing but "lip service from as many white people as you can pack into Yankee Stadium and a million more like it."[4]

In the weeks following the encounter, Yancey told the media that at no point during the meeting did she hear "a reflection on (Clinton's) part in perpetuating white supremacist violence."[5] That reflection, in fact, never came during the campaign, nor in any post-mortems of it once Trump won the election. Black women might have been disappointed, but they were hardly surprised.

What did occur in the postmortem, however, was an analysis of the ways in which white women failed to show up for Clinton. Former Slate editor L. V. Anderson (who is white) argued that white women decided that defending their position of power as white people was more important than defending their reproductive rights, their sexual autonomy, their access to health care, family leave, and child care.[6] White women bought into Trump's lies about immigrant rapists and decided they'd

[4] Merica, Dan. (2015, August 18). "Black Lives Matter Videos, Clinton Campaign Reveals Details of Meeting." CNN. https://www.cnn.com/2015/08/18/politics/hillary-clinton-black-lives-matter-meeting/index.html.

[5] Ibid.

[6] Anderson, L. V. (2016, November 9). "White Women Sold Out the Sisterhood and the World by Voting for Trump." Slate. http://www.slate.com/blogs/xx_factor/2016/11/09/white_women_sold_out_the_sisterhood_and_the_world_by_voting_for_trump.html.

rather have the respect of their angry white fathers, brothers, and husbands than the respect of literally everyone else in the world.

The bifurcations among women as expressed in the 2016 election are important to the intellectual project of American Studies, which centers the question of gender. Anderson wrote,

> The results of the election indicate[d] that most white women don't consider themselves part of the coalition of non-white, non-straight, non-male voters who were supposed to carry Clinton to a comfortable victory. Most white women still identify more with white men than they do with Black women, Latina women, Muslim women, transwomen, and every other woman who will have good reason to fear for her physical safety under a Trump regime. And while it's nonwhite and queer women who have the most to lose under Trump, white women will have to live with the consequences of their own actions in a country without a right to abortion, without access to health insurance, without an adequate family leave policy, and with a head of state who values them only insofar as he wants to fuck them.[7]

Education was also a great divide, for women as well as for men. The president-elect won 62% of white women without college degrees; Secretary of State Clinton, 34%. "Class shapes gender identity," says Nancy Isenberg, the author of *White Trash*, which examined how elites have derided rural, working-class Americans from the colonial era to this day. "I think a lot of people who support Trump think of themselves as being disinherited. They resent the fact that everything they believe in is mocked by the media elite, and Hollywood. That resentment is shared by men and women."[8]

While Clinton might have made token appearances in blue-collar communities, it could hardly be argued that Clinton was "in touch" with the 99%. Journalist Liza Featherstone noted that the campaign endlessly touted endorsements from the ranks of celebrity one-percenters, especially women. In the end, Clinton enjoyed a gender advantage only among the college-educated. Among white women without college degrees, Clinton lost to Trump by 28 points. Featherstone sarcastically

[7] Ibid.

[8] Chira, Susan. (2016, November 12). "The Myth of Female Solidarity." *The New York Times*. https://www.nytimes.com/2016/11/13/opinion/the-myth-of-female-solidarity.html.

commented, "It was almost as if waitresses in Ohio didn't care that [*Vogue* editor-in-chief] Anna Wintour was #WithHer."[9] All the talk about angry white men glossed over the fact that they were married to angry white women. This is also why class analysis is critical to the discipline of American Studies. Salamishah Tillet, an associate professor of English and Africana Studies at the University of Pennsylvania reflected, "It's not like Black people or Latino people aren't sexist and patriarchal. But when we thought about ourselves and collective best interest, we voted for Clinton."[10]

As a Black feminist, I know that I can't "lean in" to a democracy that was built on a bridge called my back. Race is a central dimension of US social, political, cultural, and economic life. The prevailing concepts of citizenship, community, freedom, and individuality in the USA contain within them deep fissures, erasures, and conflicts that depend upon particular constructions of race and racial difference. To move "past race" at this historical moment would be to ignore these conflicts and, in effect, to defuse ongoing struggles for social justice. In stressing the continuing significance of race, we take our cues from the rich and generative scholarship in African-American Studies, Asian American Studies, Chicano/Latino Studies, Native American and Indigenous Studies, Women's and Gender Studies, Queer Studies, critical race theory, cultural studies, and transnational, postcolonial and diaspora studies. We also take our cues from outside the academy, specifically from Black Lives Matter, a movement that insists that we need and deserve an elaborate strategy to eradicate both white supremacy and implicit bias toward it. We must reckon with the anti-Blackness of America's history that led to this political moment.

When I first published *Black Feminist Politics from Kennedy to Clinton* in 2008, there wasn't much scholarship on the Combahee River Collective. I mention the Collective here because of its centrality to my own thought and scholarship, as well as to the core concerns of this book. The very notion of Black feminism as something discrete

---

[9] Featherstone, Liza. (2016, November 12). "Elite White Feminism Gave Us Trump. It Needs to Die." Verso Books Blog. https://www.versobooks.com/blogs/2936-elite-white-feminism-gave-us-trump-it-needs-to-die.

[10] Chira, Susan. (2016, November 12). "The Myth of Female Solidarity." *The New York Times.* https://www.nytimes.com/2016/11/13/opinion/the-myth-of-female-solidarity.html.

and unique compared to white feminism—indeed, as something that had to arise because white feminism neither invited nor embraced it (and, in fact, often actively worked against it)—can be traced back to Combahee, as is detailed extensively and exquisitely in Keeanga-Yamahtta Taylor's 2017 book, *How We Get Free: Black Feminism and The Combahee River Collective*. In *How We Get Free*, Taylor interviews Collective founders and members Barbara Smith, Beverly Smith, and Demita Frazier about the birth of Combahee "as a radical alternative to the National Black Feminist Organization," which itself was a response to what Black feminists believed was the failure of white feminist organizations to adequately respond to racism. Combahee was also, she contends, intended to "creat[e] new entry points into activism for Black and Brown women who would have otherwise been ignored" in and by male-dominated Black and Brown liberation groups, such as the Black Panther Party. Combahee's founding principles, articulated in the Combahee River Collective Statement, presaged what we now refer to as intersectionality, understanding what white feminism has never fully grasped: that a feminist theory and practice concerned only with gender will never be of interest or value to Black women. As you read further in this book, keep this idea in mind as you think about what, exactly, Black feminism is.[11]

Black Feminist Politics in a Post-Obama Presidency

The core beliefs and values of Black feminism originally articulated by Combahee and that have been and continue to find new expressions through Black Lives Matter, and other social movements have only become more urgent since the previous edition of this book was published. Indeed, the vision of the women of Combahee could hardly be more relevant to this moment in which the president openly scorns and denigrates people of color (referring to Black urban communities as "ghettos" during his campaign being just one example) and rode into office despite a long, extensively documented history of

---

[11]Yamahtta Taylor, Keeanga. (2017). *How We Get Free: Black Feminism and the Combahee River Collective*. Chicago: Haymarket.

discrimination based on race and ethnicity.[12] Like Bill and Hillary Clinton, he bought into the notion of young Black "super-predators," even before the Clintons did; in 1989, upon the arrest of the "Central Park Five," he bought full-page ads in newspapers calling for law and order and expressing his support for the death penalty as a way to achieve social stability.[13] And once in office, he made it clear that his "police state" views had hardly changed; in fact, they'd become entrenched in the ensuing years. Six months after being sworn into office, Trump addressed a crowd of police officers on Long Island, saying that he authorized and encouraged them to not be "too nice" with suspects, especially gang members. "Like when you guys put somebody in the car, and you're protecting their head, you know, the way you put your hand over [their head], I said, 'You can take the hand away, O.K.?'"[14] Though Black women had done their best to keep him out of office, it was obvious that the work that would be required to cope with and survive the Trump administration was only just beginning.

Over 40 years after the Combahee River Collective Statement, and as movements like Black Lives Matter and the Dreamers remind us, America is still failing to provide an equal playing field for all people. And when it comes to electoral politics, even "progressive" leaders too often leave out those whose lives fall at the intersections of discrimination, such as poor black women or undocumented LGBTQ youth. Under the Trump administration, these groups are meanwhile overtly targeted for discriminatory treatment. Despite the continued abuses against marginalized people, it's important to remember that Black feminist thinkers and activists have been dreaming and fighting for nuanced solutions to systemic oppression for many years, and their work deserves our attention and consideration as we discern how best to respond to the present moment. There is no need to reinvent the wheel: The tenets of Black feminism offer us a clear, sturdy foundation upon which to carry forward the work of progressive politics in a post-Obama society in which our very lives are threatened daily.

---

[12] Desjardins, Lisa. (2017, August 22). "Every Moment in Trump's Charged Relationship with Race." PBS Newshour. https://www.pbs.org/newshour/politics/every-moment-donald-trumps-long-complicated-history-race.

[13] Ibid.

[14] Rosenthal, Brian. (2017, July 29). "Police Criticize Trump for Telling Officers Not to Be 'Too Nice' with Suspects." *The New York Times.* https://www.nytimes.com/2017/07/29/nyregion/trump-police-too-nice.html.

What are those tenets? Standing in sharp contrast to a modern version of "trickle-down" social justice where those with the most power have their interests addressed first, the Combahee River Collective instead argued the reverse: that those who are most marginalized and disenfranchised in society should be centered, and through lifting up the most disenfranchised, everyone's standard of living would in turn improve. Black women have long known that America's destiny is inseparable from how it treats us and the nation ignores this truth at its peril.

Though she is no longer First Lady, Michelle Obama certainly embodied this form of feminism in the White House, a subject that certainly deserves more critical scholarship than it has received to date. Instead, Obama's feminism has all too often been interpreted through a white feminist lens, one in which white women feel authorized and compelled to critique Obama's priorities and motives. "Are fashion and body-toning tips all we can expect from one of the most highly educated First Ladies in history?" asked Leslie Morgan Steiner, author of *Mommy Wars: Stay-at-home and Career Moms Face Off on Their Choices, Their Lives, Their Families.* She continued by adding that she had "read enough bland dogma on home-grown vegetables and aerobic exercise to last...several lifetimes."[15]

Rebecca Walker, who writes about culture, identity and motherhood, remarked that such white questioning of Obama's choices was "tedious." Beyond tedious, such questioning and critique of Black feminists' choices and priorities expose white women's lack of familiarity with and understanding of the concerns that are most central to Black women's lives.

This void in white women's understanding of Black women and Black feminism isn't limited to wider society. I see it in my own classroom each year. I teach a course on Black Feminist Thought. My syllabus includes Angela Davis, Michele Wallace, Audre Lorde, Psyche Forson-Williams, Gloria Hull, Patricia Bell Scott, Barbara Smith, Patricia Hill Collins, Patricia Williams, Beverly Guy Sheftall, Paula Giddings, Ann duCille, Adrienne Davis, Cathy J. Cohen, Evelyn M. Hammonds, Joy James, Stanlie M. James, Carol Boyce Davies, Cheryl A. Wall, and the late, great June Jordan. This list is hardly exhaustive, but even my students who are majoring in Women's, Gender, and Sexuality Studies are unfamiliar with

---

[15] Morgan Steiner, Leslie. (Undated). "Michelle Obama: Powerful or Just Popular?" ModernMom. https://www.modernmom.com/47ebe4d2-3b36-11e3-be8a-bc764e04a41e.html.

these luminaries. If white feminists were familiar with these texts, they might understand that Black women have been able to define our own feminism within the context of US racism for 200 years.

Encouraging young white women to learn about Black feminism is one of the best parts of my job, because they're hungry to learn and in the paths of Black feminists they see—often with wonder—that we have mapped out a viable path to liberation. It's a road map we made by walking, and it's one that is well-traveled by Black feminists. It's up to the Black women of my generation to pass this map down, teaching the daughters of our contemporaries that the feminism they grew up with ain't like ours, but it can be. Black, Latina, Asian, and Native American feminists have been grappling with complex questions about gender, race, class, and sexuality for decades and, in their own lives, for centuries. We know that when intersectional feminist leadership can be enacted in practice, it brings important changes about which issues are centered.

We also know that such enactment in practice is not easy and is, in fact, often painful. In the earliest feminist responses to the Trump administration and, in particular, that administration's entrenched sexism, we saw how, yet again, Black women were often marginalized, left out entirely, and then discredited or ridiculed or silenced (or, more often, all three) when they critiqued "mainstream" feminist responses. No event was more indicative of this than the Women's March that was organized as a response to Trump's election and inauguration. As white women donned pink "pussy hats" and claimed their space in Washington, DC, Black women who brought all of their concerns to the march often found themselves and their messages to be ignored. S. T. Holloway, for example, wrote about attending the 2017 Women's March as a black woman and why her experience there caused her not to attend in 2018: "[I]n a sea of thousands, at an event billed as a means of advancing the causes affecting all women, the first and last time I heard 'Black Lives Matter' chanted was when my two girlfriends and I began the chant," she recalled. "About 40 to 50 others joined in, a comparatively pathetic response to the previous chorus given to the other chants.... It represented the continued neglect, dismissal and disregard of the issues affecting black women and other women of color."[16]

---

[16]Holloway, S. T. (2018, January 19). "Why This Black Girl Will Not Be Returning to the Women's March." HuffPost. https://www.huffingtonpost.com/entry/why-this-black-girl-will-not-be-returning-to-the-womens-march_us_5a3c1216e4b0b0e5a7a0bd4b.

We can see this disregard on the part of white women in their voting patterns today, from the 57% of white women who voted for Trump—as opposed to the 89% of black women, 66% of Latina women, and 65% of Asian women who voted against him[17]—to the 63% of white women in the 2017 Alabama Senate special election who voted for Roy Moore, an alleged serial pedophile who would be comfortable jettisoning black Americans' basic human rights under the 14th, 15th, and 24th Amendments, as well as women's right to vote.[18] In that same election, 98% of black women voted against Moore and his extremist racism and misogyny in favor of Doug Jones, turning a Senate seat in Alabama blue for the first time in 25 years.[19]

It seems that although "sisterhood is powerful," as the 1970 feminist anthology of the same name would proclaim, sisterhood that excludes so many of its sisters constitutes a failed revolution. Treva Lindsey, Associate Professor of Women's, Gender, and Sexuality Studies at Ohio State University, argued in an op-ed for theGrio, "Black women show up and show out for candidates who rarely address our needs through tackling racial, gender, economic, and sexual injustice." While the GOP, argues Lindsey, is more anti-black and anti-poor than ever, even to the extent of publicly embracing white nationalism, "The Democratic Party [also] continues to largely ignore the specific demands of black women while resting upon symbolic and empty gestures of inclusion and attempting to shore up more support among the white working class."[20]

Leading black feminists today like Black Lives Matter co-founders Alicia Garza and Patrisse Cullors; trans icons Janet Mock, Cece McDonald, and Laverne Cox; author Roxane Gay; The Body Is Not An Apology social movement founder and writer Sonya Renee Taylor; and former Bernie Sanders national press secretary and political commentator

[17]CNN. Exit Poll, November 23, 2016. https://www.cnn.com/election/2016/results/exit-polls.

[18]Kaczynski, Andrew. (2017, December 11). "Roy Moore in 2011: Getting Rid of Amendments After 10th Would 'Eliminate Many Problems.'" CNN. https://www.cnn.com/2017/12/10/politics/kfile-roy-moore-aroostook-watchmen/index.html.

[19]Nilsen, Ella. (2017, December 13). "Doug Jones Is the First Democrat to Win an Alabama Senate Seat in 25 Years." VOX. https://www.vox.com/policy-and-politics/2017/12/13/16770668/doug-jones-roy-moore-alabama-senate.

[20]Lindsey, Treva. (2017, December 18). "Just a Reminder: Black Women Saved Alabama, but Not for the Reasons You Think." TheGrio. https://thegrio.com/2017/12/18/alabama-black-women-voters/.

Symone Sanders are all leading the charge in embracing Black feminism that is intersectional, considers issues of power, access, and disenfranchisement in nuanced, layered ways, and ultimately offers a higher bar to which to hold US politics.

Writes Lindsey, "Black women, and more specifically black feminists, have been trying for over a hundred years to get white feminists to address the pervasiveness of anti-blackness among white women and to proactively divest from and destroy white supremacy.... The fact that damn near everyone benefits from our 'voting' except black women speaks volumes about how we are marginalized even when we use our vote to push back against injustice. Until more black feminists are in office and black feminist policies are the status quo," adds Lindsey, "we are doomed to repeat this alarming trend."[21]

If progressives want to retake Congress in 2018, which will also likely be the only way a Trump impeachment sees the light of day, they will, with humility and grace, need to embrace the contributions of Black feminism at the national level, not as a tokenizing move to win black and brown votes but to understand and address the multifaceted forms of injustice keeping so many people from living their dreams. Crucially, this injustice also keeps marginalized groups from going out to the polls, whether they're physically barred from doing so or are too disillusioned to do so given the long history of empty promises from Democrats seeking to coax their votes.

Black feminists, and other feminists of color, have been strategizing around how to combat multiple forms of structural disadvantage for decades. It's time that existing (mostly white, mostly male) Democratic leadership finally study what they have to say, genuinely invite them to the table, and make room for a shift.

I initially wrote this book as a history, one intended to restore Black women's narratives to histories of twentieth-century feminist politics, giving Black women their rightful place in that canon. In this third edition of *Black Feminist Politics*, that goal seems even more urgent to me, and I feel compelled to extend to you an invitation: Read this book to (re)consider Black feminism. Use it to inform your own praxis and to move ever closer toward an embodiment of the kind of feminism that Black feminists have developed and practiced throughout their history. Insist upon a feminism that centers Black and Brown women and that credits them for their contributions.

[21] Ibid.

CHAPTER 2

A History of Black American Feminism

Black power, the women's movement, and feminist organizations like the National Black Feminist Organization (NBFO) and the Combahee River Collective all contributed to the emergence of a new voice for Black women in American politics and social life in the second half of the twentieth century. But the disintegration of the Combahee River Collective coincided with a conservative backlash, an era that saw the rise and fall of Vanessa Williams as Miss America and which set the stage for the Clarence Thomas/Anita Hill hearings. The roots of the conservative backlash that had such a detrimental effect on Black women can be traced to the major ideological shift that occurred in social welfare discourse during the 1960s and the supposedly liberal, progressive Kennedy administration. The Aid to Families with Dependent Children (AFDC) program had been driven ideologically by gender and class frameworks, but as a result of the social turbulence and political forces of the sixties, the discourse surrounding social welfare came to be dominated by race, with gender and class as supporting ideological frameworks.

The early part of the 1960s marked a renewed social consciousness of issues surrounding poverty. One prominent example of the heightened awareness of economic issues and class is embodied in the popularity of Michael Harrington's book, *The Other America*, which described the plight of millions of poor Americans. Harrington's book challenged a number of contemporary notions about American affluence, and though it was not an immediate bestseller, *The Other America* was read widely within academic and policy circles, attracting many favorable reviews and

© The Author(s) 2019
D. Harris, *Black Feminist Politics from Kennedy to Trump*,
https://doi.org/10.1007/978-3-319-95456-1_2

sparking strong interest in research about poverty. Harrington's book attracted the attention of both the Kennedy and Johnson administrations. In fact, the actual use of the word "poverty" to describe socioeconomic conditions of the poor did not appear in the Congressional Record or the Public Papers of the President until 1964.

There was an explosion of Americans on public assistance during the 1960s and into the early 1970s.[1] Payment to families on AFDC grew from less than $1 billion in 1960 to $6 billion by 1972. The majority of this growth occurred as a result of a massive influx of new enrollees into the AFDC program. In 1960, 3.1 million people were enrolled in AFDC; by 1969, this number had nearly doubled to 6.1 million. The annual increases between 1966 and 1969 are tallied in the following chart (Table 2.1):

Table 2.1   % increase in AFDC recipients

	1966	1967	1968	1969
% increase in AFDC recipients	4.5	11.7	13.25	17.7

By 1974, AFDC rolls ballooned to 10.8 million recipients.

This dramatic increase in social welfare spending reflected a paradox for a number of policy-makers, in that it occurred as the country was experiencing an extended period of economic prosperity. As one social services administrator noted, for the first time the expansion occurred in both good and bad years, seemingly unrelated to the state of the economy. Poverty had declined sharply throughout the 1960s. In 1959, 40 million people, almost a quarter of the American population, were living below the poverty level. By 1969, that number declined to 12.2% of the population, or 24 million individuals. Additionally, this decline was sharpest for non-white populations; in 1959, 56.2% of non-whites were in poverty, but by 1969, the number had dropped to 31.1%. Demographically, it should be noted that there was a significant change in the racial makeup of the new AFDC participants. The huge expansion

[1] US Department of Health and Human Services. (2001, March 1). "Indicators of Welfare Dependence: Annual Report to Congress." Accessed on May 20, 2018, from https://aspe.hhs.gov/report/indicators-welfare-dependence-annual-report-congress-2001/aid-families-dependent-children-afdc-and-temporary-assistance-needy-families-tanf.

of the welfare rolls disproportionately came from higher concentrations of minority groups (principally African-Americans) as the new enrollees. *The Washington Post* reported in 1970 that the AFDC rolls in the capital had grown 66%. Of that growth, over 95% of these new welfare applicants were Black. By 1970, about 48.1% of the AFDC recipients were white; 45.2% Black; and 6.7% from other races. However, it should be kept in mind that after the initial restrictions of the Social Security Act of 1935, non-white populations had enrolled in AFDC in significant numbers. Non-whites made up 32% of the welfare caseload in 1950; in 1960, that number grew to 41% and reached 46% by 1967. Thus, the face of the typical AFDC recipient was already changing quite rapidly as early as the 1950s, but the image of a single Black woman as the typical welfare recipient emerged only after the turbulent events of the 1960s: the Civil Rights movement, the Moynihan Report, and growing urban unrest.

By 1968, the sharp backlash against racial liberalism had produced its first major fruit with the election of Richard Nixon. In 1964, opinion polls showed virtually no difference on race-related issues between the two major parties. But shortly after 1964, with the turbulent events of the Civil Rights movement, the development of the War on Poverty, and the explosion of the welfare rolls, the Democratic Party would be seen as the home of racial liberalism. The Republican Party, meanwhile, would come to be considered the home of racial conservatism. In an analysis of polling data from 1956 to 1968, Rutgers political scientist Gerald Pomper found:

> The most striking change has occurred on racial issues. In 1956, there was no consensus on parties' stands on the issues of school integration and fair employment... and the Republicans were thought to favor Civil Rights as strongly as did the Democrats. By 1968, there was a startling reversal in this judgment. All partisan groups recognized the existence of different party positions on this issue, and all were convinced that the Democrats favor greater government action on civil rights than do Republicans.[2]

During this time, Democrats lost 47 Congressional seats, which effectively erased Johnson's liberal majority. Additionally, eight governorships switched over to the Republican Party in 1966. Florida elected

[2] Edsall, T. B., & Edsall, M. D. (1992). *Chain Reaction: The Impact of Race, Rights, and Taxes on American Politics*. New York: W. W. Norton, pp. 55–56.

its first Republican governor since 1872, and California voters over-whelmingly sent former actor, and future President, Ronald Reagan into his first term as the state's chief executive.[3] The Democrats' continued close association with liberal or "radical" causes, in conjunction with the growing sense of chaos and aimlessness that became the trademark of the late sixties, would prove even more disastrous in the 1968 presidential election.

THE '68 ELECTION AND THE NIXON PHENOMENON

The central element in Nixon's rise to power was his successful employ-ment of subtle, demagogic political appeals concerning race-related issues. Nixon's victory and the popularity of Southerner George Wallace, a third-party candidate who had split from the Democratic Party princi-pally on racial issues, established the framework for the successful con-servative political dominance of presidential elections throughout the 1980s.[4] From the late 1960s until the end of the 1980s, a key compo-nent of successful candidates' electoral strategies was the exploitation of racial stereotypes in connection with liberalism and "big government." As political analysts, Tom and Mary Edsall observed:

> Nixon... developed strategies essential to capitalizing on the issue of race, while avoiding the label of racism. Nixon in 1968 was among the first Republicans to understand how the changing civil rights agenda could be made to offer a politically safe middle ground to candidates seeking to construct a new conservative majority.... The Nixon strategy effectively straddled the conflict between growing public support for the abstract principle of racial equality and intensified public opposition to govern-ment-driven enforcement mechanisms.[5]

This was the crux of the messages used to court white/ethnic working-class groups in the backlash against liberalism and hence the Democratic Party. By shrewdly employing political rhetoric that was

---

[3] Edsall, T. B., & Edsall, M. D. (1992). *Chain Reaction: The Impact of Race, Rights, and Taxes on American Politics.* New York: W. W. Norton, p. 60.

[4] Edsall, T. B., & Edsall, M. D. (1992). *Chain Reaction: The Impact of Race, Rights, and Taxes on American Politics.* New York: W. W. Norton, p. 74.

[5] Edsall, T. B., & Edsall, M. D. (1992). *Chain Reaction: The Impact of Race, Rights, and Taxes on American Politics.* New York: W. W. Norton, p. 75.

heavily racially coded, Nixon was able to cultivate the bitterness against liberalism that was emerging chiefly from the white ethnic and working-class groups, thereby developing a powerful and effective political coalition.

Welfare abuse, particularly embodied in the stereotype of the welfare queen, was an extremely potent political tool to court white ethnic and working-class voters. This group was a crucial segment in the New Deal coalition that had allowed the Democratic Party to dominate the national political scene since the 1930s. As E. J. Dionne commented, "Repeated claims of liberal solicitude for the common people had been key to Democratic triumphs under Franklin Roosevelt. Thus, the New Deal slogan, 'If you want to live like a Republican, vote Democratic.'"[6] But with the seemingly "liberal" excesses over civil rights and the War on Poverty emanating in the late sixties, this crucial bloc of white working-class voters had become increasingly alienated within the Democratic Party. The Machiavellian brilliance of the welfare queen trope was that it immediately brought forth connotations of deeply embedded racial stereotypes without ever explicitly doing so, thereby evading claims of racism. Welfare and crime had become racial code words in a new political language that was developed in the late sixties and utilized by conservatives like Nixon.

The chaotic political climate of the late 1960s was perfect for exploitation based on racially coded words and symbols. With rising urban violence, crime in major cities, and burgeoning public assistance rolls, crime dependency and welfare dependency were permanently racialized and deemed "Black" within the mainstream political culture. A variable further complicating the increasingly racialized dynamics of American politics was the controversy that resulted from the 1965 Moynihan Report, which directly linked welfare dependency to pathological behavior of the "poor." According to Senator Moynihan, there was a "ghetto" pathology among African-Americans in the depressed inner cities that was producing an alarming rise in single-mother households and dramatic increases in the rate of illegitimate births and, consequently, a rise in welfare dependency.[7] The vitriolic response to the Moynihan Report and

---

[6]Dionne, E. J. (1991). *Why Americans Hate Politics*. New York: Simon & Schuster, p. 79.

[7]Moynihan, D. P. (1965). *The Negro Family: The Case for National Action*. Washington, DC: Office of Policy Planning and Research United States Department of Labor.

subsequent liberal acquiescence to critics' claims, without addressing some of the substantive findings of the report, served to further alienate liberals from the mainstream. As Edsall and Edsall stated:

> The reluctance of liberalism and of the Democratic party to forthrightly acknowledge and address the interaction of crime, welfare dependency, joblessness, drug use, and illegitimacy with the larger questions of race and poverty reflected not only an aversion to grappling with deeply disturbing information, but compounded the political penalties the party would pay for its commitment to racial liberalism.[8]

These political penalties would appear in full force in the 1968 presidential contest and would hamper Democratic presidential candidates from Nixon onward. Democratic dominance in capturing the Oval Office would decline dramatically after 1964, with only one victory in the two decades prior to 1988.

A BLACK FEMINIST RESPONSE
TO THE CONSERVATIVE MAJORITY

In 1975 feminist, scholar, and author Michelle Wallace tackled the issue of power relations between Black people and white people and described how, in a capitalist society where white people have power, Black people are left to fight each other for the leftovers. Wallace described the resulting dynamics in the following way. The Black man does not receive enough power to change the situation of the race, but he is made to believe that the Black woman is to blame. Black women, in turn, have learned that feminism is for white women, so they are left with no way of empowering themselves. Wallace pointed out that problems arise when white women choose to look at Black women as fellow victims; instead of critiquing the society that pits Black men against Black women, and where the remaining way to assert their manhood, is to oppress Black women. Wallace observed that white women stand against white men much more often than Black women are allowed to criticize Black men. With her 1975 essay, "A Black Feminist's Search for Sisterhood," published in the New York weekly, *Village Voice*, Wallace encouraged Black

---

[8] Edsall, T. B., & Edsall, M. D. (1992). *Chain Reaction: The Impact of Race, Rights, and Taxes on American Politics*. New York: W. W. Norton, p. 55.

women to stand up for themselves and form an organization that dealt with their issues. Wallace, who was one of the founding members of the National Black Feminist Organization, warned against Black women copying white feminists and getting stuck on the same issues that had divided white feminists. Wondering if the time might be right for a Black feminist movement, she urged Black women to unite and find out.

Wallace's essay in the *Village Voice* was a preview of ideas that she would go on to develop more fully in her later books, including *Black Macho and the Myth of the Superwoman*. The book contains two essays, "The Black Macho" and "The Myth of the Superwoman." One of the most important parts of the book is Wallace's critique of the 1965 Moynihan Report and, specifically, Senator Moynihan's scapegoating of Black women for the plight of Black people. Moynihan wrote, "[I]n essence, the Negro community has been forced into a matriarchal structure which, because it is so out of line with the rest of American society, seriously retards the progress of the group as a whole and imposes a crushing burden on the Negro male."[9] Moynihan failed to point out the conditions that created this "matriarchy," successfully projecting the problems in the Black community on Black women instead of white racism. The Moynihan Report was a thinly veiled political agenda, but it was still received with praise, influencing both the policies of government and the sentiment of the American public. Even Black men were affected. Wallace wrote, "[J]ust as Black men were busiest attacking Moynihan, they were equally busy attacking the Black woman for being a matriarch."[10] Wallace criticized the fact that even if Black men wanted to reject the notion of Black women being too domineering and loud, the Moynihan Report and its ripple effects in society prompted Black men to feel threatened by Black women and their social role. The Moynihan Report tried to provoke Black men to control their women in order to regain their "manhood." Few Black men questioned what whites might gain from the report and its stereotyped assumptions. The Moynihan Report came at a crucial time in Black history. During the Civil Rights movement, Black women fought to gain the same rights as Black men. Black men who felt threatened by Black women's assertion of

[9]Wallace, M. (1976). *Black Macho and the Myth of the Superwoman*. New York: Verso, p. 109.

[10]Wallace, M. (1976). *Black Macho and the Myth of the Superwoman*. New York: Verso, p. 110.

equality felt safer with white women, and the Moynihan Report provided evidence that Black men had reason to feel this way. As Wallace concluded, "The Black man needed a rest. No wonder he wanted a white woman. The Black woman should be more submissive and above all keep her big Black mouth shut."[11]

The title of Wallace's book reflected the author's intent to shatter the myths that surround Black people, both men and women. Wallace claimed that even during slavery, Black men and women were equal and there were reasons why patriarchy did not characterize Black family patterns. Wallace historicized the notion of the Black macho and the ways in which white society tried to spread such myths in order to handle Black men and control them even after slavery was abolished. Lynching was a successful method that white men used to punish Black men who had excelled in their own societies. After lynching became socially and legally unacceptable, the white dominant society tried other ways to disempower Blacks through stereotyping. For Black men, stereotypes such as "coons" and "Toms" were prevalent and were perpetuated through movies and books. Black men either were unthreatening fools who missed the good old days of slavery or were hyper-threatening, uncontrollable aggressors who had to be curbed, lest they unleash social unrest and disorder.

For Black women, similar dichotomous stereotypes existed with the Mammy and Jezebel images. When Wallace wrote her book, she criticized Black men for starting to internalize and believe in the stereotypes of Black women as Jezebel and Sapphire. Black men felt that Black women caused their own disempowerment and poverty. Wallace wrote that "the Americanized Black man's reaction to his inability to earn enough to support his family, his impotence, his lack of concrete power, was to vent his resentment on the person in this society who could do least about it—his woman."[12] Wallace showed why these stereotypes started to appear in the American society and how they have lived on in official policies and documents such as the Moynihan Report. She claimed that Black men and women started having problems in their relationships when they started to copy white couples and internalize their problems. Wallace further

---

[11]Wallace, M. (1976). *Black Macho and the Myth of the Superwoman*. New York: Verso, p. 11.

[12]Wallace, M. (1976). *Black Macho and the Myth of the Superwoman*. New York: Verso, p. 24.

claimed that Black men and women also internalized the stereotypes that existed about each other and about themselves. While Black women felt that they needed to be tougher on Black men because they were "no good," Black men, especially in the early seventies, wanted to embody the "buck" stereotype, which was highly sexual and provocative, but was still created by white people. One of the issues that Wallace discussed is the highly taboo issue of the relationship between Black men and white women. She argued that within this white, racist, patriarchal society, it is not strange that the symbol of power and achievement for Black men has been to have a white woman. Indeed, "the notion of the Black man's access to white women as a prerequisite of his freedom was reinforced."[13] The notions of the stereotypes, the Moynihan Report, and the sudden trend for Black men to be with white women all culminated in the Black Power movement in the 70s, which Wallace calls "the Black man's struggle to attain his presumably lost 'manhood.'"

Wallace offered examples of the role of Black Power movement leaders such as Malcolm X and Stokely Carmichael, noting that they represented the new "model" of what a man should be. The macho men were supposed to replace the so-called matriarchy with a much-needed patriarchy. Wallace claimed that very little was gained during the Black Power movement except further disempowerment of Black women and separation of Blacks along class lines. In the second part of her book, Wallace concentrated on the reactions of Black women with respect to the Black Power movement. There was a feeling that Black women's place was behind their men, that they had already been liberated, and that being Black was more important than being female. In this section, Wallace shifted her focus from ordinary Black women to radical activists such as Angela Davis, whom Wallace admired although she was critical of the picture of her that the Black Power movement portrayed: a woman acting because of love and not because of political convictions. "For all her achievements, Davis was seen as the epitome of the selfless, sacrificing 'good woman'—the only kind of Black women the movement accepted."[14] Wallace argued that there was an unwillingness to see a woman for her political convictions and actions. Women within the

---

[13]Wallace, M. (1976). *Black Macho and the Myth of the Superwoman*. New York: Verso, p. 27.

[14]Wallace, M. (1976). *Black Macho and the Myth of the Superwoman*. New York: Verso, p. 119.

Black Power movement were supposed to find their place behind their men or their male leaders, but Wallace urged Black women to criticize Black men when criticism was necessary. Wallace's frustration with the isolation and misunderstanding experienced by many Black feminists was articulated clearly in passages such as,

> If a Black female celebrity is pretty, or sexy or is married to a White man, she is called a talent less whore. If she's elegant or highbrow or intellectual, she's pronounced funny looking, uptight, and in need of a good brutal fuck. If she happens to appeal to a White audience, she is despised. If she's independent, physical or aggressive, she's called a dyke.[15]

Wallace did not stop her criticism with the Black male leaders of the sixties and seventies, but continued with Black male authors, such as Ishmael Reed, whose work Wallace charged as being "talky, bitter, complicated, [and] accusatory."[16] She also criticized filmmaker Spike Lee for his treatment of Black female characters. Thus, Wallace was one of the first Black intellectuals to link the political with the social and to examine—and, importantly, to forcefully articulate—the ways in which racism in the political and social sphere impacted cultural productions in the creative and artistic sphere.

Shortly before Wallace published *The Black Macho*, the poet Ntozake Shange had created a new literary genre with her "choreopoem," which she titled "for colored girls who have considered suicide/when the rainbow is enuf." The choreopoem, which debuted at the New Federal Theatre on Broadway in 1976, is a collage of pieces delivered by seven women in which they convey their individual experiences in African-American society and with Black men in particular. The women are named after the colors of the rainbow; significantly, they do not have their own names. Shange's "for colored girls" attracted strong criticism as a production that was naïve, immature, and anti-male.[17] Yet the fact that Shange asserted women's right to have their own narratives and,

---

[15]Wallace, M. (1976). *Black Macho and the Myth of the Superwoman*. New York: Verso, p. 120.

[16]"A Black Feminist Commentary." (1991, February 24). *The San Francisco Chronicle*.

[17]Peters, E. (1978). "Some Tragic Propensities of Ourselves: The Occasion of Ntozake Shange's 'For Colored Girls Who Have Considered Suicide/When the Rainbow Is Enuf.'" *Journal of Ethnic Studies* 6 (1): 79–85.

moreover, the right to tell those narratives opened a door to a new type of creative cultural production that expanded opportunities for Black women to explore, discuss, and understand the issues that affected their lives, as well as present these issues before a broader and more diverse audience.

Shange's choreopoem and its subsequent revivals also served as a way to further illuminate both the shortcomings of sociopolitical movements constructed around identity, as well as misunderstandings of them. For instance, on April 24, 1994, *The Washington Times* reviewed a revival of "for colored girls," with the critic proclaiming, "Black men and white people will find absolutely no redeeming images of themselves here." These lines, which appeared in the beginning of the review, came 20 years after the play was written and first performed. The reviewer tries to find something redeeming within the play but still situates it only during the 70s, as if Black women, or other women of color or marginalized people, cannot see themselves in the play today. At the same time, the critic also failed to put "for colored girls" into an appropriate sociohistorical context. As a result, Shange's best-known work continues to be misinterpreted and misunderstood.

Robert Staples critiqued both Wallace and Shange in his essay, "The Myth of Black Macho: A Response to Angry Black Feminists," which was published in the March–April 1979 issue of the *Black Scholar*. Staples wrote that "watching a performance of 'for colored girls' one sees a collective appetite for Black male blood."[18] Even Black women scholars such as Jacqueline Trescott insisted that Shange's men "are scheming, lying, childish, and brutal baby-killers, they are beasts humiliated for the message of sisterly love."[19] Critics like Staples and Trescott did not stop and ask themselves *why* these two Black women wrote as or what they did; instead, they judged and condemned these women writers and tried to protect the men's behavior in the texts. Staples wanted to persuade his readers to accept the men's behavior since he thought that, "there is a curious rage festering inside Black men, because, like it or not, they have not been allowed to fulfill the roles (e.g., breadwinner, protector) society

[18] Lester, N. A. (1992). "Shange's Men: For Colored Girls Revisited, and Movement Beyond." *African American Review* 26 (2): 319.

[19] Lester, N. A. (1992). "Shange's Men: For Colored Girls Revisited, and Movement Beyond." *African American Review* 26 (2): 319.

ascribed to them."[20] Is this a valid reason why Black women should sit back and accept it if Black men treat them badly? How does this reasoning improve the situation? If copying a white patriarchal system and behavior has not worked and does not work for Black men, why not put it aside and find a new and more just pattern of relationship that does not oppress Black women? Nowhere in his essay did Staples engage any of these questions.

It is true that Black men have been and are victims within a racist, capitalistic system, but they also have their own responsibilities within it. Staples, for his part, did not acknowledge that people could be both victims and oppressors at the same time. In opposition to Staples, Neal Lester argues in his essay, "Shange's Men: 'for colored girls' Revisited, and Movement Beyond," that Shane attacked the abusive behavior in some Black men but not all because the characters in the play long for closeness and relationships with Black men despite their poor treatment. Neither Shange nor Wallace demanded abstinence, lesbianism, or a move away from Black men as a political action. They both expressed their love for Black men, but that love is not without conditions. Even if Shange showed the brutal side of some Black men through her characters, she did not minimize the victimization of Black men in this society. As Sandra H. Flowers wrote in "'colored girls' Textbook for the Eighties," "I believe that Shange's composition for Black men surfaces most noticeably in this poem and that her portrayal of Beow Willie recognizes some of the external factors which influence relationships between Black men and women."[21]

Shange's play showed what kinds of ideals Black women were searching for. Shange insisted "[M]y target in 'for colored girls' is not Black men per se, but the patriarchy in general, which I view as universal in its oppression of women."[22] Shange also resisted the notion that she glamorized Black women at the expense of Black men, and insisted that her treatment of Black women was neither glamorizing nor uplifting, but rather a reflection of how she viewed reality. Black men, and some Black women, were not accustomed to seeing Black women stand

---

[20]Lester, N. A. (1992). "Shange's Men: For Colored Girls Revisited, and Movement Beyond." *African American Review* 26 (2): 319.

[21]Flowers, S. H. (1981). "Colored Girls: Textbook for the Eighties." *Black American Literature Forum* 15 (2): 51–54.

[22]"A 'Colored Girl' Considers Success." *Essence* (1982), p. 12.

up for a Black autonomous feminism that not only questioned racism within white feminist movements but also went against sexism within Black society. Such a stance is central to Wallace and Shange's writing, since they did not attack all Black men—only the ones who abuse and oppress women and those who let other men do so without educating them to act otherwise. It is clear that the Black establishment was not ready for Wallace or Shange, since both women were so unapologetic for their strong feminist views and their insistence on sharing these views publicly.

There are many similarities between Shange's play and Wallace's book, both of which criticize the way Black men have been socialized to oppress Black women in order to exert their own manhood. Both authors tried to create a sisterhood and a way for women to comfort one another and feel close to one another. The women in Shange's play sing, "I found God in myself, and I loved her!" An important aspect of Shange's play, unrecognized by male critics in particular, is that it opened the discourse about Black feminist theater and revealed a whole new—indeed, alternative—meaning to black power. It seems as though Shange's play and Wallace's book came before their time, since not only Black men but also some Black women could not understand them. Nonetheless, both texts were—and are—critical cultural products because they helped situate women in the political sphere and, as historical documents, help current readers to understand the sociopolitical realities of the 1970s for Black women.

Wallace and Shange were not seen as isolated examples of angry Black feminists. John Cunningham wrote an article in *The Guardian* on August 13, 1987, titled "The New Black Man's Burden." In this article, Cunningham argued that "the revenge of the women" had gone too far and that people like Ntozake Shange, Michele Wallace, Alice Walker, and Maya Angelou all owed their fame and fortune to Black men, since it was through bashing men that these authors gained the reading public's attention. The author accused the women of reinforcing racial stereotypes and dividing the Black community by portraying some Black men as abusive. Cunningham also quoted Ishmael Reed, who suggested that Black feminists were conspiring behind Black men's backs with white conservatives in order to further marginalize and demonize Black men. Clearly, Cunningham's failure to both contextualize and analyze these writers and their works thoughtfully was representative of a larger problem with sociopolitical movements of the day.

While I do not wish to suggest that scholars, Black or white, should restrain themselves from articulating their beliefs, what is problematic about Cunningham's framing of Black women writers' work is that it was both shallow and lacking context. Furthermore, these types of limited analyses only served to further complicate and divide communities already sorely in need of unification. Similar problems were evident in the aforementioned essay by Robert Staples. In the essay in which Robert Staples responded to the controversy over Wallace's book, Staples claimed that Shange and Wallace were influenced by white media, and he justified the behavior of Black men that Shange and Wallace criticized by arguing that Black men were socialized to behave in such a manner by the country's capitalist system. Staples alleged that both Shange's and Wallace's work was limited in value because neither examined capitalism and its impact critically. He wrote,

> To completely ignore capitalism's systemic features and its role in Black oppression is to adopt the normative approach of neo–conservative social analysis and bias no different than Whites, which makes [these texts] an example of the rightward turn in America.

Staples also claimed that Black men did not have the institutional power to oppress Black women except in two areas—the church and the family, as if either of these institutions is a negligible aspect of Black women's lives. Staples further claimed that Black men do not inherit anything from male supremacy since they are the truly disadvantaged, which, he asserted, cannot be said of Black women. According to Staples, Black women have more education, and their mortality rate is lower. He also claimed that since more than half of Black women are divorced, widowed, or never married, "this aloneness is a factor in the anger of Black women toward Black men." Staples' argument was reflective of an ideological framing of responses to Black women's intellectual and cultural production during the period. In several articles by other critics, the phrase "angry Black feminists" was used frequently as if to suggest that Black feminists suffer from a disorder, that they are irrational, and therefore cannot be taken seriously. This attitude is a remnant of Victorian times, which is, sadly, still common whenever women try to go against the status quo and critique patriarchy. Male academics and critics were not, apparently, familiar with the practice of "theorizing from the self," and if they were, they did not want to acknowledge such a practice as a rigorous academic approach. Instead, male critics such as Staples dismissed Black feminists' theories wholesale, casting the female intellectuals as hysterics, traitors, and unqualified academics.[23]

Despite the publication of many reviews and critical essays on Wallace and Shange, no Black male intellectual was ready to stand up for these Black feminists and say that there is at least something redeeming in them and their work. Additionally, almost half of the women scholars reviewing their work went against Wallace and Shange in a way that suggests they had internalized the negative sentiments against these two Black feminist writers. One example was the economist Julianne Malveaux, who wrote,

[W]hile Wallace can be credited with bringing the social politics of Black people out of the closet, she does little to evaluate the discussion past those late evening conversations that happen often when we get together. Emotionally charged, bandying about lots of accusation, her book resolves nothing.[24]

Yet Malveaux seemed to have missed the point entirely. Neither Wallace nor Shange intended to *resolve* any questions. Rather, they intended to pose questions that each reader was invited to answer from his or her own personal experience. Neither Wallace nor Shange claimed that they had answers; instead, they raised taboo issues and encouraged social dialogue to engage those issues.

The critics, male and female alike, could find little praiseworthy about Wallace's or Shange's work. Malveaux even accused Wallace of having written an "emotionally charged" book, privileging the cool detachment of traditional academic writing as a more legitimate narrative posture. Wallace, in particular, writing from within the establishment, railed against the notion that a work is considered more valid if the author is detached and dispassionate. Malveaux also condemned Wallace's work as "hyped up" and the effect of manipulative white media. Based on the volume and tone of critical response, it seems that Wallace and Shange touched a raw nerve. Critic Terry Jones suggested that the content of

---

[23] Staples, R. (1979). "Myth of Black Macho: A Response to Angry Black Feminists." *The Black Scholar* 10 (6/7): 24–33.

[24] Malveaux, J. (1979). "The Sexual Politics of Black People: Angry Black Women, Angry Black Men." *The Black Scholar* 10 (8/9): 32–35.

Black Macho and *for colored girls* offered one of the most serious threats to Black people since the slave trade. He considered the works to constitute "[a] threat from within" the Black community. The not-so-subtle underlying message of the hostile criticism lodged against Wallace and Shange was that these women should "stop dwelling on the negative aspects of our existence."

Fifteen years after *Black Macho* was first published, Michelle Wallace wrote a new foreword for the 1990 edition. Her views had changed, and she admitted some mistakes, including her failure to acknowledge the Black women who had written before her, as well as the problems of "nationalism as a liberation strategy for women." Wallace also confessed in the new foreword that if she were to write the same book again, she would not claim that *Black Macho* was "the crucial factor in the destruction of the Black Power movement." Even though this construct remains important, Wallace acknowledged that it is difficult to back such a claim with hard evidence and data. Nonetheless, *Black Macho* remains a well-articulated account of the betrayal and frustration that was felt by many women in the Black Power movement at the time. Wallace's book was one of the first published productions of Black feminist thought, in the same way that Shange's choreopoem was one of the first Black feminist plays. Wallace's "A Black Feminist's Search for Sisterhood," which paved the way to the book *Black Macho,* is quoted in the Combahee River Collective's *A Black Feminist Statement,* which came out just a few years before her book was published:

> [W]e exist as women who are Black feminists, each stranded for the moment, working independently because there is not yet an environment in this society remotely congenial to our struggle because, being on the bottom, we would have to do what no one else has done, we would have to fight the world. ("A Black Feminist's Search for Sisterhood")

The inclusion of Wallace's writing in the Collective's statement affirmed that Wallace had accurately taken the pulse of the Black feminist movement—at least a significant part of it—and had articulated its concerns. Analyzing Wallace's essay, the CRC wrote that Wallace "is not pessimistic but realistic in her assessment of Black feminists' position, particularly in her allusion to the nearly classic isolation most of us face.

We might use our positions at the bottom, however, to make a clear leap into revolutionary action."[25]

The work of Michelle Wallace and Ntozake Shange shook Black academe and the predominantly male establishment, creating necessary controversy that advanced the Black feminist movement. Without the debates the works engendered, Black feminism and Black women's writings would not be as developed as they are today. Wallace's and Shange's works were also necessary since they were articulations not only *about* Black women, but *by* Black women, offering a narrative that diverged considerably from the limiting stereotypes of the Moynihan Report, as well as those in books such as *Soul on Ice* by former Black Power leader Eldridge Cleaver. Black men had a long way to go before grasping Black feminism and its concerns, but Wallace's and Shange's work also revealed that Black women had a great deal of thinking to do and action to take as well.

Without Wallace and Shange, would there have been bell hooks' book, *Ain't I a Woman,* or *Black Feminist Thought* by Patricia Hill Collins? One thing is certain, and that is that Black feminist studies would not have been able to create its own identity and criticism if the ideas of self-love and the knowledge of self-hatred and sexism had not been articulated by Wallace and Shange. If it were not for early Black feminists' writing that explicitly critiqued Black men's sexism, many Black lesbian feminists would have felt very alienated and distanced from their straight sisters. Books like *Black Macho* and plays like *for colored girls* helped people like Barbara Smith of the Combahee River Collective to come back into the feminist movement after having been disenchanted, disenfranchised, and disempowered by the Black Power movement\. Perhaps more women would agree with Wallace and Shange today than 20 years ago, but there is still a noticeable trend among Black men to stand up for other Black men in spite of obvious sexism during the Million Man March and the controversy over Anita Hill. This shows that some Black men still distance themselves from "those angry Black feminists" and are not willing to engage on a deeper level with the issues that Wallace and Shange brought up in their work.

[25] Hull, G. T., Scott, P. B., & Smith, B. (1982). *But Some of Us Are Brave.* New York: Feminist Press, p. 18.

RONALD REAGAN AND THE CULTURE OF POLITICS

As Wallace and Shange were busily stimulating conversation on the cultural scene with radical works, the political climate in the USA was growing increasingly conservative. The backlash movement against liberalism that emerged with Nixon was finally consummated with the election and presidency of Ronald Reagan in the 1980s. As Edsall and Edsall commented, "In many respects Ronald Reagan, in his quest for the presidency, updated and refined the right-populist, race-coded strategies of Wallace and Nixon."[26] Reagan had made bids for the presidency in 1968 and 1976, but it was not until 1980 that the political environment was ready for the California governor's explicit, racially driven, ideological rhetoric. In making his case to voters in 1980, Reagan made it clear that his planned assault on government would rely primarily on the means-tested programs (i.e., "welfare") that disproportionately served minorities.[27] Reagan's concentrated attack on AFDC and other means-tested programs was in alignment with the growing public support and sympathy for the plight of Blacks and other minorities. In 1979 and 1980, national support for increased spending to improve the conditions of Blacks and other minorities fell to a record low of 24%. Opposition to welfare spending swelled to its highest level in 1976 and remained intense through 1980. In addition, the 41% of respondents in 1980 who thought, "Blacks and other minorities should help themselves" versus those saying that "Government should improve the social and economic position of Blacks" (19%) was an all-time high, compared to 37 and 29%, respectively, in 1976 and 38 and 31% in 1972.[28] The emerging racial conservatism within the electorate cut across racial lines, as a chasm developed between the views of Black and white Americans. Just as Wallace and Shange had oppressive social structures, the increasingly oppressive and highly racialized economic structures and policies of the nation prompted intellectuals and cultural creatives to explore issues related to Black poverty in their work. No work was more seminal during this period than Alice Walker's novel, *The Color Purple*.

[26]Edsall, T. B., & Edsall, M. D. (1992). *Chain Reaction: The Impact of Race, Rights, and Taxes on American Politics*. New York: W. W. Norton, p. 10.

[27]Edsall, T. B., & Edsall, M. D. (1992). *Chain Reaction: The Impact of Race, Rights, and Taxes on American Politics*. New York: W. W. Norton, p. 148.

[28]Edsall, T. B., & Edsall, M. D. (1992). *Chain Reaction: The Impact of Race, Rights, and Taxes on American Politics*. New York: W. W. Norton, p. 152.

UNDERSTANDING ALICE'S GARDEN:
THE COLOR PURPLE CONTROVERSY

In 1981, Alice Walker wrote *The Color Purple*, which won both the Pulitzer Prize and the American Book Award for fiction. The novel was one of the most controversial books written by a Black woman and sparked years of discussion. Walker's third novel, published after *The Third Life of Grange Copeland* and *Meridian*, *The Color Purple* is centered on the subject of Black relationships and a clear critique of patriarchy, as well as an examination of the social and economic structures that perpetuate such conditions. The novel is set in the South, a region with which Walker was familiar. She was born in Eatonton, Georgia, in 1944, the youngest of eight children. She attended Spelman College in Atlanta and was offered a scholarship to attend Sarah Lawrence College; instead, Walker took a leave of absence and travel to Africa. She came back from Africa pregnant, contemplated suicide, but had an abortion instead, and wrote her first poetry book, *Once*. Walker was extremely influenced by her family and their lives. "She makes no bones about loving her grandfathers and the stories they'd tell." Her family and her surroundings influenced Walker when writing *The Color Purple*, and that is why she used Black vernacular and why Anglo American culture was so absent from the book. The author said, "[W]riting *The Color Purple* was not so much a struggle – but it was more a letting go, of just trying to clear my channels enough."

Before discussing the implications of the novel and the political message that it conveyed, it is important to place the book in a historical context that helps us to understand the significance of its arrival in the early 1980s. *The Color Purple* continued the tradition of Ntozake Shange's 1976 choreopoem *for colored girls who have considered suicide/ when the rainbow is enuf* and Michele Wallace's 1979 book *Black Macho and the Myth of the Superwoman*, both of which were catalysts for discussions of sexism within Black society. *The Color Purple* was influenced not just by Wallace and Shange, but also by other "troublemakers" such as Lorraine Hansberry, who was dismissed by Black male critics in the 1960s, and countless other Black women writers like Zora Neale Hurston, similarly important to but marginalized during the Harlem Renaissance.

One of the problems with the discussion that resulted from Walker's book and the movie adaptation of *The Color Purple* is that few people are aware of the difference between the two. Most of the critique that Walker received was in response to the movie, and most of the people who criticized her felt that she was to blame for all the shortcomings of the film. The media also focused on the negative aspects of the movie instead of showing that most Black women enjoyed the movie and felt that it was both an accurate reflection of their experiences and a positive portrayal of Black women in general. As Jacqueline Bobo stated,

> in reaction to Black women's favorable responses to the film, Black male criticism of the film began to attain much more media space. In January 1986 *The New York Times* reported that the film was the dominant topic of conversation on radio and talk shows.[29]

The film reached its audience in several stages, and each time it induced a strong reaction. It was released during the holiday season in 1985, but was re-released theatrically at the beginning of 1987. The movie grossed $100 million by 1986, which is much more than the book's profits, so it is safe to say that more people saw the movie than read the book; however, many people equated the two synonymously and talked about them as such.

The critique of the movie extended from the producer and director to Walker herself, whose own version of the screenplay had not been used for the movie. Even people who had not read the book started critiquing it and the author, calling Walker a "man hater." One of the most vicious condemnations of Walker came from *The Washington Post* columnist Courtland Milloy, who wrote that some Black women would enjoy seeing a movie about Black men shown as brutal bastards. Furthermore, he wrote, "I got tired a long time ago of White men publishing books by Black women about how screwed up Black men are." The problem was that Milloy had not read the book, but still felt justified in commenting about the novel and its author. Even Spike Lee declared in *Film Comment* that "the reason that Hollywood elected Alice Walker's novel to make into a film was that Black men are depicted as one-dimensional animals." Such a comment is particularly curious coming from Lee, whose movies are widely considered to portray women

[29]Bobo, J. (1988). "Black Women's Responses to *The Color Purple*." *Jump Cut* 33: 43–51.

unidimensionally and, often, negatively. The wide range of criticism reflected fear, especially among Black men, of a popular book by a Black female author in which they are being criticized. This fear existed in the white society as well, since the media and the talk shows are controlled by the white dominant society. It was a fear which would characterize another event that was about to unfold, and one which was far more visible to pop culture enthusiasts: The scandal involving Miss America, Vanessa Williams.

VANESSA WILLIAMS, "EXEMPLARY QUEEN"

While Alice Walker's novel may have represented a highbrow threat to Black masculinity and to dominant culture, Sarah Banet-Weiser argued that "... the [1983] crowning of Vanessa Williams is a particularly visible instance of the politics of the 1980s and Reaganism," accessible to anyone with a television, radio, or a newspaper.[30] To understand exactly what it was that Vanessa Williams represented and how her fall from grace constituted a threat to her symbolic accomplishment, it is first necessary to understand some of the dominant tropes deployed by politicians that cast Black women into the unidimensional role of the welfare queen.

One of Ronald Reagan's favorite anecdotes on the campaign trail, in multiple campaigns, was the story of a Chicago "welfare queen" who had "80 names, 30 addresses, 12 Social Security cards and a tax-free income of over $150,000."[31] This supposedly true story represented a melding of resentments against the poor. At its most extreme, the image of the welfare queen conjured up a picture of a gold-clad, Cadillac-driving, promiscuous Black woman living off the government dole and buying steak and beer with food stamps. The food stamp program, another means-tested program, was a target of Reagan's ire and also became an important part of the welfare queen narrative. Food stamps, according to the Hollywood actor-turned-President, were a vehicle to let "some fellow ahead of you buy T-bone steak while you were standing

[30]Banet-Weiser, S. (1999). *The Most Beautiful Girl in the World: Beauty Pageants and National Identity.* Berkeley, CA: University of California Press.

[31]Reagan, R. (1976). "Campaign Speech." Slate Voice. Retrieved on May 20, 2018 from https://soundcloud.com/slate-articles/ronald-reagan-campaign-speech.

in a checkout line with your package of hamburger."[32] Reagan's depiction of the welfare queen was based on a woman from Chicago, Linda Taylor, who had been charged with welfare fraud in 1976. She was actually charged with defrauding the state of $8000, not $150,000.[33] Not only was Taylor misrepresented, but also the President's extensive use of the welfare queen narrative served to permanently consolidate racist stereotypes of Black women within contemporary political discourse. As a result of this shrewd manipulation of racist caricatures, social welfare discourse during the 1980s became fundamentally structured around the "welfare queen" trope, with race as its central ideological organizing axis. As Patricia Williams remarked, "Somewhere during the Reagan-Bush years the issue of race [became] more firmly wedded to the notion of welfare than ever before, and the rest is history" (Rooster's Egg, year, 5).

Vanessa Williams was the first Black Miss America and, like many other "first" Black Americans, was truly positioned as a test case for the viability of competing racial discourses in the context of emerging multiculturalism and New Right politics. Williams "was marked as a race-transcending American icon, and the pageant itself participated in marketing diversity as it happened, thereby incorporating it–and Williams herself–as a crucial element fueling the national imagination." When Williams was first crowned, her success at crossing the historical color line of the Miss America pageant was read as evidence that Black women could be included within the parameters of white femininity. Former US Representative Shirley Chisholm said at the time of Williams' coronation, "My first reaction is that the inherent racism in America must be diluting itself…. I would say, thank God I have lived long enough that this nation has been able to select a beautiful young woman of color to be Miss America." Chisholm continued by emphasizing the significance of Williams' victory for Black communities in the USA, claiming that "because it didn't 'put bread on the table' people might say 'So what?' when considering the importance to the civil rights movement of a Black woman's winning of the crown…. [But the event was] not trivial because it shows a sense that the country, for whatever the motivation

---

[32] Edsall, T. B., & Edsall, M. D. (1992). *Chain Reaction: The Impact of Race, Rights, and Taxes on American Politics.* New York: W. W. Norton, p. 148.

[33] Zucchino, D. (1997). *Myth of the Welfare Queen: A Pulitzer Prize Winning Journalist's Portrait of Women on the Line.* New York: Scribner, pp. 54–55.

might be, seems to be trying desperately to move toward an egalitarian set of circumstances."[34]

Williams' success and the narrative constructed around it were not to last, however. In July 1984, *Penthouse* ran an issue that featured Vanessa Williams engaged in sexual acts with a white woman. These photographs, taken three years before the pageant, were the reason the Miss America pageant commission asked Williams to relinquish her crown and title. Banet-Weiser observed:

> Just as she was granted individual personhood when she won the Miss America crown, she was summarily denied this same category when the photographs were published: she became all Black women in U.S. society, and she affirmed mass-mediated representations of this identity.
>
> The "exposure" of Vanessa Williams recalled and foregrounded historically powerful narratives about Black women and sexuality, and it confirmed racist beliefs embedded within beauty pageants concerning 'questionable morals' purportedly held by all Black women. It can also be seen as an instance of a broader discourse about race and difference, and we should consider the story of Williams a particularly instructive instance of the ways the discourse of diversity works in U.S. culture.

Jackie Goldsby added:

> [T]he telling and retelling of Vanessa Williams's impressive victory and equally impressive downfall provided an opportunity –a lost opportunity– to engage in public conversation about the various ways race conditions and intersects sexuality. Without interrogating the racial specificity of the context in which Williams was positioned, her story could not be told– indeed, there was no available social narrative for the telling. Like the [White] feminist reaction to Anita Hill, the elative silence that greeted events precipitating Williams's downfall was a result of America [stumbling] into a place where African-American women live, a political vacuum of erasure and contradiction maintained by the almost polarization of "Blacks and women" into separate and competing political camps.[35]

---

[34]"Black Leaders Praise Choice of First Black Miss America." *New York Times*, September 19, 1983.

[35]Goldsby, J. (1993). "Queen for 307 Days: Looking B(l)ack at Vanessa Williams and the Sex Wars." In *Sisters, Sexperts, Queers: Beyond th Lesbian Nation*, ed. Arlene Stein. New York: Plume Books.

Vanessa Williams became an Icarus figure who flew too high and fell. Once she lost her crown, many members of the Black community felt betrayed. One woman journalist wrote, "That [Williams] had been hailed as a particularly 'exemplary' queen, one who injected new life into the homogeneously bland pageant, only makes her fall more keenly felt by Black women who are trying hard to exert a sense of self."[36] Williams's subsequent exploitation is the quintessential act of resistance against Black women in the 1980s. The "exemplary" queen of the '80s is quickly and efficiently replaced by the welfare, quota, and condom queens of the '90s.

---

[36] Gilliam, D. (1984, July 26). "A Sad Lesson." *The Washington Post.*

CHAPTER 3

Black Women's Relationships with Party Politics

THE CLARENCE THOMAS/ANITA HILL HEARINGS

During the month of October 1991, Anita Faye Hill, a law professor, gave sworn testimony before the Senate regarding her allegation of sexual harassment that she experienced while working for Supreme Court Justice nominee Clarence Thomas at both the Department of Education and the Equal Opportunity Commission in the early 1980s.[1] Hill's statement recounted sexually explicit conversations and references allegedly made by Thomas to her on several occasions. Revisiting the 1991 Congressional saga of the confirmation process of Thomas to the Supreme Court reveals a context in which both race and gender identities were influential, particularly because the Hill-Thomas conflict was intra-racial rather than interracial. The shared racial identity of Thomas and Hill, as well as the Congressional Black Caucus (CBC) members, created an environment in which gender became a more salient factor than race, providing a strong example of when and where gender can trump race for Black women in political positions and how gender remains even more divisive a political wedge than race.

---

[1] Miller, A., ed. (1994). *The Complete Transcripts of the Anita Hill-Clarence Thomas Hearings*. Chicago: Academy Chicago Publishers.

© The Author(s) 2019
D. Harris, *Black Feminist Politics from Kennedy to Trump*,
https://doi.org/10.1007/978-3-319-95456-1_3

Yet race was not an unimportant element of the Hill-Thomas conflict. As Paula Giddings has observed, certain issues, especially those of a sexual nature, are considered taboo subjects for discussion within the African-American community.[2] As a result, social pressures and fear of ostracism work against speaking out, as they might have in the Hill-Thomas case had Hill not been assertive and persistent in her insistence that Thomas's behavior was egregious and needed to be exposed. According to Giddings, at the particular moments when racial rhetoric and gender rhetoric come into conflict, Black women are compelled to choose between the two. The Thomas-Hill case, by raising an issue that related specifically to women—sexual harassment—is a situation in which racial rhetoric was used both to support and to oppose Thomas within the African-American community.

The public was largely supportive of the confirmation of Thomas—more than 38% of people polled after Hill's allegations were made public advocated Thomas's confirmation as a justice in the country's highest court.[3] What makes this statistic particularly compelling is a statistic which seems contradictory: More than 51% of respondents in the same survey expressed the opinion that they believed the Senate had not taken Hill's claims as seriously as the allegation warranted.[4] Yet the support of Thomas may be understood by the judge's clever manipulation of the narrative he constructed about the conflict and his role in it. By claiming to be a victim of a "high-tech lynching," Thomas was able to control the story being told in such a way as to prime the racial consciousness of most African-Americans, appealing to the highly charged metaphor of lynching. Through the use of racial characterizations regarding the charges against him as a group attack by someone with greater power rather than simply an attack against one man who happened to be African-American (and one who had behaved inappropriately and illegally), Thomas successfully swung public support away from Hill and toward himself.

The public support of Thomas and the successful deployment of the lynching image may be further explained by Dawson's Black Utility Heuristic,[5] which states that group interests will be used as a proxy for

[2] Giddings, P. (1992). *When and Where I Enter.* New York: HarperCollins.

[3] Kolbert, E. (1991, October 11). "The Thomas Nomination: Sexual Harassment at Work Is Pervasive, Survey Suggests." *The New York Times.*

[4] Kolbert, E. (1991, October 11). "The Thomas Nomination: Sexual Harassment at Work Is Pervasive, Survey Suggests." *The New York Times.*

[5] Dawson, M. C. (1994). *Behind the Mule: Race and Class in African American Politics.* Princeton, NJ: Princeton University Press.

individual interests when making decisions. According to Mansbridge and Tate,[6] the racial imagery of lynching grouped with the "symbolic status [and authority] of [Thomas's position and potential] office" activated the racial consciousness of most African-Americans. Because of Thomas's appeal to the strong and unapologetically racial image of lynching, the general public may have thought that Thomas would make legal decisions on the Court that reflected his racial consciousness, despite evidence that Thomas exhibited positions on certain issues that differed from those of the African-American community in general. The real question regarding Thomas was, if he did feel some type of affinity toward any demographic group, which group would that be? It is entirely possible that Thomas may have been thinking of group benefits that were not based upon his racial group identity, but on his gender or class identity. This reliance upon descriptive representation, without regard for substantive representation, ultimately left the mass public disillusioned and without adequate representation, and left Hill without the ability to adopt either the conventional racial narrative or the conventional gendered narrative. Such were the complicated dynamics underlying the Thomas-Hill conflict.

Thomas's narrative effectively silenced and simultaneously discredited Hill. Thomas had usurped the narrative of racial solidarity, leaving Hill the solitary option of adopting a gendered narrative. However, gender-based rhetoric has long been associated with white feminists, and, in Hill's case, the conventional gendered narrative would have been limiting, both ignoring her race and preventing her from garnering support from white feminists who have traditionally "owned" the gendered narrative. Hill's intersectionality—the combination of her race and her gender— illuminated the ways in which the marginalization of Black women "within dominant discourse of resistance limits the means available to relate and conceptualize [the] experiences [of] Black women."[7] Despite the linked fate and shared consciousness among African-Americans, certain segments within the group hold positions of privilege with regard to political discourse, while other members—namely, women—are relegated to the margins. Specifically, "issues affecting men are often presented as

[6]Mansbridge, J., & Tate, K. H. (1992). "Race Trumps Gender: The Thomas Nomination in the Black Community." *Political Science and Politics* 25 (3): 488–492.

[7]Crenshaw, K. (1996). "Whose Story Is It, Anyway? Feminist and Antiracist Appropriations of Anita Hill." In *Applications of Feminist Legal Theory to Women's Lives: Sex, Violence, Work, and Reproduction*, ed. D. Kelly Weisberg. Philadelphia: Temple University Press.

representative of the condition of [the] entire community and thus worthy of a group response."[8] Racial solidarity has provided a united front for the advancement of African-Americans as a people, while at the same time silencing critiques *within* the group regarding the vast difference between substantive and descriptive representation and the failure to address issues of gender oppression that perpetuate self-destructive political outcomes such as the Thomas-Hill saga.[9] Racial solidarity can provide a cohesive agenda for African-Americans as a group, but it should be possible to include within this discourse the voices of those marginalized within its boundaries, thus allowing Black women in power the opportunity to bring public attention to gendered issues.

Although Hill was not competing for a political position, the dynamics of the Hill-Thomas case are illuminated by theoretical constructs about opportunities available to Black women in American politics. First, a Black woman's success in politics appears to be closely tied to the support that Black men receive in the same state or locality; in this way, the electoral success of Black women is tied to that of Black men.[10] When the intra-racial alliance is threatened, then, as it was in the Hill-Thomas debacle, the chances of the woman's success are diminished. There are other theories that are important, too, and which also help to explain the kinds of dynamics underlying situations faced by Black women as described in previous chapters. In "Gender, Race, and the State Legislature: A Research Note on the Double Disadvantage Hypothesis," Moncrief, Thompson, and Schuhmann[11] discussed the issue of the "double disadvantage" hypothesis, which contends that Black women are politically disadvantaged both by gender and race. This hypothesis suggests that due to the double disadvantage, Black women experience difficulties

---

[8]Cohen, C. J. (1999). *The Boundaries of Blackness: AIDS and the Breakdown of Black Politics*. Chicago: University of Chicago Press.

[9]Crenshaw, K. (1996). "Whose Story Is It, Anyway? Feminist and Antiracist Appropriations of Anita Hill." In *Applications of Feminist Legal Theory to Women's Lives: Sex, Violence, Work, and Reproduction*, ed. D. Kelly Weisberg. Philadelphia: Temple University Press.

[10]Prestage, J. (1977). "Black Women State Legislators: A Profile." In *A Portrait of Marginality: The Political Behavior of the American Woman*, eds. Marianne Githens and Jewell Prestage. New York: David McKay.

[11]Moncrief, G., Thompson, J., & Schuhmann, R. (1991). "Gender, Race, and the State Legislature: A Research Note on the Double Disadvantage Hypothesis." *The Social Science Journal* 28 (4): 481–487.

competing in electoral politics in the USA. Supplementing the double disadvantage hypothesis is the "double whammy" theory, which posits that stigma are attached to both the gender and the racial identities of Black women in positions of leadership. It may be that in order for Black women to gain success in politics, they have to downplay gender issues to preserve racial solidarity. This compromise may also have implications for the types of positions that Black women are able to defend in the political arena when race is in conflict with any other variable.

Still other theories, especially those drawn from the political science literature, have long acknowledged that Black women in general, and in the political arena in particular, are often forced to make a choice between being Black and being female, deciding where to align their loyalties when social conflicts arise that make both identities salient.[12] The particular ways in which this choice played out for Anita Hill have been analyzed, yielding compelling results. While a graduate student at the University of Michigan, DeAunderia Bryant used the Lexis-Nexis Congressional Universe to analyze representatives' floor statements, cross-referencing the 102nd Congress (1991–1992) with the name of each CBC member, as well as with the names of each white female representative. Bryant then combed through the dates to find any reference to Clarence Thomas during the month of October 1991; there was only one such statement for each representative who chose to speak.

Next, Bryant cross-referenced Clarence Thomas with the same representatives' names, examining statements reported by all major newspapers during October 1–31, 1991. The dates are significant because the first two weeks of October were when Thomas's confirmation was in question, and the last two weeks of October followed Thomas's confirmation to the Supreme Court, which occurred on October 15, 1991. Bryant categorized each newspaper article by content. Articles that mentioned race (including the apparent negation of race, as articulated in statements such as "This is not about race"), racism, segregation, Black Civil Rights, or the Civil Rights Movement were put in a "race" category. Articles categorized as having "gender" content included such references as sexual harassment, statements about Anita Hill specifically, and various statements about men not understanding or taking Hill's allegations seriously. A third category Bryant devised was "ideology."

[12] Mansbridge, J., & Tate, K. (1992). "Race Trumps Gender: The Thomas Nomination in the Black Community." *Political Science and Politics* 25 (3): 488–492.

Examples from this category included references to the right wing, conservatives, the Bush administration, "vision and viewpoint," and constitutional views. Bryant screened out statements—and there were many—regarding policy and partisanship, as well as those statements that made no specific references to race or gender.

In October 29, 1991, women were serving in the House; of these 20 were Democrats and nine were Republicans; four of the Democrats were African-American. There were 21 African-American men; 20 were Democrats and one was Republican. In order to control for party differences, only Democrats were used in Bryant's sample. Therefore, the study involved 20 female representatives (four of them Black) and 20 male CBC members. All data consisted of direct quotes only and numbers correspond to one set of categorization scores per newspaper or floor statement; therefore, a single statement could be assigned to more than one category (for instance, if the speaker addressed issues of both race and gender, then the statement would be classified in both categories). Bryant uses the terms "categorization" and "imagery" interchangeably because each statement brings to mind images of the race, gender, or ideology categories that are being referenced.

The results of Bryant's content analysis indicated that Black women used both race and gender to oppose Thomas, but their racial statements were an attempt to negate the role of race, such as, "This is about sex and not about race." The statements of the female representatives differed dramatically from the types of racial statements made by male CBC members. For example, one male representative said, "We hope the administration gives the same type of attention and support to the Civil Rights Bill as they did the nomination of Clarence Thomas." Note that this representative also deployed the strategy of speaking for the collective, using the word "We," as if he represented all of his male colleagues. The male representatives' acknowledgment of gender was minimal. Texas representative Craig Washington anticipated that the confirmation of Thomas would further restrict women who feel that they "can't come forward because they're fighting against the odds and they're not going to win." The only other gender reference made by a male was by New York representative Major Owens. Although Owens criticized Thomas for the judge's apparent lapse of memory about his stance with respect to *Roe v. Wade*, Owens avoided mentioning sexual harassment, the subject at hand.

The statements made by female CBC members were substantively different and tended to resemble the types of statements made by white female representatives. Most of the female representatives' statements analyzed by Bryant articulated the women's criticism of what they viewed as male colleagues' failure to view the Thomas-Hill debacle as an obvious matter of sexual harassment. Almost all of the women's statements avoid the mention of race. The one exception was a statement made by Connecticut representative Barbara Kennedy, who negated race:

> Mr. Speaker, the compelling case for the nominee to the Supreme Court was not legal expertise, and it was not race. It was character, that out of the crucible of life experience, a man emerges with vision and a viewpoint that cannot be duplicated on the Supreme Court.

Of 16 white female House members, 12 spoke out in floor statements, newspaper articles, or both. More statements were made by the senior women in the House, Patricia Schroeder (D-CO) and Barbara Boxer (D-CA). At the time, Boxer was in the process of campaigning for a seat in the Senate. Both Schroeder and Boxer made one floor statement and received eight newspaper references. Schroeder was appalled by the entire confirmation process and stated:

> ...it was like in *The Wizard of Oz* when the curtains were drawn back. Women saw...what a men's club it has become.... The Senate is richer than the norm and may not understand women's reactions to sexual harassment as much, because they've never needed a job. They say, 'Why didn't you just walk out?' You can say that if you have a trust fund....' Our whole culture is going through this traumatic, cataclysmic time when rules are changing. So I hope the men find out quick. There is going to be a real crash course in the Senate on sexual harassment.

Schroeder's statement reflected female representatives' perception that the overwhelming majority of men in the Senate did not understand the issue of sexual harassment and were showing insensitivity in addressing the issue as it was playing out in the Senate confirmation hearing of Clarence Thomas.

Barbara Boxer also made references to the appearance of the confirmation process as an all-male club run by the Senate:

If there had been charges of fixing a ballgame against this man, they may have given it more attention.... This is about women, and there's no women over there but two.... And one thing I know is that there just aren't enough women on Capitol Hill to represent the women in our democracy and there should be more. If there were, then the seriousness and the scope of these issues would be better understood.

Other statements made by female representatives addressed the taint left by the Thomas-Hill affair on the prestigious position of Supreme Court justices. In reference to the qualifications expected of a Supreme Court justice, Nancy Pelosi (D-CA) stated that judges "should be like Caesar's wife – above suspicion." She continued, "Clarence Thomas squeaked by the Senate with 52 votes. The Senate has confirmed a person who received the lowest rating ever from the American Bar Association and about whom serious doubts have been raised." Pelosi also made statements that focused on the ideological stance of the Bush administration and how the Thomas confirmation was one example among many of insensitivity to women's issues. "This administration is already anti-choice and anti-family leave," she remarked. "[The Thomas-Hill case] may be viewed as adding to a certain perception of the Bush administration."

The female members of the CBC raised similar issues as their white peers. In 1991, only four members of the House were African-American women. Out of this group of four, only two chose to speak out regarding the Thomas-Hill controversy. Bryant found no remarks made by the female representatives that could be classified as belonging to the "race" category. The similarity between the statements made by white and Black women shows that their ideological framing of the Thomas-Hill case focused on the issue of gender and how sexual harassment, usually perpetuated by a male boss, is simply pushed aside by men in positions of power. Congresswoman Eleanor Holmes Norton (D-DC), the former head of the Equal Employment Opportunity Commission where the alleged harassment took place, explained how sexual harassment does not appear to be taken seriously by men:

This is a once in a lifetime opportunity to sensitize millions of men about sexual harassment.... Sexual harassment is the most widely practiced form of sex discrimination today, by men who think it's all fun and games. If it stops, you don't Harrumph! And march out. You go on thinking you can do your work in a relationship that's what you wanted all along.

In reference to race, Holmes Norton stated, "This [the Thomas-Hill case] is about sex and not about race. A Black woman raised these questions, not a question, not a White woman, or White men. I don't think we can conclude anything about stereotypes about Black men based on allegations made by a Black woman." Holmes Norton's discursive strategy was to negate the role of race in order to raise the saliency of gender within the debate.

Maxine Waters (D-CA) made a similar point: "Clarence Thomas has allowed himself to be a pawn of the right wing. I resent very much how he interjected race in this debate." Waters went on to discuss the real issue, adding, "Women are saying, 'It's about time.' Every male boss in America is reassessing whether he is in line for a sexual harassment suit." Waters' statements exemplify the concerns of both the racial and gendered context in which the Thomas-Hill saga unfolded. Waters opposed Thomas on the grounds of his ideologically conservative stance, as well as the allegations of sexual harassment made by Hill.

Of the twenty male Democrats within the CBC, only four chose to speak against Thomas after the allegations of sexual harassment came to light. Had Bryant established the starting point of her analysis in September, when Thomas was first nominated, she would have discovered only two more statements from male CBC members, Alan Wheat and Ron Dellums. When examining all statements made by the 24 CBC members, only 25% (four male, two female) chose to speak out regarding the Thomas-Hill controversy during Bryant's research period of October 1–31, 1991. The statements by Black men differ dramatically from those of Black and white women in that racial and ideological considerations took precedence over gender. The major exception was Craig Washington (D-TX), who spoke directly about sexual harassment. In his statement, Washington addressed sexual harassment and race. "It's not Black women who have lynched Black men," Washington said, engaging the narrative trope of lynching that Thomas had deployed so successfully, adding, "it is White racism that has been tolerated for so long by many of Judge Thomas's supporters."

Although Major Owens (D-NY) made references to Thomas's silence with respect to whether his views on abortion in a floor statement, race and the ideological difference exhibited by Thomas were the paramount concerns in Owens's press statement:

This guy [Thomas] is a danger. He is the highest-placed Black in the country. Conservative Blacks will rally around him. They will be coming out of the woodwork and asserting themselves. We are in for some difficult days in the African American community.

The same ideological concerns were voiced by Edolphus Towns (D-NY), but were directed specifically toward the Bush administration. "We hope the administration gives the same type of attention and support to the Civil Rights Bill as they did the nomination of Clarence Thomas. I hope the President will also look at the Civil Rights Bill and see the same support" (cite). John Lewis (D-GA) chose to attack Thomas's use of racial rhetoric in order to gain Black support. As a veteran of the Civil Rights Movement, Lewis stated that Thomas had "shamefully invoked the race card" in such a way that was "entirely inappropriate and irresponsible." Lewis called Thomas's "high-tech lynching" comment a "shameful affront to the legacy of the Civil Rights Movement." It would appear that Lewis's main concern was the use of racial imagery by a man who appeared to stand ideologically juxtaposed to all that the Civil Rights Movement stood for. Lewis mentioned nothing about the matter of sexual harassment.

CAN BLACK FEMINISM BE QUANTIFIED?

Until recently, most of the scholarship on Black feminist thought has been qualitative. Evelyn Simien, however, has been doing groundbreaking work to develop an empirical model that would take into account the interlocking effects of race and gender by examining the 1993 National Black Politics Study (NBPS).[13] Simien's objective is clear: to advance the study of Black women and politics within the discipline of political science by documenting the development of Black feminist consciousness. With this objective in mind, Simien makes purposeful choices. First, she rejects the singular approach that dominates the group consciousness literature because there is a need to account for the simultaneous effects of race and gender. Second, Simien begins with Black feminist tenets developed from the ideas and experiences of Black women as opposed

---

[13]See, for example, Simien, E. (2004). "The Intersection of Race and Gender: An Examination of Black Feminist Consciousness, Race Consciousness, and Policy Attitudes." *Social Science Quarterly* 85 (3): 793–810.

to white women because the sex roles of Black and white women have been defined differently. Third, Simien makes an effort to examine intragroup differences because this practice has long been omitted from feminist scholarship and Black politics research. Finally, Simien contends that Black feminist consciousness is a "politicized group identification" embracing interrelated attitudes and beliefs that capture the essence of Black feminist thought. More specifically, she asserts, Black feminist consciousness involves the following attitudes and beliefs: (1) an acute awareness of interlocking oppression, which suggests that the struggle to eradicate racism and sexism is rooted in yet another "ism" that plagues humanity—classism; (2) a commitment to gender equality or equality of the sexes; (3) an acceptance of the belief that feminism benefits the Black community; and (4) a sense of belonging or conscious loyalty to the group in question (i.e., Black women) on account of shared experience, referred to here as "common fate" because the individual who identifies with the group label has come to realize that individual life chances are inextricably tied to the group.

Thus far, other scholars have emphasized several themes underlying Black feminist consciousness, among them, intersectionality, gender equality, Black feminism as it benefits the Black community, and "linked fate" among Black women. From a theoretical perspective, the concept of Black feminist consciousness is rich and well developed. Unfortunately, empirical assessments of Black feminist consciousness have been more limited. The 1993 NBPS was a unique study in that it contained questions that measured Black feminist consciousness. Participants were selected in one of two ways: (1) from a national random digit dial sample or (2) randomly selected from a list of households in Black neighborhoods. The response rate was 65%, resulting in 1206 Black respondents, all of whom were voting eligible. A full description of the survey may be found in the codebook compiled by the principal investigators, Michael C. Dawson, Ronald E. Brown, and James S. Jackson.

Since no one definitive measure of Black feminist consciousness is used in survey research with African-American respondents, six items were selected from the 1993 NBPS to construct this measure. It is important to note here that the same items were asked of Black women and men, and all items were rescaled to a 0-to-1 format, with 1 indicating high group consciousness, specifically Black feminist consciousness. One item asked whether racism, poverty, and sexual discrimination are linked and should be addressed by the Black community. Other items asked whether Black women should share equally in the political leadership of the Black community and as a larger percentage of the clergy in Black churches. Respondents were asked if they thought Black feminist groups help the Black community by advancing the position of Black women or whether these groups divide the Black community. Respondents were also asked whether they thought what generally happens to Black women in this country will have something to do with what happens in their own lives. Those who responded affirmatively were asked, "Will it affect you a lot, some, or not very much?" Finally, Black citizens were asked whether Black women suffered both from sexism within the Black movement and racism within the women's movement. These six items were used to determine the respondents' level of group consciousness.

The first stage of Simien's project involved factor analysis. Factor analysis is a statistical technique used to delineate the principal components of a highly abstract construct. In this case, the goal of factor analysis is to reduce the data by classifying a number of interrelated variables—a total of six used here to measure Black feminist consciousness—into a limited number of factors (or dimensions). This method is most useful when constructing multi-item scales. While many questions or items can be used to construct a scale that measures Black feminist consciousness, Simien relies on factor analysis to explain the total amount of variation between and among individual survey items. Here, in an effort to determine the dimensionality of the common factor space, she focuses on explaining the total amount of variation in positions taken by African-American men and women on the six items that tap Black feminist consciousness. The principal components are ordered with respect to their variation so that the first few account for most of the variation in the original variables.

While the relationship between Black feminist consciousness and the "feminist feeling thermometer" is statistically significant ($p \leq .01$), the two variables are weakly correlated (Pearson's $r = .195$). Simien turns to the relationship between Black feminist consciousness and the feminist identification measure. This relationship is not statistically significant. Moreover, the two variables are weakly correlated (Pearson's $r = .056$). Notice the relationship between the "feminist feeling thermometer" and the feminist identification measure. The relationship is statistically significant ($p \leq .01$), and the correlation between the two variables is moderate (Pearson's $r = .37$). These results clearly demonstrate that items designed to tap feminist consciousness among white women are problematic because they yield a measurement of support for white feminism among Black women—not Black feminist consciousness. Given that there are many differences, both historically and in contemporary times, between the ways in which Black women and white women experience sexism in this country, it is fair to say that white feminism is not comparable to Black feminism.

We turn now to the relationship among Black feminist consciousness, the "feeling thermometer" for Blacks, and the Black identification measure. The relationship is statistically significant ($p \leq .01$); however, the two variables are weakly correlated (Pearson's $r = .077$). Similarly, the relationship between Black feminist consciousness and the Black identification measure is statistically significant ($p \leq .01$), and the correlation between the two variables is moderate (Pearson's $r = .335$). Likewise, the relationship between the "feeling thermometer" for Blacks and the race identification measure is statistically significant ($p \leq .01$). However, the two variables are weakly correlated (Pearson's $r = .096$). Most striking is the relationship between Black feminist consciousness and the interaction term. This relationship is statistically significant ($p \leq .01$) and the correlation is moderate (Pearson's $r = .366$), which is what one would expect when considering that the interaction term assumes that race and gender are separate, mutually exclusive categories and Black feminist consciousness emphasizes the simultaneity of oppression.

In sum, the relationship between Black feminist consciousness and the respective "feeling thermometers" for feminists and Blacks was statistically significant. However, the variables were weakly correlated. While the relationship between Black feminist consciousness and the feminist identification measure was not statistically significant, the relationship between Black feminist consciousness and the race identification measure was statistically significant. Although Black feminist consciousness and the feminist identification were weakly correlated, Black feminist consciousness and the race identification measure were moderately correlated. Most striking was the relationship between Black feminist consciousness and the interaction term because this relationship reached statistical significance and the two variables were moderately correlated. All things considered, the empirical findings bolstered Simien's claim that Black feminist consciousness is distinct from both feminist consciousness and Black identification.

The second stage of factor analysis delineated the principal components of Black feminist consciousness for Black women and men separately. It is believed that the "both movements" item may be the most difficult for respondents to answer because this item in particular activates the sense of internal conflict often experienced by Black women when they feel that they must choose between race and gender. Black men are expected to experience a similar sense of internal conflict when considering the hierarchy of interest within the Black community that assigns priority to race over gender. This internal conflict is what Gay and Tate have referred to as a double bind, which suggests that Black women will support their interests as women, but their support can be muted or even overwhelmed when those interests collide with race.

It would appear on the basis of the factors cited here that there is a distinct group of Black female respondents who favor more Black women leaders as well as support the idea that Black feminism benefits the Black community; however, this distinct group of Black women reports a lower sense of linked fate with Black women and accepts the position that Black women suffer from mostly the same problems as Black men when considering the "both movements" item. In light of their doubly bound situation, these women uphold the hierarchy of interest within the Black community by placing more emphasis on race than gender. For this reason, the second dimension (or factor) is titled "Hierarchy of Interests." The proportion of variance explained by the first dimension was 25% and its eigenvalue was 1.49, which meant a certain amount of variance (16%, eigenvalue of .988) was added by the second dimension. Taken together, these two dimensions account for 41% of the total variance.

The results of this analysis bolstered Simien's claim that the "both movements" item is the most difficult for Black respondents to answer because it activates the sense of internal conflict often experienced by Black women when they feel that they must choose between race and gender. Similarly, Black men must also consider the hierarchy of interests within the Black community. The factor analysis cited here shows that all Black respondents experienced some sense of internal conflict or crisis. However, it is critical to point out that the hierarchy of interests within the Black community does not produce the same divisive outcome for Black men as it does for Black women. In short, gender matters.

GENDER MATTERS

Why do we care about the different identities held by Black women in political positions and how they are engaged and, at times, come into conflict? Specifically, whether Black women can take stands on "Black issues" as well as "women's issues" is a question of representation. In *The Concept of Representation* (1967), Hannah Pitkin states that the very nature of representation is an action on constituents' beliefs in an informal capacity. A representative may seek her own preferences, but also make decisions in the best interest of constituents, despite what they say they want. There must be a fine balance between trusteeship, where the representative acts on behalf of her constituency without their expressed consent, and role of a delegate, where the representative acts on behalf of the expressed wishes of her constituency.

In *The Paradox of Representation* (1997), Lublin stated, "African American voters support the election of Black representatives not just to gain a new role model, but because they believe that Black representatives will work harder for real substantive gains for their community."[14] The real issue, according to Swain (1995), is that the increase of Black faces in political positions (descriptive representation) may not necessarily correlate with increased tangible goods (substantive representation) for African-Americans. She implies that symbolic representation, even though public officials may not advance those interests deemed important by their constituency, may be the result of wholehearted efforts to elect representatives who share demographic aspects of identity. It has long been known that representatives are self-interested, that they have a strong need to be reelected, and that much of their activity is unknown to most constituents and takes place behind closed doors of negotiation and compromise.[15] The question is whether substantive representation alone is enough for the kind of changes that still need to be made with regard to racial equality, or whether descriptive representation is needed as well. Put succinctly, is it enough that a representative claims to believe in most things that constituents believe in and has a voting record to support it, even though the representative may be white?

---

[14]Lublin, D. (1997). *The Paradox of Representation: Racial Gerrymandering and Minority Interests in Congress*. Princeton, NJ: Princeton University Press, p. 101.

[15]Fenno, R. (1978). *Home Style: House Members in Their Districts*. Boston: Little, Brown.

Can substantive symmetry be enough to ensure this representative will still espouse the same ideals behind closed doors as he or she does in public? Framing the question in racial terms, should African-Americans simply trust in either substantive or descriptive representation alone?

When examining the confirmation process of Thomas, there was great division within the African-American community about whether descriptive representation or substantive representation was most needed. The question for the public quickly became whether African-Americans could take the chance that another African-American would be nominated for such a high position in the future, rather than a question of the current nominee's ideological stance. Swain highlights the weakness in this calculus by pointing to the various appointees who did not support the majority of issues supported within their racial/ethnic communities, Thomas being the exemplary case. The question, then, is how Black progressive politics are undermined when Black women use racial solidarity as their cue, rather than gender.

Similar issues also came to the forefront in the O. J. Simpson trial, which could be subtitled, "The Erasure of Marguerite." Although most empirical studies reflect Black women's disdain for interracial marriages between Black men and white women, most Black women supported O. J. Simpson, a man who left his Black wife for a younger Barbie-like white woman. Black women were able to forgive Simpson (particularly since he was accused of killing the white wife). The Simpson case bears certain similarities to the allegations against Thomas in that the issue to be resolved was not one of guilt or innocence, but rather an opportunity to "beat the legal system." Most Black women refused to demonize Clarence Thomas or to censure him for his grossly inappropriate behavior. Instead, just as they did with Simpson, many Black women including, the esteemed writer Maya Angelou, chose to play it safe by effectively turning their heads and letting Thomas off the hook, considering it more important to take a Black hero where one could be found, however flawed he might be.

The important exception was Black female academics, many of who were brave enough to state publicly that they believed Hill. Their public outrage toward the all-white male judiciary had significant political implications, resulting in a record number of female candidates being elected to Congress in 1992. This election was popularly dubbed "the year of the woman," and for Blacks the woman of the year was Carol Moseley Braun. In late 1991, before the Clarence Thomas confirmation hearings took place, Carol Moseley Braun decided to run for the US Senate. She would attempt to unseat the incumbent, Senator Alan Dixon, in the Illinois Democratic primary the following March. Wealthy Chicago lawyer Albert Hofeld also declared his intention to run for the Democratic nomination, turning the primary into a three-candidate race.

It is rare for an incumbent senator to be unseated in a primary election, and Dixon's campaign benefited from many of the advantages of incumbency, including a long list of political contributors and the support of the Democratic Party establishment. Chicago Mayor Richard Daley, Senator Paul Simon, Representative Dan Rostenkowski, and other Illinois Democratic and labor leaders supported Dixon. Hofeld's advantage—indeed, the only thing that made him a legitimate candidate—was his personal bank account. He spent $4.5 million of his own money campaigning, most of which paid for television commercials that were highly critical of Dixon. Though Moseley Braun had less money to spend than either of her opponents, she had a number of advantages in the race. First, Dixon's decision to break ranks with most Senate Democrats by voting to confirm Clarence Thomas received a great deal of scrutiny, incensing women activists, who threw their support behind Moseley Braun. Hofeld's commercials attacking Dixon also advantaged Moseley Braun. Not only did they diminish Dixon through allegations and Hofeld through his posture as a mudslinger, but also they boosted Moseley Braun's stature as the candidate who refused to stoop to negative campaign tactics. Dixon had angered many union workers with his initial reluctance to back a bill that would have outlawed the permanent replacement of striking workers, and though he eventually decided to support the bill and labor leaders eventually lent him their official support, the backing Dixon received from labor voters was less than enthusiastic. Additionally, the country was in an economic recession in 1992 and the House of Representatives had just witnessed a banking scandal, both of which may have made voters less likely to vote for incumbents. Moseley Braun's personality was also an asset. "I just wish we had a Republican with the charisma and dedication Carol has," said one of Braun's former opponents, state Representative Virginia Fiester Frederick, a Republican from Lake Forest. "...I've listened to women who are ecstatic over her win, and these are Republican women calling my office."[16]

[16]In *St. Louis Post Dispatch*, March 22, 1992, p. 8.

Moseley Braun's status as a Black woman was also a factor, especially after the nation's consciousness had been refocused on race and gender by the Clarence Thomas hearings. In campaign speeches, Moseley Braun frequently mentioned that the Senate should more accurately reflect the diversity of America's population. She did not, however, appear to play the race or gender card overtly, considering diversity more broadly, as in the following quotes reported by journalist Robert Novak:

> Braun... insists that her decision to challenge Dixon was not based on his vote for Thomas, or Anita Hill's allegations that Thomas had sexually harassed her. "The campaign started before our senator voted on the confirmation," Braun said in an interview after her [primary] victory. "It wasn't an issue in this campaign. What was an issue was that the Senate unlocked its doors... and it needed to more closely reflect our society. Democracy is supposed to mean the people govern. Our institutions have to reflect the people's concerns, not just the narrow interest of millionaires talking to each other."

Moseley Braun's candidacy was clearly aided by the potential that she could make history by becoming the first African-American woman ever elected to the US Senate. However, this history-making potential was recognized by the media more frequently in the general election campaign than it was before the primary. Moseley Braun's platform was liberal. She promised to be a voice in Washington for people who were underrepresented there. She advocated increasing taxes for the top one percent of wage earners. She also proposed to cut $100 billion in defense spending—twice as much as incumbent President George Bush proposed—and to use the freed-up money to repair roads and bridges, providing jobs.

The week before the primary, a *Chicago Sun Times*/Fox News Chicago poll showed Dixon with the support of 41% of Democrats who planned to vote, compared to 29% for Moseley Braun and 21% for Hofeld. A poll for Peoria television WEEK had Dixon at 37%, Hofeld at 35%, and Moseley Braun at 18% (Ritter). With three candidates in the race and turnout in primary elections notoriously hard to predict, the only reasonable prediction worth making was that the race would be close.

The Democratic primary took place on March 18, and Moseley Braun unseated Dixon as the party's nominee. Moseley Braun won half the vote in Chicago, handily outperforming Dixon's 30%, and also won Cook

County suburbs and the Chicago "collar counties." Dixon won in less populated areas downstate, but those areas also gave significant support to Hofeld, taking away from Dixon votes he needed badly. The day after Moseley Braun's primary victory, the national media honed in on the possibility that a Black woman could be elected to the Senate. Moseley Braun was thrust into the national spotlight, becoming a star overnight, and the potential that she would make history attracted support from across the country. "Ms. Braun was transformed from the little-known Cook County recorder of deeds – the county's chief file-keeper – to a national celebrity who counts people like Gloria Steinem and Bill Clinton as her new best friends."[17] A week and a half after the primary, Moseley Braun flew to Washington, where she received pledges of support from the AFL-CIO and Jesse Jackson, and met with other potential backers. In fact, the entire Democratic Party seemed to throw its support behind Moseley Braun. As Freivogel observed,

> Don Foley, of the Democratic Senatorial Campaign Committee said Braun had been swamped with offers of assistance.... The [DSCC] has not yet said how much money it will give Braun, but Foley described the race as uniquely important. Foley said the party "had a special responsibility to her because of the historic nature of her race." Moreover, Foley noted, the Democrats need to win Illinois to have a shot at winning the presidential race.[18]

Moseley Braun had raised less money than her opponents in the primary, but she had been told that she would need to spend $5 million to $6 million to win the general election, so she set to work raising funds that would be necessary to defeat her opponent, Republican Richard Williamson. Unlike many of the campaigns that take place today, in which both major party candidates rush to the center and attempt to portray themselves as mainstream moderates, there were clear ideological differences between Moseley Braun and the conservative Williamson, a lawyer who had once been an advisor to President Ronald Reagan. Williamson, who was considered the underdog—the last Republican

[17]Wilkerson, I. (1992, November 4). "Milestone for Black Woman in Gaining U.S. Senate Seat." *The New York Times.*

[18]Wilkerson, I. (1992, November 4). "Milestone for Black Woman in Gaining U.S. Senate Seat." *The New York Times.*

senator elected from Illinois was Charles H. Percy in 1978—had a two-pronged strategy to overcome Moseley Braun's early lead in the polls: portray her as ultraliberal and criticize her as being unethical.

One tactic Republicans employed was to attempt to link Moseley Braun to US Representative Gus Savage (D-IL), an African-American known for holding controversial views regarding Israel and Jews. On September 23, Cook County GOP Chairman Manny Hoffman criticized Moseley Braun for having participated in a March 7 rally that Savage also attended. After Moseley Braun left the rally, Savage showed up and gave a speech in which he criticized American Jews supporting his opponent in the primary. Hoffman called on Moseley Braun to denounce Savage, and Williamson's campaign attacked Moseley Braun with campaign ads criticizing her sponsorship of a 1979 legislative resolution that honored Savage as a "model of public service."

Reports of scandals escalated. In late September, Chicago's WMAQ-Channel 5 reported that Moseley Braun had dispersed $28,750 of her mother's inheritance without first applying it to her public aid bills. Moseley Braun kept about $10,000 of the money without reporting it to state officials. In an October 2 opinion piece in the *Chicago Sun-Times*, Steve Neal was highly critical of Moseley Braun's treatment of her mother's inheritance and her ethics in general:

> In her 14-year public career, Braun has missed few opportunities for personal gain. She knows all the tricks of parlaying political influence into cash. As a legislator, she was also a $103,450 bond counsel for the city of Chicago, though she had no experience in the field. As recorder of deeds, Braun registered as a lobbyist with the local officials on behalf of her pal [state Rep. Alfred G.] Ronan. Braun collected a $30,000 lobbying contract to one of Shea's partners, Billie Paige. Special interests get special consideration from Braun.

Moseley Braun's alleged ethical violations were a point to which Williamson would return throughout the campaign, both in television ads and debates. In fact, in the second public debate of the campaign, which took place October 22, "Williamson, as in most of his campaign, tried to turn the one-hour forum into a discussion of Moseley Braun's ethics and to portray her to the left of Bill Clinton." The candidates also clashed on a number of policy issues. Particularly prominent was the question of how to deal with crime, the debate having occurred just days after a seven-year-old Chicago

boy, Dantrell Davis, had been killed in a shooting that drew public attention to the issue of violence. Moseley Braun said that in order to keep the
guns off the street, Congress should pass the Brady Bill, which would place
new restrictions on the purchasing of guns. Moseley Braun also criticized
Williamson for his links with the National Rifle Association. Williamson
said Moseley Braun was soft on crime and criticized her opposition to the
death penalty and her support for decriminalizing marijuana. Williamson
also argued in favor of a voucher system that would give parents money
to send their children to private school, noting that Moseley Braun's son
attended a private school. Moseley Braun criticized Williamson for bringing
her son into the debate and stated her opposition to vouchers. Williamson
responded that Moseley Braun's proposal to spend more federal money on
education was "a goofy liberal idea."

As the election neared, the campaign became increasingly negative,
with the candidates attacking each other on almost a daily basis. The
day before the election, the candidates traded barbs that highlighted
the themes of their campaigns. Williamson urged voters to elect "somebody they don't have to be embarrassed by – someone who is honest."
Moseley Braun said, "We don't need any more arrogant rich boys in the
Senate, and that's what this campaign is all about." A week earlier, she
had paid more than $15,000 to the Illinois Department of Public Aid
to settle the question about her mother's inheritance, but Williamson
continued to hammer her on the issue, claiming she had broken the
law. Illinois Governor Jim Edgar, a Republican supporting Williamson,
said that though he thought "somebody broke the law" in regard to
the inheritance situation, prosecution would be inappropriate because it
was not the standard approach to such cases. Despite Williamson's vigorous attacks, his exposure of Moseley Braun's alleged ethical deficien-
cies never produced the surge in the polls he had hoped, and Moseley
Braun won the November 3 election by a significant margin. "Despite
miserably cold and damp weather over the state's most populous areas,
election officials were predicting a record turnout of at least 5.2 million
of the state's 6.6 million registered voters." Exit polling indicated that
Moseley Braun captured about half the white vote and "virtually every
Black voter" in an election that *The New York Times* said had been "a
race where symbolism was as important as strategy."[19]

[19]Wilkerson, I. (1992, November 4). "Milestone for Black Woman in Gaining U.S.
Senate Seat." *The New York Times*.

After her election, Moseley Braun toured the Southern part of Illinois to reassure voters that she wouldn't forget about them in Washington. She said her priorities, intended to benefit the entire state, were to attract investment to Illinois, to create more job opportunities, to give law-enforcement authorities strong federal support, and "education, education, education." Recognizing the symbolic value of her election, Moseley Braun said the best way she could live up to the expectations that others across the country might have of her was to be the best senator in Illinois history.

Moseley Braun was just one of the many women and racial minorities who won election to Congress in 1992, the "year of the woman," although the vast majority of the membership continued to be white and male. Of 110 new members in the House of Representatives, 24 were women, 16 were Black, and eight were Hispanic, making the incoming Congress the most diverse in American history. The Senate also admitted four new women into its ranks, a small percentage considering that there were 33 Senate races in 1992, but a larger number than ever before. Moseley Braun headed to Washington planning to further the many causes she had advocated on the campaign trail, but she was not able to leave behind the ethical questions that had plagued her campaign in Illinois. Even before she was sworn in as Illinois' junior senator, the press honed in on a number of questions about the behavior of her campaign manager, Kgosie Matthews and a possible romantic relationship between the two, and on the way her campaign funds were spent. Questions about her ethics would continue to dog Moseley Braun throughout her six-year term.

Moseley Braun's first few months in the Senate were "rocky," according to an article that appeared April 5, 1993, in *Crain's Chicago Business.* "The senator started in office with a series of political miscues, organizational delays, and ethical question marks; efforts... to erase her relatively high $543,871 campaign debt should indicate whether she is generating more support than dismay...." Because of the perceptions that Moseley Braun had had a difficult beginning in Washington, many Chicago area businesses were reluctant to contribute money to erase her debts, preferring a wait-and-see approach. However, Moseley Braun was receiving financial backing from Chicago's futures exchanges, for which she had "gone to bat early and often with the Clinton administration over its proposed trading tax and other issues." According to the article, some potential contributors were reluctant to help Moseley Braun pay off her debts because they sensed she had spent more money than she needed to defeat a lackluster opponent. They also questioned the $15,000 monthly salary she paid campaign manager Matthews during the race. Her relationship with Matthews continued to draw attention through the spring, with Moseley Braun disclosing in April that she and Matthews were engaged to be married in the summer. The wedding never took place, but the summer of 1993 was important for Moseley Braun nevertheless.

In July 1993, Moseley Braun took to the floor of the Senate, persuading her colleagues to vote against renewing a design patent held by the United Daughters of the Confederacy for a symbol that included the Confederate flag. Her speech, and the following vote, drew national press coverage and praise. A bill that would have renewed the Daughters of the Confederacy's patent had failed to make it out of committee that spring, so on July 22, Senator Jesse Helms (R-NC) proposed amending a national service bill to include language that would renew the patent. Many senators were unaware what they were voting on, and Helms won a test vote for the amendment, 52 to 48. But then Moseley Braun took the floor and delivered a passionate speech denouncing the flag as a symbol of slavery and arguing that the Senate had no place renewing a patent that included it. "On this issue there can be no consensus," she said. "It is an outrage. It is an insult. It is absolutely unacceptable to me and millions of Americans, Black or white, that we would put the imprimatur of the United States Senate on the symbol of this kind of idea."[20]

After Moseley Braun's speech, Senator Bob Bennett (R-UT) offered a motion to allow the Senate to reconsider Helms's amendment. Moseley Braun returned to the floor, saying, "This is no small matter," that a flag symbolizing slavery should not be "underwritten, underscored, adopted by this United States Senate."[21] A number of other senators then went to the floor and sided with Moseley Braun. In the second vote, Helms's amendment was killed, 75 to 25. In a Senate where positions are almost never influenced by floor speeches, Moseley Braun's oratory had swayed 27 senators to change their votes. The next day, in an editorial, *The New York Times* praised Moseley Braun's actions:

[20]Clymer, A. (1993, July 23). "Daughter of Slavery Hushes Senate." *The New York Times.*

[21]Clymer, A. (1993, July 23). "Daughter of Slavery Hushes Senate." *The New York Times.*

On Thursday, Carol Moseley Braun woke up a sleepy Senate to the unthinking way the White majority can offend minority Americans.... Senator Jesse Helms studiously missed her point when he said, "Race shouldn't have been introduced" into the floor debate. Once the full Senate realized that race was already implicated in the symbolism of the Civil War emblem, the affront to Black Americans was clear. Using the time-honored threat of the filibuster, Senator Moseley Braun claimed full membership in the Senate club. Several weeks ago she had used conventional techniques to bury the measure in the Judiciary committee. Only after Senators Helms and Strom Thurmond broke the norms of courtesy and tried to sneak the amendment past the entire Senate did she resort to high drama.... On the Senate floor, she matched reason to passion, with splendid results.[22]

Moseley Braun's "majestic moment"[23] was important, but it was also fleeting. Later that summer, Moseley Braun's campaign debt again became an issue when she missed a filing deadline for federal disclosure forms and instead released a summary showing that her campaign debt had climbed to over $600,000. An August 13 *Chicago Sun Times* article mentioned Moseley Braun's debt and reviewed what she had achieved over halfway into her first year in office:

> "The debt is very upsetting to me," she said. She said the bills eventually would be settled.... The senator said that amongst her biggest accomplishments so far were helping to expand flood-relief coverage for Illinois victims and having a hand in killing a tax on commodities trades. She said she was "most proud" of not having missed a single vote.

Two weeks later, the Federal Election Commission announced its plan to conduct an exhaustive investigation into Moseley Braun's finances and reported that she continued to pay Matthews as a fund-raising consultant, raising the question, "Is paying Matthews a form of subsidizing her own lifestyle?"

As Moseley Braun settled into her job as a senator, the country's political climate began to shift dramatically. Republicans successfully portrayed President Bill Clinton's proposal for government-provided universal healthcare coverage as a liberal attempt to make government bigger.

[22] *The New York Times.* (1994, July 24). "Ms. Moseley-Braun's Majestic Moment."
[23] *The New York Times.* (1994, July 24). "Ms. Moseley-Braun's Majestic Moment."

The failure of the Clinton healthcare plan was the basis on which House minority leader Newt Gingrich (R-GA) led the Republicans in their reactionary 1994 campaign, centered around a platform called "The Contract with America," which proposed reducing the size of the national government and returning power to states. The way in which women candidates were perceived had also changed in 1992. According to an October 2, 1994, *New York Times* article, women were having a much tougher time campaigning than they had two years earlier. The article said that Moseley Braun and other women "rode the sex card to the United States Senate in 1992"[24] but since they "left a complicated legacy for those running this year, many agree that being a woman is not the advantage it was two years ago and may even be a handicap."[25] The article continued:

> Since the raw anger over the Supreme Court confirmation hearings of Clarence Thomas...has subsided, many female candidates say they do not think it helps to emphasize their sex. In a turnabout from two years ago, it is the men who now see the benefit of playing up the sex of their female opponents. Crime rather than the economy has become the central issue in many races, leaving women to suffer from a stereotype that they are not as tough as men on crime.[26]

The November election was dubbed "the Republican Revolution" after the Republicans won by a landslide, capturing control of both houses of Congress for the first time since the 1950s and shifting what was considered the political center significantly to the right. In 1995, the Republican leadership began trying to implement many of the points of their Contract with America. President Clinton, fearing his reelection prospects were in jeopardy, was initially reluctant to take on the Republicans, who seemed to have a strong electoral mandate for their proposals. The Democratic leadership in the Senate was, in many cases, also unwilling to risk angering voters by strongly opposing Republican

[24] Berke, R. L. (1994, October 3). "In '94 'Vote for Woman' Does Not Play so Well." *The New York Times*.

[25] Berke, R. L. (1994, October 3). "In '94 'Vote for Woman' Does Not Play so Well." *The New York Times*.

[26] Berke, R. L. (1994, October 3). "In '94 'Vote for Woman' Does Not Play so Well." *The New York Times*.

plans. However, a few of the Senate's more liberal members, including Moseley Braun, held steadfast to their beliefs and actively fought the Republicans. One example of opposition came in July, when Moseley Braun and Senator Paul Wellstone (D-MN) were the only two senators to oppose a bill that would have cut $16.4 billion in spending previously approved by the Senate.

> Parting company with President Clinton and other Party elders, Sens. Paul Wellstone of Minnesota and Carol Moseley-Braun of Illinois prevented a final vote on the bill to cut $16.4 billion from previously enacted spending while funding aid to victims of the California earthquake and other disasters. "The people of my state would not want to see me just lay down on this railroad track and get run over without saying anything," said Moseley Braun. She and Wellstone objected to cuts in job training, heating assistance for the poor, and other domestic programs.

Making a formal alliance with Wellstone, considered one of the most progressive legislators to vote on the Senate floor, worked against Moseley Braun almost as much as her controversial trip to Nigeria the following summer. During that 1996 trip, Moseley Braun visited with the Nigerian dictator, Sani Abacha. She had not consulted with the State Department before the trip, nor had she informed most of her staff about where she was going. Moseley Braun's visit to Nigeria provoked widespread criticism and led to the resignation of her chief of staff, who was upset about not having been informed of Moseley Braun's plans. The trip to Nigeria and Moseley Braun's interaction with Abacha again raised questions about whose interests she represented. The lead of a *Boston Globe* editorial placed her trip in the context of her race and gender: "Carol Moseley Braun has made some missteps since becoming the first Black woman elected to the US Senate in 1992. But none of her previous errors has been as damaging to the national interest as her recent visit with the dictator of Nigeria, Sani Abacha." The article continued:

> Moseley-Braun has described her sojourn variously as a "vacation," a bid to offer condolences to the Abachas after a recent death in their family, and a legitimate fact-finding voyage (though she spoke with none of the many prosecuted Nigerian democracy advocates). The most disturbing possibility is that she had no concrete rationale at all. She just went.... Besides Louis Farrakhan, Moseley Braun is the most prominent apologist for Nigeria in

America. Why she has spoken in the Senate against sanctions for the big-gest subjugator of Black people in the world (Nigeria is Africa's most pop-ulous nation) is a mystery. We only hope that it has nothing to do with the fact that her former fiancé, who accompanied her on this visit, was once a registered lobbyist for the Nigerian government in Washington.

The *Globe's* comparison of Senator Moseley Braun to Minister Louis Farrakhan evoked ideas of separatism and otherness within the USA. Although the Senator had numerous episodes of questionable judgment, her mistakes and subsequent support were attributed to race as opposed to any other reason, including lack of federal legislative experience. One statement representative of this approach to analyzing Moseley Braun's time in office was articulated in a *New York Times* article written by long-time Moseley Braun watcher, Richard L. Berke, who wrote:

> The turnabout among Democrats reflects the sensitive politics of race rather than the accomplishments of Ms. Moseley Braun. Many Democrats said they would be wary of the backlash if they took her on, particu-larly since this state has no other highly visible Black politicians. Several Democrats also said they had no appetite to reopen the racial tensions of a decade ago, when a Black mayor, Harold Washington, was elected in Chicago over two White challengers and the politics of race upended the city's once monolithic Democratic machine. Some said they were acting out of self-interest; if Black voters were alienated, they might not turn out for other Democratic candidates.[27]

It wasn't until the third-to-last paragraph of the almost 2000-word article that Moseley Braun's accomplishments as a senator were men-tioned, and briefly at that. The article stated that she had a liberal vot-ing record and had been an "eloquent" advocate for minorities and women, pointing specifically to her 1993 speech against renewing the Daughters of the Confederacy patent. Berke also mentioned that, "as she vowed in her campaign," Moseley Braun had spent a significant amount of time working on education issues and had focused on improving the "nation's crumbling schools."[28] The *Times* article concluded by quoting

---

[27]Berke, R. L. (1997, July 4). "Racial Politics Lets Flawed Candidate Find Allies." *The New York Times.*

[28]Berke, R. L. (1997, July 4). "Racial Politics Lets Flawed Candidate Find Allies." *The New York Times.*

Loyola political science professor John P. Pelissero as saying Moseley Braun's biggest challenge was that she was known for "all these character issues."[29] Ironically, this article and the others like it that had focused on Moseley Braun's character rather than her legislative record not only identified the political challenge facing her, but also perpetuated it by keeping the public's attention focused on her character.

In addition to those problems mentioned already, a high turnover rate among Moseley Braun's Senate staff had contributed to a widespread public perception that she was not doing a good job. In a four-year span, her office had hired and then lost four chiefs of staff and four press secretaries, perhaps the two most important positions in any Senate office. Polls showed that prospective voters viewed Moseley Braun as dishonest and unethical. At the advice of her new political consultant, Moseley Braun began to address questions about her character more concretely. For most of her term, she had maintained that the concerns others had expressed about her were blown out of proportion, should be off-limits because they related to her private life, and were irrelevant to her senatorial duties. Her new response to ethical questioning was that the criticism of her resulted from "public relations disasters" which would have been of far less significance had she handled them in a "more sophisticated way." Moseley Braun seemed to be alluding— though she never overtly expressed as much—that she lacked mentoring and role models from other legislators with more experience. There were not, in fact, any role models for Moseley Braun, and it seems that no one took her under their wing to prompt her as to Senate protocol, whether formal or informal.

Given the lack of support, Moseley Braun relied upon the defense that her missteps had been exaggerated by the media, which exploited her political naiveté. She insisted that her trip to Nigeria wouldn't have been nearly as much of an issue if she had only the presence of mind to hold a press conference beforehand to announce she was going. Her trip, she said, was not very different from many taken by other senators. "Understand, colleagues go to China and meet with Chinese officials. That country has an absolutely abominable human rights record.

---

[29] Berke, R. L. (1997, July 4). "Racial Politics Lets Flawed Candidate Find Allies." *The New York Times.*

So I ask the question, what's the difference?" Rather than dwelling on the negatives, as the press had for much of her time in the Senate, Moseley Braun's strategy was to focus on her achievements and to talk about these more effectively. She was candid about her lack of experience, reflecting:

> I started off thinking I had to be a good legislator and the rest would take care of itself, and that's just not the case.... The rest does not just take care of itself any more than being a good legislator doesn't just take care of itself. You have to invest energy, you have to invest thought, you have to be invested in the portrayal and the symbolism around what you do as much as the substance.

With the goal of distracting voters from the ethical questions by giving them something positive to think about instead, Moseley Braun formulated a campaign script that included fighting against automated teller machine surcharges, working to attract more federal funds to fix deteriorating school buildings, pointing out her role in bringing community policing and 3000 new police officers to Illinois, and taking some credit for the country's economic turnaround because of her votes to cut taxes and balance the budget. Moseley Braun sought to draw attention to her record, which included expanding minority ownership of television stations and fighting cuts to social programs of the poor. She had also taken moderate stances on certain issues, championing Illinois business interests and voting in favor of the constitutional amendment to require a balanced federal budget. Moseley Braun finally began to address significant fund-raising issues facing her campaign. It had taken her years to eliminate debt remaining from her 1992 campaign, and though she raised $1.1 million over the summer of 1997, she was well behind her targets and needed to raise more in order to run television ads to promote herself and answer charges raised by her opponents. Her need to raise funds increased when it became clear that she was one of three female Democratic senators up for reelection who were key targets of the national Republican Party.

The March 17th Republican primary was, of course, of interest to Moseley Braun as it determined her November opponent, conservative Peter Fitzgerald, a 37-year-old multimillionaire from a wealthy banking family. His opponent, Loleta Didrickson, had the support of most Republican Party insiders because they thought Fitzgerald—who opposed abortion in all cases, supported legalizing concealed weapons, and was against gay rights—was too conservative to be a viable candidate in the general election. Republican leaders, including 1996 presidential nominee Bob Dole, came to the state to campaign for Didrickson. Ultimately though, Fitzgerald won the primary by spending $7 million of his own money on a television campaign and attracting the support of religious conservatives. Moseley Braun's campaign was happy to hear the primary results, as they seemed to have improved her own reelection prospects. "As Bob Dole says," Moseley Braun said, referring to Dole's arguments against Fitzgerald and on behalf of Didrickson, "it's a difference between the mainstream and the extreme."[30]

By May however, it became clear that Fitzgerald's victory hadn't solved all of Moseley Braun's problems. Fitzgerald's personal wealth, estimated at $40 million, would prove a significant asset to his campaign, especially since Moseley Braun's campaign was still having trouble raising money. President Clinton, Vice President Al Gore, and First Lady Hillary Rodham Clinton, who would eventually wage her own successful Senate campaign in New York, all came to Illinois to campaign on Moseley Braun's behalf and to help her raise funds. By the end of the summer, Moseley Braun's campaign had $1 million on hand and more money was coming in, but she had still been unable to effectively defend against Fitzgerald's steady barrage of negative advertising. An August *Chicago Tribune* poll showed Moseley Braun trailing Fitzgerald 46 to 39% with a four-point margin of error. An early September poll by the *St. Louis-Dispatch* showed Fitzgerald leading by 11 points, 46 to 35%, also with a four-point margin of error.

At a Labor Day event, Moseley Braun found herself once again attracting negative press coverage after she got angry and lost her composure, charging racism in response to an article by syndicated columnist George F. Will, who criticized her personal and political conduct. "I think because he could not say 'nigger,' he said the word 'corrupt,'" Moseley Braun said,[31] though Will had not actually used the word "corrupt" in his article. "George Will can just take his hood and go back

---

[30] Jeter, J. (1998, March 18). "Conservative Wins GOP Primary for Senate Seat." *The Washington Post.*

[31] Belluck, P. (1998, September 9). "Beleaguered Illinois Senator Accuses a Critic of Racism." *The New York Times.*

to wherever he came from," she added.[32] Shortly after the outburst, Moseley Braun apologized publicly and faxed an apology to Will, but it was too late to keep the media from giving wide coverage to the episode. As the election neared and it became clear that Fitzgerald had a significant chance to oust Moseley Braun from office, the campaign turned ugly. According to an October 8 article in *The New York Times*, "with less than a month to go, the candidates have dropped all pretense of keeping the gloves on."[33] Moseley Braun referred to Fitzgerald as "duplicitous," a "wolf in sheep's clothing," and a candidate who resorts to "scuzzball" campaign tactics.[34] Fitzgerald called her "shrill," said Moseley Braun had "nothing positive to say about her own record," and complained that her career had been "obscured by numerous scandals and controversies."[35] Polling continued to show a roughly 10 point percentage gap in Fitzgerald's favor and indicated that voters believed he was the more honest and trustworthy candidate. The day before the election, Moseley Braun continued campaigning vigorously. "Most polls over the last few months have shown Ms. Moseley Braun trailing badly," wrote *The New York Times*.[36] Even at this late juncture in the campaign, though, analysts still believed Moseley Braun might be able to eke out reelection, given that "Ms. Moseley Braun... appeared frequently... with notable campaigners like Hillary Rodham Clinton and running an aggressive series of advertisements, [and] three polls published in the last few days show her gaining ground and, in one case, running even with Mr. Fitzgerald."[37]

---

[32] Belluck, P. (1998, September 9). "Beleaguered Illinois Senator Accuses a Critic of Racism." *The New York Times*.

[33] Belluck, P. (1998, October 8). "Democrat Loses Ground in Illinois Senate Race." *The New York Times*.

[34] Belluck, P. (1998, October 8). "Democrat Loses Ground in Illinois Senate Race." *The New York Times*.

[35] Belluck, P. (1998, October 8). "Democrat Loses Ground in Illinois Senate Race." *The New York Times*.

[36] Belluck, P. (1998, November 3). "Moseley Braun, Trailing, Pushes Hard." *The New York Times*.

[37] Belluck, P. (1998, November 3). "Moseley Braun, Trailing, Pushes Hard." *The New York Times*.

Even though Moseley Braun managed to significantly narrow the gap between herself and Fitzgerald over the last few weeks of the campaign, she was ultimately unable to overcome the questions about her character that had persisted since her 1992 campaign, and she lost by four percentage points in the November 3 election, 47% to Fitzgerald's 51%. The first Black woman ever elected to the Senate was about to join a sisterhood of Black women who could not survive the Democratic Party. She would not, however, be the last.

CLINTON'S CABINET OF CURIOSITIES: LANI GUINIER AND DR. JOYCELYN ELDERS

Carol Moseley Braun's unsuccessful Senate term occurred during the Clinton era. Many Black women were hopeful about the possibilities for their own expanded involvement in the political arena in January 1993 with the inauguration of President Bill Clinton, his choice of Maya Angelou as his inaugural poet, and his attempt to put Blacks in his Presidential cabinet. Shortly after his inauguration, Clinton nominated his friend and former classmate Lani Guinier to the prestigious and crucial post of Assistant Attorney General for Civil Rights. Guinier's nomination sparked an immediate firestorm of criticism from the right, which labeled Professor Guinier as the "Quota Queen" and assailed her for ideas expressed in her publications, most of which her opponents had not read, or which they had taken out of context and misunderstood. In the face of this opposition—what one friend of Guinier's called a "low-tech lynching"—Clinton backed down, not only withdrawing her nomination, but also refusing to afford Guinier the opportunity to speak out in her own defense (and, of course, his). The result was a civil rights setback of monumental proportions.

Unfortunately, the Guinier embarrassment was followed by the scandal that engulfed Dr. Joycelyn Elders, nominated by Clinton in July of the same year, to be the Surgeon General. Elders was confirmed by the Senate with a vote of 65-34 as the nation's 16th surgeon general. She succeeded Antonia Novello, the first woman to be named to the post, making her the second woman and the first Black to serve in this capacity. Elders was sworn in and just a little over a year later, on December 9, 1994, was asked to resign. Her brief tenure exemplifies Black women's struggle to gain stature in the Democratic Party in general, but in William Jefferson Clinton's cabinet in particular.

In 1991, then presidential candidate Bill Clinton emphasized as one of his key campaign themes that he would "end welfare as we know it."[38] Five years later, with his fall reelection looming, President Clinton signed into law the Personal Responsibility and Work Opportunity Act, representing the most comprehensive, landmark welfare legislation since the New Deal. The bill, which had been strongly endorsed by Congressional Republicans, ended six decades of the government safety net that had served as the fundamental basis for social welfare programs. The legislation dismantled Aid for Families with Dependent Children (AFDC), the program most associated with the welfare system, and created a new, more restrictive program called Temporary Assistance for Needy Families (TANF). Many policy analysts believed that this was a "centrist" move on the part of President Clinton to ensure reelection. Passing this legislation helped solidify the contemporary political discourse on social welfare reform that prioritized race and depicted Black women according to the "Welfare Queen" narrative that had been crafted by President Reagan.

The welfare queen is the defining social stereotype of the Black woman: a lazy, promiscuous, single Black mother living off the dole of society. She poses a threat to the Protestant work ethic that drives America and the American Dream of social advancement and acceptability. The welfare queen trope is a complicated social narrative in which race, gender, and class are interlocked. The welfare queen metaphor does not simply embody images of Black women; its broad-ranging scope is deeply embedded in almost every facet of our social and political discourse. The episodes recounted here of Vanessa Williams, Anita Hill, Carol Moseley Braun, Lani Guinier, and Joycelyn Elders were all heavily influenced by the welfare queen narrative. Noted legal scholar Lani Guinier was branded a "Quota Queen" by conservative political groups in their effort to block her nomination to a top position in the Justice Department. As Patricia Williams observed, "'Quota Queen' evoked images of welfare queens and other moochers who rise to undeserved heights, complaining unwarrantedly all the way. Lani Guinier, the complex human with a distinguished history, was reduced to a far-left 'element'...."

[38] http://www.issues2000.org/Celeb/Bill_Clinton_Welfare_+_Poverty.htm.

The queen trope was perpetuated by the media. The day after Professor Guinier was nominated to the subcabinet post, *The Wall Street Journal* published an opinion piece by Clint Bolick, the litigation director of the right-wing organization, The Institute for Justice. Bolick's piece was titled "BILL CLINTON'S QUOTA QUEENS," of which Guinier was one. Bolick's piece—and most articles in the media—failed to give Guinier the opportunity to contest the dominant narrative. In fact, Guinier was effectively silenced until five years are her retracted nomination, when she wrote her own book.

In her memoir, Guinier addressed the pervasiveness and the problem of the quota queen trope, observing

> Though "Quota Queen" was coined in the plural the day after the formal nomination, the term was quickly used to target me alone. After all, as a law professor I was the only one with a paper trail. Many of my ideas were complex and thus easily distorted through sound bites. In my law review articles, I expressed reservations about unfettered majority rule – Madison's majority tyranny – and about the need sometimes to disaggregate the majority in order to ensure fair representation for all substantial minorities. Some columnists who attacked me praised remarkably similar ideas, but in a different context. George Will for example, had opined in a newspaper column: 'The Framers also understood that stable, tyrannical majorities can best be prevented by the multiplication of minority interests, so the majority at any moment will be just a transitory coalition of minorities.' The difference was that what I used to illustrate my academic point about the limitations of winner-take-all majority rule was not, as it was in George Will's example, the minority of well-to-do landlords in New York City. I wrote instead about the political exclusion of the Black minority in many local county and municipal governing bodies in the United States.

Guinier traced the roots of the welfare queen image right back to their origins, adding,

> I became Reagan's welfare queen tooling around the neighborhood in her Cadillac, mocking the hard work of others and the hard labor undertaken to produce this Democratic system. The image of the undeserving poor was transformed into the image of the undeserving voter who would benefit by me – their champion – manipulating the rules to distort democracy in favor of my chosen few. I was not only asking for what they didn't deserve or hadn't earned. I was willing to corrupt the entire democratic system to get it for them.

During May and June 1993, I was displayed in cartoon and narrative in more than 330 articles as a "Quota Queen." *Newsweek* magazine used the term in a headline, CROWNING A QUOTA QUEEN?, to signal a story in which the term 'welfare' was also featured prominently. The subtext was that of the welfare mother, with one hand outstretched palm-up, the other resting saucily on her hip as if to say, 'I dare you not to give me what is *mine, mine, mine.*' It no longer mattered that I had not even written on welfare. No one cared that, in fact, I did not believe in quotas. That I was a democratic idealist became irrelevant. No one bothered to try to understand my vision of dispersed and shared power.

Guinier wrote astutely and incisively about the way in which she was turned into a queen by the media, but she was not the only Black woman who suffered that fate. Similarly, Surgeon General Joycelyn Elders was unceremoniously marked a "Condom Queen" as a result of her position in which she advocated the availability of condoms in public schools as a public health strategy for halting the spread of HIV/AIDS. What made Elders' position untenable, of course, and which ultimately led to her resignation, was that Elders' advocacy of condoms (as opposed to the less realistic strategy of advocating abstinence) was sexually evocative, setting her up as a sex queen, who is not, after all, unrelated to the welfare queen. Rather than understand Elders' position as a realistic and potentially useful manipulation of the erotic, as articulated by Audre Lorde in her essay, "Uses of the Erotic," Elders was lambasted for her alleged call for adolescent sexual promiscuity and, indeed, promiscuity.

Elders recognized the power of the erotic. She spoke out publicly in 1993–1994 about issues that the Black women of Combahee spoke about behind closed doors 15 years earlier. She was also unafraid to publicly address the racialized and sexualized aspects of public health that prevented optimal well-being for all Americans and minorities in particular. In a speech at the annual meeting of the National Family Planning and Reproductive Health Association, representing about 4000 clinics, Elders said:

> The Medicaid system must have been developed by a White male slave owner. It pays for you to be pregnant and have a baby, but it won't pay for family planning…. [I]t fails to provide services to poor women to prevent unwanted pregnancies, and this failure contributes to poverty, ignorance and enslavement. White male slave owners wanted a lot of healthy slaves, people to work. We don't need slaves anymore. We need healthy, educated, motivated children with hope. We need to really invest in family planning.

After people took offense at her remarks, Elders offered a supplementary explanation:

> What I meant was, if you're poor and ignorant, with a child, you're a slave. Meaning that you are never going to get out of it. These women are in bondage to a kind of slavery that the 13th Amendment just didn't deal with. The old master provided food, clothing, and health care to slaves because he wanted them to get up and go to work in the morning. And so on welfare you get food, clothing, and shelter – you get survival, but you can't really do anything else. You can't control your life.

The following comments led to her being called the "condom queen":

> Condoms are not the government's solution to the teenage pregnancy crisis. But we want to make condoms available to those who choose to be sexually active. I am not in the opinion that just because you have a condom, you are going to go out and have sex. There is not a person in this room that does not have car insurance, but you're not going to go out and have a wreck because of it.

When asked at a press conference in 1987, when she was chosen to head the Arkansas Health Department, whether she would pursue the distribution of condoms in school-based clinics as a means of reducing teenage pregnancy, she replied, "Well, we're not going to put them on their lunch trays, but yes." Asked about being called the "condom queen," Elders replied, "If I thought it would help persuade young people to protect themselves, I'd wear a crown with a condom on it." Elders' remarks were dramatic, stirring controversy and alienating a more conservative public afraid to talk openly about sexuality from her views, even if they shared them. Finally, it was the Surgeon General's suggestion that the topic of masturbation be included in the public school curriculum about sexuality that led to her ultimate downfall in the Clinton administration. President Clinton misconstrued Elders's comments on masturbation *information*, saying that she called for *instruction*. On December 9, 1994, Clinton asked her to resign after Elders answered a physician's question at a professional meeting. She had said that teaching the facts about masturbation might well be included in educating schoolchildren about their sexuality. Clinton's response was, "Well, I'm sorry but we can't just have any more of this and I want your resignation by 2:30 P.M."

An ousted official normally is permitted to maintain the illusion that she has voluntarily stepped aside, and there is a polite exchange of letters. The White House took pains to make clear that Clinton had demanded that Elders leave.

Elders was in the unique position of being a Black woman in a presidential post like the Kennedy Commission women, but Elders publicly articulated the radical feminist theories espoused by the Combahee women. The PCSW women might argue that Elders was fired because she was Black, and the National Black Feminist Organization might argue that she was fired because she was a Black woman. The women of the Combahee River Collective would have been likely to argue that a far more complex dynamic was at play. Born in poverty, Dr. Joycelyn Elders was an educated, eventually upper-middle-class Black woman who spoke out about the erotic. To understand contemporary Black feminism and Black women's experiences in politics, one must turn toward the history of Black feminist political groups as discussed earlier in this book.

As Patricia Williams so aptly concluded: "The use of the term 'queen' to describe Dr. Elders, another Black woman ultimately driven from her post in a doggedly-waged smear campaign, highlights the extent to which the connotations of the term demand some explicit consideration" (Egg, 145–146). Finally, one often-ignored element of Clarence Thomas's testimony before the Senate confirmation committee was his shameful invoking of the welfare queen stereotype in denigrating his sister, Emma Mae Martin, for his own political advantage. Although the welfare queen trope did not hold anywhere near the prominent public position in the 1990s that it did with the Reagan administration, the welfare queen still played a disturbing, significant role within the Clinton administration. Welfare reform was a major theme of Clinton's electoral message in both 1992 and 1996. In 1992, Clinton's promotion of welfare reform positioned him as a new, different kind of Democrat not beholden to the traditional Democratic special interests. As Nancy Fraser (1993) noted: "Clinton's winning electoral strategy involved muting so-called claims of so-called special interests, especially Blacks and organized labor." Clinton's positioning away from the "liberal interest groups" such as minorities, feminists, and labor was a blatant attempt to appeal to the disenchanted working-class and white ethnic groups that had defected from the Democratic Party as part of the backlash against liberalism in past presidential elections. By publicly reprimanding Black leaders, including Jesse Jackson, Clinton was attempting to market himself as a "new Democrat" who was indeed "independent" from and not bound to these liberal special interests.

The use of welfare as a wedge issue was a crucial element in this strategy. As a result of the political restructuring of social welfare discourse, welfare by the 1980s had become a medium beyond public assistance and relief. As Fraser (1993) stated, "During the 1980s in the United States 'welfare' increasingly served as a vehicle for expressing such stresses, while also coding antagonisms of gender, race, and class." Clinton's shrewd self-promotion under the "new Democrat" label was an attempt to counter the advantages conservatives had been able to exploit on the racially charged issues involving welfare, poverty, and race. Numerous campaign advertisements in 1992 were aired espousing the Clinton-Gore ticket as a "different kind of Democrat." One television spot showed Clinton speaking from the governor's mansion in Arkansas and saying:

> For so long government has failed us, and one of its worst failures has been welfare. I have a plan to end welfare as we know it – to break the cycle of welfare dependency. We'll provide education, job training and childcare, but then those who are able to work must go to work, either in the private sector or in the public service. I know it can work. In my state we've moved 17,000 people from welfare rolls to payrolls. It's time to make welfare what it should be – a second chance, not a way of life.

This strong emphasis on welfare reform by the Clinton-Gore ticket was an attempt to break the Democratic Party's connection to the current welfare system, which had severely weakened the party's overall credibility. The liberal silence on a number of these complicated social issues involving race and poverty has been deadly. As Edsall and Edsall stated:

> In political terms, such a fundamental omission from the social policy debate by liberals has opened the door for conservatives to profit by focusing public attention on morality-laden 'values' issues – issues running the gamut from the lack of labor-force participation in the ghetto, to sexual promiscuity, to drug abuse, to teen pregnancy, to crime and so on.[39]

[39] Edsall, M. D., & Edsall, T. B. (1991). *Chain Reaction: The Impact of Race, Rights, and Taxes on American Politics.* New York: W. W. Norton.

Clintonism can be seen as an attempt to address this omission from social policy by Democrats, but as Fraser noted: "Welfare reform a la Clinton continues to target and stigmatize the poor."

Clinton's utilization of welfare reform to distinguish his "new Democrat" credentials also exposed his acceptance of the conservatives' negative construction of welfare and welfare recipients and allowed the President himself to endorse and perpetuate, albeit indirectly, the welfare queen narrative. The strong emphasis on punitive measures such as time limits and strict work requirements within the PROWRA illustrates the measure's focus on the behavior of recipients, rather than structural explanations, as the fundamental cause for welfare dependency and poverty. The popularity of work requirements "implies that recipients are *shirkers* who stay on the rolls longer than necessary in order to avoid work" (ibid.). Additionally, the Clinton slogan "welfare should be a second chance, not a way of life" implies that there was strong misuse and abuse of the system by recipients. The "second chance" phrase also seemed to hark back to the original, idealistic, ideological basis of poor relief, which relied heavily upon the distinction between the legitimate, deserving poor and illegitimate, non-deserving poor. The second chance language also simplistically reduces the plight of welfare recipients to "chance" opportunities in life. Additionally, it implies that AFDC recipients already had, and *blown*, their first chance.

Furthermore, Clinton's espousal of welfare reform maintained the distinction between social entitlement and obligation, with Social Security and Medicare falling in the former category, while AFDC, food stamps, and Social Security Insurance (SSI) fall in the latter. The maintenance of the dichotomy between "good" social insurance (i.e., universal welfare programs that are not typically designated as "welfare") versus the means-tested "bad" welfare programs further stigmatizes the welfare recipients as undeserving, while social insurance recipients are deserving. As Fraser and Gordon noted: "Such programs were constructed to create the misleading appearance that beneficiaries merely got back what they put in." For all Clinton's talk about "welfare reform," his administrative actions continued the two-tier welfare system that has been dominant within American social and political landscape since the Social Security Act of 1935. As Fraser commented: "Campaign promises to 'end welfare as we know it' never contemplated eliminating the division between social insurance and public assistance."

One of the greatest concerns with the popularity of Clinton's welfare reform package was its maintenance of a conservative social welfare discourse that upheld the exploitation of racial stereotypes and marginalized disadvantaged minority groups. The so-called welfare reform measure that was passed in 1996, like other "behavioral" policy solutions (family cap, workfare, and the like), shifted the entire burden and fault of the poverty and the system onto those who were most disadvantaged themselves. The entire political and ideological brunt of PROWRA was principally concentrated on flawed misperceptions of the "welfare system" and racist stereotypes of its recipients.

Contrary to the dominant welfare queen stereotype, the typical welfare recipient is neither Black, nor has numerous additional children to receive benefits. According to a December 15, 1996, *Minneapolis Star Tribune* article on welfare reform, in 1995 AFDC had 13.6 million recipients, including 9.3 million children and 4.3 million adults, virtually all of whom were single mothers. Demographically, about 37% of AFDC parents are white; 36% are Black, 20% Hispanic, about 3% Asian, and about 1% Native American. Additionally, the average AFDC family size was actually shrinking over the last 20 years of the program, from 3.6 in the early 1970s to about 2.8 in the 1990s. Furthermore, there has been no empirical evidence to date to substantiate claims that availability of welfare has provided incentives and motivation for having additional children. Finally, in terms of spending, the biggest increases in outlays (besides the "special insurance programs") in the means-tested welfare programs are found in Medicaid, medical insurance for the poor, and SSI, which have tripled and doubled in spending respectively since 1980. Once adjusted for inflation, AFDC spending actually held *flat* for 15 years. Spending on food stamps had also been held flat from 1980 to 1990, but has since increased by one-third due to a 30% increase in eligible recipients.

The typical duration on welfare is difficult to determine because many recipients cycle on and off the AFDC program. If we were to count first-time applicants, 56% leave AFDC within a year and 70% leave within two years. But counting all return spells, about 52% of applicants stay on AFDC less than three years in a lifetime and about 35% will be on AFDC for five years or more.[40] As two prominent social scientists and welfare

---

[40] *Minneapolis Star Tribune*, December 5, 1996, A37.

policy architects, Mary Jo Bane and David Ellwood, commented in *Welfare Realities*,[41] welfare durations are not just a short-term situation depicted by liberals, nor are they a long-term "narcotic" as described by conservatives.

A most troubling concern with neoliberal Clintonism was that minority groups continued to be shortchanged within the political process as their interests were sacrificed in appeals to the "swing" Reagan Democrats, namely, working-class whites. Adding insult to injury, racist caricatures of minorities, and especially that of the welfare queen, were used to appeal to these voters, even if only subtly. The Clinton Administration did not establish a stellar record of interactions with outspoken Black women. Additionally, it was also particularly ironic and paradoxical that this convergence of the passage of welfare reform and continued manipulation of racist caricatures (especially Black women) occurred within a "Democratic" administration. The emergence of the New Democrat philosophy can partly be attributed to the sense of liberal "inevitability" that developed in the late 1980s in response to continued defeat of national Democratic candidates. This position, espoused by a number of influential "liberal" writers and thinkers, seems to argue that the resulting disastrous interaction between race and social policy, politics, and liberalism was inescapable.

Is Bill Clinton Black?

So what can we learn from this? Blacks in general and Black women in particular have been blindly devoted to the Democratic Party. This has led to disappointment at best, and mistreatment at worst. Black women have been labeled condom queens, quota queens, and welfare queens and have not been defended by those who have claimed to be our greatest allies, such as President Clinton. An example of this blind devotion is Toni Morrison's claim that Bill Clinton was our first Black President. In a 1998 *New Yorker* article, Morrison argued that when Clinton committed a "profound, perhaps irrevocable, error in judgment, ... the Republicans smelled blood, and a shot at the totalitarian power they believe is rightfully theirs." She went on to say:

---

[41]Bane, M. J., & Ellwood, D. T. (1996). *Welfare Realities: From Rhetoric to Reform.* Cambridge, MA: Harvard University Press, p. 42.

...[T]his is our first Black president. Blacker than any actual Black person who could ever be elected in our children's lifetime. After all, Clinton displays almost every trope of Blackness: single-parent household, born poor, working-class, saxophone playing, McDonald's loving boy from Arkansas.

Morrison's framing was problematic. Jazz and junk food are not what make people Black. In fact, it was precisely Clinton's "white skin privilege" (a term that Bill Bradley learned from Cornel West), that allowed him to remain in office despite sex, lies, and audiotape, while making his Black appointees disappear.

Morrison held onto this position until 2008, when Senator Barack Obama competed to become the Democratic nominee for the President of the USA against rival, Senator Hilary Rodham Clinton. Vijay Prashad observed that,

When Bill Clinton ran for the White House in 1992, I was deeply annoyed. He represented so much that we, on the left, despised: The reaction within the ranks of the Democratic Party's elite that wanted to "save" the party form what it saw as the excesses of a combination of the New Left, the already declining trade unions, and, most importantly, the Rainbow cultivated and mobilized by Jesse Jackson's two runs for the presidency (1984 and 1988). Clinton was despised by the rank and file trade unionists, most of who turned out to vote for Jerry Brown and Paul Tsongas (who had already left the race O in the Connecticut primary. Brown opposed NAFTA and endorsed the concepts of a living wage, both positions anathema to Clinton. Few of us on the left went into that general election, and into the Clinton years with any illusions.[42]

Prashad goes on to write that once Clinton is in office,

The braying of the right was so abhorrent and hypocritical that Clinton gained some measure of forgiveness from those who were otherwise livid with him. It was in this context, that Toni Morrison said that he was being treated like a Black man: given no quarter, shown no mercy, but treated guilty as charged without any consideration or process. (ibid.)

---

[42] Prashad, V. (2008, May 22). "The Revelation of Bill Clinton," Znet.

Prashad explains how things have changed between 1998 and 2008.

> But now, finally Clinton has given us some honesty. He has opened his heart during this primary season, joining Hilary Clinton in pandering to the Old South, the hard core racist bloc that was never reconciled to Civil Rights, that continues to blame Blacks for the vivisections of their economic fortunes. It is this bloc that handed Hilary Clinton the primaries of Pennsylvania, Indiana, West Virginia and Kentucky. After her loss in the South Carolina primary, where the Democratic electorate is substantially Black, Hilary Clinton's husband, Bill, told the press, "Jesse Jackson won South Carolina in 1984 and 1988. Jackson ran a good campaign and Obama ran a good campaign here." (ibid.)

It was after these remarks were made that I predicted that Toni Morrison would take back her invitation of Bill Clinton into the Black family, and indeed she did.

CHAPTER 4

The '90s in Context: A History of Black Women in American Politics

As far as many Blacks were concerned, the emergence of the women's movement couldn't have been more untimely or irrelevant. Historians trace its roots to 1961, with the President's Commission on the Status of Women chaired by Eleanor Roosevelt. At a time when Black students were languishing in southern jails, when Black full time working women were earning 57 percent of what their White peers were earning, the Commission concentrated its attention on the growing number of middle-class women who were forced to enter the labor market in low skill, low paid jobs.[1]

The emergence of the women's movement was untimely for Black women in general, but for a select group it *was* relevant. Black women, who had largely been left out of civil rights politics and, especially, leadership, hoped, if only briefly, that they would be able to stake a place within the women's movement where they could promote their concerns as people who were both female and Black. As this chapter will demonstrate, that hope was both heady and intense, though short-lived. The first section of this book compares the ideological positions and political agendas of the Black women who were appointed to the Fourth Consultation of President John F. Kennedy's Commission on the Status of Women (PCSW) to those of the National Black Feminist Organization

---

[1] Giddings, P. (1984). *When and Where I Enter: The Impact of Black Women on Race and Sex in America*. New York: William Morrow and Company, p. 299.

© The Author(s) 2019
D. Harris, *Black Feminist Politics from Kennedy to Trump*,
https://doi.org/10.1007/978-3-319-95456-1_4

(NBFO) and the Combahee River Collective (CRC). By examining the ideological and political perspectives of these three Black women's groups, the evolution of Black feminism from 1961 to 1980 can be documented.

The first group, the PCSW, was composed of financially and educationally privileged Black women chosen by officials of the federal government to serve on a national commission of women that was charged with the task of identifying and articulating women's concerns. The NBFO and the CRC, by contrast, included middle- and working-class Black women who had been active in civil rights and grassroots Black organizations. The varied experiences of Black women activists served as the crucible for the development of Black feminist ideologies during that period. Despite differences in education and social class, these Black women and their organizations were aware of three overlapping realities: (1) There were inextricable links between gender and racial identity; (2) Their socioeconomic status was, at least in part, determined by both their gender and racial identity; and (3) There was a need to organize collectively to redress the injustices of these realities.

Close examination of the political activities of these Black women and their organizations reveals that each group's ideological perspectives represented an evolution of thought that grew out of the preceding group's work. The Black women on the Kennedy Commission, for instance, articulated more conservative notions about gender than the women of the NBFO, who, in turn, articulated more conservative notions about female sexuality and the disadvantages of the capitalist system than the women of the CRC. Unlike the women of the PCSW and the NBFO, members of the CRC agreed that sexual orientation was distinctive and separate from gender and racial identity, and they organized around that realization, a third characteristic that contributed to the condition of multiple oppressions.

Each of these three groups struggled with defining their priorities and determining their strategies accordingly. As the result of the pressures of political expediency, both external and internal, the groups were often forced to adhere to a single-item agenda, singling out race *or* gender *or* sexuality as the issue around which they would organize and act. While the Black feminist movement can be seen as evolving from the relatively liberal and single-minded focus on gender of the Kennedy Commission to the more radical and multifaceted focus on gender, race, class, and sexual orientation of the CRC, race work often trumped other aspects of individual and collective identity. I am not presuming that the predecessors of twenty-first-century Black feminism were *solely* concerned with race work, but as Jeanne Noble points out, the women of the PCSW, the NBFO, and the CRC all strategically deprioritized gender depending on available openings in the social movement and political opportunity structures. Later efforts were more successful, however, at integrating multiple issues into a single activist agenda. The later groups existed as a result of the efforts of the earlier ones; in fact, there was significant overlap in their membership. Furthermore, the ideological and strategic development among Black feminists coincided with the growth of the Civil Rights, Black Power, and Women's Liberation movements, to which they made important contributions.

Each new generation of Black feminists was more radical than the preceding one, and each new generation revitalized the organizational structure of its group to reflect a more progressive and more inclusive movement. The PCSW had been formal, convened as a panel of experts by a government entity, but the NBFO and the CRC were grassroots organizations that experimented with the structure of small consciousness-raising (CR) groups rather than the formation of large formal institutions. This model of organizational work sprung out of the experiences of the young participants, many of who came from middle-class backgrounds and had worked in the South in the Student Nonviolent Coordinating Committee (SNCC). Some of these Black feminists had also been members of Students for a Democratic Society (SDS) and other radical student organizations in the North, thus, the structure or a grassroots organization with an activist bent was both familiar and transferable to the ideologies and missions of the emerging NBFO and CRC.

ORAL HISTORY AS EVIDENCE

Oral histories and analysis of archival data are used here to document the evolution and activity of the PCSW, the NBFO, and the CRC. The minutes from the Negro Women's Consultation for the PCSW were reviewed at the John F. Kennedy Library in Boston, and the minutes from the NBFO were provided by Margaret Sloan, the organization's founding director. The minutes from the CRC retreats were provided by Gloria Akasha Hull, as were mission statements, pamphlets, and other unpublished materials. The Pauli Murray papers from the Schlesinger Library and materials from the Black Women's Oral History Project

provided additional valuable information, as did secondary sources, journal articles, and newspapers. The archival data are important because
they contain the public records of these groups; however, one limitation
is that these public statements often do not indicate the personal experiences and responses of the people involved.

To fill this gap between the organizational histories and the personal
histories of the women who comprised the organizations, oral histories
were collected from 11 Black women who participated in these history-making groups. These interviews of Black women's lived experiences
are treated as primary sources in this book. Albert Memmi[2] has noted
that what is central to race theory is the interpretation of differences and
what inferences may be drawn from such differences. Taking Memmi's
suggestion, I asked the interviewees for their interpretations of political
organizing between 1961 and 1980 and drew my own inferences from
the transcripts. Like historian Evelyn Brooks Higginbotham,[3] I found
that race served as a "metalanguage" for the construction and representation of other social and power relations, namely those based on gender,
class, and sexuality. Oral history becomes an important source of evidence
because it allows us to examine what theorists have described as the particular epistemological position of Black women in American society,
a position that sociologist Patricia Hill Collins refers to as the "outsider
within."[4] Using a Black feminist theoretical framework to understand the
roles of Black women allows us to determine *whose* knowledge defines
Black women. According to C. S'thembile West,[5] ontology is the essence
of being: "How I be; Who I be; What I be; not how I am or who I am
or what I am."[6] The Black woman must decide how she defines herself.
To outsiders, this conjugation of the auxiliary verb "be" appears to be
improper grammar, but West argues that only the Black woman can tell
us what is improper about her defining her being.

[2] In *The Colonizer and the Colonized*. Boston: Beacon Press, 1965.

[3] In "African-American Women's History and the Metalanguage of Race." *Signs* 17 (2):
251–274, 1992.

[4] In "Learning from the Outsider Within: The Sociological Significance of Black Feminist
Thought." *Social Problems* 33 (6) (October/December): 14–32, 1986.

[5] In "Afrocentricity: Moving Outside of the Comfort Zone." *The Journal of Physical
Education, Dance, and Recreation* 65 (5): 28, 1994.

[6] As cited in Barbara Omalade's. (1994). *The Rising Song of the African American
Women*. New York: Routledge, p. 35.

If Black women reject others' definitions of them, they must then define or redefine their own being and provide their own ontologies, or theories of being. Historically, Black women's being has depended on the balance between self and community, for without the individual there is no community, and without the community there is no individual. Black women's resistance to being defined by others is documented here through an examination of their personal narratives. Letters, autobiographies, oral histories, and personal narratives provide a rich source of data for understanding and interpreting Black feminists' ontologies. Research that reveals the social, political, and economic context for these narratives provides the historical background for explaining Black feminist theory, which is thus grounded in Black women's experiences.

The narratives offered by the members of the three Black women's groups included in this study—the Fourth Consultation of the PCSW, the NBFO, and the CRC—examine the transformation in Black feminist ideologies from the community organizing of the civil rights era to the preoccupation with the politics of identity in the 1970s and 1980s.

ENTER JFK: THE FORMATION OF THE PRESIDENT'S COMMISSION ON THE STATUS OF WOMEN

By the time the 1960 presidential campaign began, John F. Kennedy's clear liberal theme—his exhortation to "get the country moving again"[7]—resonated strongly for many Americans, and Black Americans in particular. During Kennedy's campaign for the presidency, the Black community's political power was demonstrated in the election of five Blacks to the House of Representatives and Kennedy's own crucial margin of votes in his narrow victories in Illinois, Michigan, and South Carolina. Once Kennedy was in office, he began to implement programs to address the problems American society was confronting. One of the central issues in Kennedy's social justice agenda was addressing the racial divide that existed, and, in particular, to rectify the historical exclusion of Black women within the national agenda.

When President Kennedy entered office, his national reform agenda did not include women; however, a well-developed program concerning and involving women—one that squared with the President's own

[7] Kennedy, J. F. (1960). Remarks. Allentown, PA. http://www.presidency.ucsb.edu/ws/index.php?pid=74265. Retrieved on May 19, 2018.

views and the rest of the liberal agenda—emerged from a coalition led by the administration's Women's Bureau. Kennedy's ties to the progressive labor community made him especially receptive to the coalition's plan of action; the internal politics of Kennedy's administration gave a particular shape to the development of a strategy of which the PCSW was the centerpiece. Ideas for what came to be called the Kennedy Commission came from many sources. The New York Business and Professional Women's Clubs had written to the President on inauguration day to request the creation of a panel to discuss utilization of mature women's skills. Kennedy turned the letter over to Esther Peterson, director of the Women's Bureau, who replied that a similar plan was already being considered. In addition to Peterson's vigorous support, Katherine Ellickson, formerly assistant director of the Social Security Department of the AFL-CIO, and Dollie Rowther Robinson, a longtime union employee at the Women's Bureau, pressed the President for the establishment of a commission specific to the concerns of women. Robinson, a Black woman, urged that the President expresses the same concern for women's opportunities as he had about racial discrimination, and she argued that the commission would be such a vehicle. Labor Secretary Arthur Goldberg took the women's plan to the President.

Although ideas for the President's Commission came from many areas, it was, above all, the brainchild of labor union women. Because the labor movement had a history of attempting to achieve goals for women at least partially through federal legislation and executive action, a presidential commission seemed to be an appropriate avenue for change to Peterson and her colleagues. Kennedy, more closely allied to the labor movement than his immediate predecessors, heeded the voice of a woman with a labor union background instead of one with political debts to repay. As a result, in 1961 federal policy toward women veered in a new direction.

THE PCSW AND NOW:
PRECURSORS TO NBFO AND COMBAHEE

Women have basic rights that should be respected and fostered as part of our Nation's commitment to human dignity, freedom and democracy. It is appropriate... to set forth before the world the story of women's progress in a free democratic society, to review recent accomplishments, and to acknowledge frankly the further steps that must be taken.

This is a task for the entire nation. It is my hope that the Commission's report will indicate what remains to be done to demolish prejudices and outmoded customs which act as barriers to the full partnership of women in democracy. The Commission will welcome recommendations from all groups on this crucial matter. Progress will require the cooperation of the whole community.

President John F. Kennedy, December 14, 1961

The labor women's proposal was approved by President Kennedy and the PCSW was convened into being by executive order in December, 1961, a full four years before the moment historians mark as the beginning of the feminist movement. The establishment of the PCSW was significant because it not only represented a tangible sign of concern about women's issues from the highest authority in the land, but it would also pave the way for significant policy and program legislation that would have a dramatic impact on women's political involvement. The enactment of equal pay legislation in 1963 and the passage of fair treatment and non-discrimination laws as codified in Title IX of the Education Amendments of 1972 are just two examples of the long-term implications of the work that was performed by the women of the PCSW in 1961. The creation of the PCSW gave a new legitimacy to the struggle against discrimination based on sex. As Betty Friedan wrote in 1963,

> the very existence of the President's Commission on the Status of Women, under Eleanor Roosevelt's leadership, creates a climate where it is possible to recognize and do something about discrimination against women, in terms not only of pay but of subtle barriers to opportunity.[8]

The members of the PCSW initiated a national discussion that continued into the 1990s.

The membership of the PCSW and its subsidiary bodies represented many constituencies. Fifteen women served with eleven men on the commission itself, with ten members of the commission coming from the federal government, including the Attorney General, the Chairman of the Civil Services Commission, and the secretaries of Commerce, Agriculture, Labor, and Health, Education, and Welfare. The director

---

[8]As quoted in Cynthia Harrison. (1988). *On Account of Sex: The Politics of Women's Issues, 1945–1968.* Berkeley: University of California Press, p. 160.

of the Women's Bureau, Esther Peterson, along with Labor Secretary Arthur Goldberg, oversaw the selection procedures, choosing members from women's organizations, labor unions, educational institutions, and governmental agencies to supply more than 120 participants for the commission and its seven technical committees. No official of the National Women's Party was invited to join the commission, although Peterson did include two women identified with the pro-ERA National Federation of Business and Professional Women's Clubs. Recognizing that a commission without ERA support would lack credibility, Peterson cleared the way for the two aforementioned groups' participation by omitting a statement of purpose indicating a preconceived position on the amendment.[9]

The PCSW considered four topics to be of particular importance and focused its energies on addressing these issues in its meetings: private employment opportunities, new patterns of volunteer work, portrayals of women by the media, and the problems of Negro women. The inclusion of the last topic reflected the Commission's acknowledgment of the problems of dual discrimination borne by Black women. This acknowledgment was promising, but the promise was ultimately not born out: The written report that represented the culmination of the PCSW's work failed to incorporate the resulting recommendations.

THE FOURTH CONSULTATION

The Fourth Consultation brought together educators, editors of Black magazines, representatives of the New York Urban League, and government officials. Although the Black women who participated on the commission were in no way economically or educationally representative of most Black women, their voices were relevant and their agendas were significant. One of the most compelling figures of the PCSW's subcommittee on the problems of Negro women was the Chair of the Fourth Consultation, Dorothy Height. Height, who was born in Richmond, Virginia on March 24, 1912, had an interesting background in professional development and activism that prepared her to understand and convey some of the unique needs of American black women. During her formative years, her family moved to Rankin, Pennsylvania.

---

[9]Harrison, Cynthia E. (1980). "A 'New Frontier' for Women: The Public Policy of the Kennedy Administration." *The Journal of American History* 67 (3): 630–646.

After completing Rankin High School, Height applied to Barnard, a women's college, in New York City. She was informed by the school, however, that they already had two Black students and therefore she would have to wait a term or more.[10] Rather than suffer the wait, Ms. Height opted to attend New York University. She graduated in 1924 after three years of study and received her master's degree in educational psychology the following year. Height became an investigator for the New York City Department of Welfare and eventually rose to the position of district supervisor. One of the first elected officers of the United Christian Youth Movement and active in the Harlem Christian Youth Council, Height participated in a select planning group with Eleanor Roosevelt for the 1938 World Youth Congress. Her long affiliation with the YWCA began in 1937 when she became the assistant director of the Emma Ransom House in Harlem. Later, as the executive director of the Phyllis Wheatley YWCA in Washington, DC, her involvement in the 1947 YWCA Convention led to the adoption of its first interracial charter; she thereafter became director of the YWCA's Center for Racial Justice.

In 1947 Dr. Height became the national president of Delta Sigma Theta Sorority, Inc. During the nine years she held the position, according to Paula Giddings' history of the organization, "neither the direction nor the substance of the initiatives changed under her leadership, but the breadth and interest in them did."[11] Under her leadership, the sorority started a bookmobile to serve Black communities in Georgia and held a series of nationally broadcast town meetings. In 1950, Height organized the sorority's first international chapter in Port-au-Prince, Haiti.

Dr. Height's leadership was not limited to the already impressive resume with local organizations in New York City and the presidency of the sorority, however. Height's affiliation with the National Council of Negro Women began in the 1930s, and she eventually became President in 1957; she still held this position when she chaired the Fourth Consultation. The council, created by Mary McLeod Bethune, was conceived as a means of uniting women from disparate groups, as well as those who did not identify with any social or political organization, with the ambitious goal of representing the "national and international

[10] Height, D. (2005). *Open Wide the Freedom Gates: A Memoir.* Washington, DC: Public Affairs.

[11] Giddings, P. (1988). *In Search of Sisterhood: Delta Sigma Theta and the Challenge of the Black Sorority Movement.* New York: William Morrow and Company, p. 219.

concerns of black women."[12] The organization voiced concerns for protective labor legislation and in 1964 went on record opposing the Equal Rights Amendment (ERA). One member warned against the council's being led astray by the promise of equal rights: "We are being rocked to sleep by a trick phrase—one dear to us and to under-privileged groups, therefore calculated to dull our ability for discriminating between what is good and what appears to be good."[13] Although the NCNW adopted a position against support of the ERA, Dorothy Height was herself in favor of the ERA.

Throughout the 1960s and 1970s, the National Council of Negro Women attempted to be aware of its position as an organization that would benefit all Black people. Although Height had served as a member on the US Department of Defense Advisory Committee on Women in the Services during World War II,[14] during the peak of the civil rights movement, her concerns for women as a group became subordinate to her concerns for Black rights. Under her direction, the NCNW worked primarily to promote a new concept of equality for Black women, reflecting the approach taken by the Kennedy Commission.

Height was interested in the way in which the PCSW framed its approach to discussing equality. She observed that the PCSW treated women not as a political cause, but as integral players in political and social life whose opinions and ideas needed to be heard and integrated into the dominant discourse. The Fourth Consultation addressed the Black woman specifically, acknowledging in its discussions that virtually every form of discrimination affected Black women more severely than white women. Among extant written materials is a paper penned by the members that described how pending PCSW recommendations, such as the extension of minimum wage laws, would assist minority women in particular. Other matters for which the women of the advocated were better, Black-run community programs and the inclusion of Afro-American history and culture in the elementary school curriculum

[12]National Council of Negro Women, Inc. http://www.ncnw.org/about/index.htm. Retrieved on December 20, 2007.

[13]As cited in Franke, K. M. (1995). "The Central Mistake of Sex Discrimination Law: The Disaggregation of Sex from Gender." *University of Pennsylvania Law Review* 144 (1): 1–99.

[14]As cited in Berry, M. F. (1982). "Twentieth-Century Black Women in Education." *The Journal of Negro Education* 51 (3): 288–300.

to provide role models for Black children. The participants also raised an objection to the idea of forcing mothers who received Aid to Families with Dependent Children (AFDC) to work outside the home. In general, the consultation revealed that the Black women considered racial bias, not sex discrimination, their major handicap. Despite the fact that the Commission recognized the special hardships of Black women, it rejected an analogy between discrimination and remedies based on racism and those based on sex bias.

Patricia Bell-Scott is one of the few scholars to provide insight into Pauli Murray's hesitance to participate in the PCSW. She writes:

> John Kennedy's charm held no sway with Murray. Yes, she could not ignore the importance of the commission's charge or its stature. That Eleanor Roosevelt, Caroline Ware, and National Council of Negro women president Dorothy Height were part of this powerhouse ensured that the work would be of high quality and taken seriously.... Because Murray had more than twenty years of experience as a scholar and an activist in the areas of race and sex discrimination, the group asked her to draft an informational memorandum on women's constitutional rights that considered the feasibility of a constitutional amendment. To be working with the PCSW under Eleanor Roosevelt's leadership and to be appointed tutor of law at Yale, which gave her junior faculty status, made Murray as excited as a "puppy with two tails," which was her favorite expression.[15]

In Brittney C. Cooper's groundbreaking book, *Beyond Respectability: The Intellectual Thought of Race Women*, she provides new insight into the leadership of Pauli Murray. Cooper argues that Murray's personal papers at the Schlesinger Library and her two autobiographies, *Proud Shoe: The Story of an American Family* and *Song in a Weary Throat*, teach us that Murray's conceptualization of Jane Crow is one of the earliest conceptualizations of intersectional theory within Black Feminist thought.

When she served on one of the subcommittees of President Kennedy's Commission on the Status of Women, Murray wrote a memorandum and personally walked it around to key senators on Capitol Hill, whose votes were necessary to make sure the word "sex" remained in

---

[15] Scott, P. B. (2016). *The Firebrand and the First Lady: Portrait of a Friendship: Pauli Murray, Eleanor Roosevelt, and the Struggle for Social Justice*. New York: Vintage, pp. 306–307.

the 1964 Civil Rights Act. Not only did Murray's advocacy on behalf of the Civil Rights Act help ensure the inclusion of legal protection against sex discrimination, but she also laid the legal scaffolding for Kimberle Crenshaw's intersectional arguments about Black women's status as a protected legal class a quarter-century later.

Her contributions were invaluable to the Fourth Consultation. The report of the Fourth Consultation addressed five issues: (1) Negro family patterns, (2) employment opportunities, (3) vocational guidance, (4) community service and participation, and (5) adult education—and presented several relevant suggestions to enhance the roles of Black women in American society. The following section discusses these five issues and includes relevant background information about the women who participated in discussions and the formulation of recommendations regarding each issue.

Negro Family Patterns

One of the concerns of the PCSW was the matter of what it referred to as Negro family patterns. Drawing upon empirical and qualitative studies, the PCSW articulated how larger social trends, including educational access and utilization, shaped relationships, particularly within Black families. The report of the PCSW subcommittee cites a study of Negro women by Dr. Jeanne L. Noble, a doctoral dissertation titled "The Negro Woman's College Education," which contended that Negro women generally based their educational choices on perceived and actual vocational opportunities. Noble, herself a graduate of Howard University, served as president of Delta Sigma Theta Sorority from 1958 to 1963. She completed her master's and doctoral degrees at the Teachers College of New York's Columbia University. According to Paula Giddings, in the early fifties Dr. Noble contended that significant tensions existed within Black communities that could be attributed to gender differences. Giddings argued that the tension was exacerbated by the tendency of middle-class Black women to make independent decisions about engaging in relationships, irrespective of the marriage and childbearing trends of the period. Noble's study indicated that 75% of the college graduates she studied got married three to four years after graduation, while 16% waited more than seven years to marry. At the time, deferred marriage was unusual because the national median age for women to marry was 20.

Giddings also concludes that in a period when the average Black mother had four children and the average white mother had three, 38% of the women in Noble's study had one child. Fifteen percent had two children, and only six percent had three to six children. An overwhelming 41% had no children. Noble's explanation of these childbearing patterns among college-educated Black women is that the women in her study rejected the pressure to conform to dominant social expectations about the sexual and domestic "obligations" of women.

This pressure and expectation was a real one, and the members of the Commission had themselves adopted and perpetuated these norms. The participants in the Fourth Consultation blamed Black women for the destruction of the Black family, caused by their own "selfish" academic and professional ambitions. Commission members articulated their concern that the Negro male would be unable to assume the expected masculine role of defender, protector, and provider of the family under such conditions, particularly when his options were already limited by the constraints imposed by societal racism.

One of the most vocal members of the Fourth Consultation to express discontent with the status of the Negro family was Alice Allison Dunnigan. Dunnigan was the first Black woman to receive a prominent position in a presidential administration. Born in 1906, she was an educator, politician, and journalist. She received a teaching certificate from Kentucky State College and continued her studies in 1930 at West Kentucky Industrial College, where she received the first home economics certificate ever awarded by that institution. Dunnigan became a federal employee and worked her way through the ranks of the civil service. She also became chief of the Washington Bureau of the Associated Negro Press, the first Black woman to be admitted to the Capitol and White House Press Corps, and the first Black correspondent to travel with a President of the USA when she accompanied President Truman during the 1948 campaign. Her background in education, government service, and news reporting led to her appointment as education consultant to President Kennedy's Commission on Equal Employment Opportunity. In this position, Dunnigan conferred with labor and industry representatives about how best to assure equal job opportunities for minorities.

In the April 19, 1963, meeting of the Consultation on Problems of Negro Women, Dunnigan articulated a different interpretation of Negro family patterns that challenged the majority opinion of the PCSW.

Dunnigan surmised that Black families were inherently more matriarchal than white families because Black men were often prevented from obtaining gainful employment congruent with their skills and qualifications due to entrenched racism. Curiously, Black women had a comparatively easier time obtaining employment—while affected by racism, Black women were viewed as uniquely qualified for certain types of jobs, especially domestic work. As a result of this strange mechanism of the intersection of racism and sexism, Black women often became their families' breadwinners. Dunnigan's theory was met with resistance from the other members of the commission, including Dorothy Height.

Despite the commission's reluctance to admit the possibility of the legitimacy of Dunnigan's ideas, she did, in fact, have some support. Deborah Wolfe and Inabel Burns Lindsay were in agreement with Dunnigan's argument regarding the matriarchal family among Black communities. Wolfe served as education chief for the US House of Representatives Committee on Education and Labor from 1962 to 1965. In this position, she was instrumental in the development, passage, and implementation of some of the most innovative educational legislation written. She graduated from New Jersey State Teachers' College in 1937 with a degree in education. She earned her master's degree in rural education from Columbia University Teacher's College in 1938, and her doctorate from Columbia in 1945.

Inabel Burns Lindsay (1900–1983) served for 22 years as the dean of the Howard University School of Social Work, which she helped establish in the late 1930s. She received her master's degree from the University of Chicago in social work in 1937 and her doctorate from the University of Pittsburgh in 1952. In the April 19, 1963, discussion about the female-headed household, Wolfe and Lindsay indicated their receptivity to Dunnigan's ideas and challenged the Commission to think more deeply about the potential impact of women's breadwinner roles on all members of Black families and, by extension, Black communities. These women concluded that the responsibility of the Commission was to acknowledge the reality of Negro family patterns and to devise policy and program recommendations that would alleviate stressors on all family members.

The Commission did acknowledge the complexity of social influences upon the Negro family. Within the meetings it was acknowledged that more Negro women attended college and held college degrees than Negro males and because of these circumstances, Negro women frequently married below their educational standard. This phenomenon may have resulted in the woman earning more money than her husband. In such cases, the Black male partner often felt insecure or envious, feelings, which potentially precipitated the dissolution of families, thereby perpetuating the matriarchal family pattern. The consultation concluded that the matriarchal family type, in turn, caused problems for Negro children, both boys and girls, in developing their masculine or feminine roles.

On a practical level, the consultants expressed the strong hope that the Commission would advocate for more community childcare facilities, open to children of all economic levels and through all means—public, cooperative, and private. However, several participants stated that the establishment of additional childcare services should not be part of a program to try to force mothers of young children into the labor market by taking away public assistance. The final suggestion was that public assistance legislation be further improved to strengthen family life. Amendments were passed in 1961 to provide federal funds on a matching basis to states whose laws provided AFDC based on need, regardless of whether there was an employable male in the household. This remains an important issue because many states have not accepted the effort to maintain and strengthen family life during periods of economic dislocation. In fact, in many jurisdictions the unemployed father is, in effect, encouraged to desert his family in order for the family to be eligible for public aid.

Employment Opportunities

The PCSW subcommittee on Negro women's issues considered two facets of employment opportunity. The first was a look at white-collar, semi-professional, and professional opportunities; the second explored the issues of domestic household workers. One of the major problems identified was that Negro women often found that jobs were available to them only at the lowest economic and professional levels, whereas sales and clerical jobs were closed to them. The report explained, for example, that Negro women had difficulty obtaining secretarial jobs, since a major means of entering the secretarial field at that time was through graduation from a recognized business or secretarial school. Many of these schools, however, did not admit Negroes. The consultants' suggested remedy for this problem was vocational legislation. They advocated that the Manpower Training and Development Act be broadened so that the preparation and placement of Negro women workers in its programs for job training and retraining were expanded.

As was the case with family patterns, the topic of employment opportunities was a point of divisiveness among the members, and their diverse views resulted in fragmentation with respect to both philosophical and pragmatic treatments of the subject of employment. Some participants emphasized the widespread desire among Negro workers to move upward out of what they considered to be undesirable occupations. Others said that since many Negroes undoubtedly would continue to be in household work, upgrading skills and improvements in employment conditions was desirable.

In a discussion of the basic need for broadening opportunities for those in household employment, two additional approaches were suggested: (1) unionization of household workers to establish decent wages, hours, and standards of working conditions, and (2) facilities to help those who were qualified or desired further training gain and access better employment opportunities. It was anticipated that both of these efforts could lead to greater interest and incentives on the job, while simultaneously increasing the sense of dignity necessary for good job performance.

The subcommittee also pointed out that Negro women employed in household service often lacked Social Security coverage, partly because many employers failed to pay contributions to old-age, survivors', and disability insurance. The group urged that the federal government take further steps to enforce compliance with the law requiring that employers make Social Security contributions for these women and also to educate the Negro household worker about her rights and benefits under this program.

Vocational Guidance

Vocational guidance for youth was a significant concern of the consultation members. Following *Brown v. Board of Education* (1954), many Negro youth were enrolled in schools where only white high school guidance counselors were available to them. The guidance provided for Negro youth was often based on misconceptions of the intellectual abilities Black students, as well as a lack of awareness and knowledge about Black adults' academic and professional opportunities and accomplishments. Participants in the Fourth Consultation felt that guidance counselors needed to promote opportunities for upward mobility among Negro youth and provide inspiration for setting and achieving higher goals. To this end, the Commission recommended that guidance coun-selors familiarize themselves with the academic and vocational resources available to *all* youth, and that the availability of those resources be made known and accessible to Negro youth.

The Commission seemed to understand that there were vocational guidance concerns that were specific to young Black females. Wolfe noted that there were likely overlaps between the organization of Negro family patterns and the academic opportunities and vocational guid-ance provided to Negro youth. Wolfe suggested that the disempowered Negro man, essentially emasculated by his breadwinner wife, was largely uninvolved in his children's academic and vocational lives, and that the Negro woman, already overextended with her own professional obliga-tions, was confronted with the double bind of choosing between work and family or trying to be a woman who could juggle all of her obli-gations and fulfill her priorities with equal attention and effort. Wolfe even surmised that Negro women's participation in the work was a fac-tor that accounted for their lack of participation in community life in the roles of volunteers. According to Wolfe's postulation, the Negro woman's absence from public life, then, implied a variety of negative outcomes with respect to vocational guidance for Negro youth, albeit unintentionally.

Community Service and Participation

The Commission viewed community service and participation as a mat-ter of importance because its members believed that if Blacks—and Black women, in particular—played a more visible role in public and political life, their concerns would organically work their way onto local, state, and federal agendas. One of the major recommendations of the consult-ants was for Negro women to participate on policy-making boards at local, state, and federal levels. They argued that it was particularly impor-tant for Negro women to serve on decision-making bodies on behalf of the community, which would benefit not only them and their chil-dren, but also many white children. Many white children at that time had seen Negroes only as domestic workers, and therefore grew up to be white adults who had never had a peer relationship with Negroes. The subcommittee anticipated that revitalized policies could result in improved community relationships.

Adult Education

Adult education was an area of great pertinence to Negro women and was another central concern of the committee. Of the 3.8 million functionally illiterate citizens in the USA at that time, many were Negroes. Although a recommendation intended to remedy the problem of the paucity of educational opportunities for adults was not offered by the Fourth Consultation, a reference to the fact that the issue was discussed extensively leads one to think that more information may be available in the transcripts of the meetings. What can be surmised with confidence is that the very appearance of this issue on a federal-level commission's agenda brought the issue to the consciousness of policy-makers and just a decade later, significant educational reform was legislated that improved educational access and equality for women and men alike.

BIOGRAPHY AS HISTORY: THE BLACK WOMEN ON THE COMMISSION

In order to understand the context in which the work of the commission occurred and the people and personalities who shaped its discussions, decisions, and recommendations, it is important to examine the personal histories of the Black women who served on the commission. Alice Allison Dunnigan, Inabel Burns Lindsay, Geraldyn Hodges Major, Lillian Holland Harvey, and Lorraine Hansberry are introduced here, with their personal biographical information and significant political and social contributions—both to their communities and to the commission—highlighted. The reader sees that as diverse as these women's backgrounds and demographic characteristics were, they shared some common concerns that arose from similar experiences, and thus, they were able to engage in fruitful discussion and action in their collaborative work on the commission.

Alice Allison Dunnigan, a member of the Consultation on Problems of Negro Women, was the first Black American woman reporter to gain access to the press galleries of the US Capitol and be accredited to the White House and the State Department. The daughter of a sharecropper, Dunnigan, was born on August 27, 1906, in Russelville, Kentucky, the youngest child of Willie and Lena (Pittman) Allison. In the Black Women's Oral History Project, she referred to her parents as common laboring people. She grew up in a rural area, about two miles from what she called a very small village. Because her father was a sharecropper, he didn't receive money until the end of the year when the tobacco crop was sold. To help out with the family financial situation, Alice's mother did laundry.

When Dunnigan completed the ten years of education available to Blacks in the segregated Russelville Schools as valedictorian, she wanted to continue her schooling and pursue a career as a teacher, but her parents did not concur. As Dunnigan recalled:

> My mother had to do the laundry work throughout the year to keep the family going, but she didn't make more than five dollars a week. She'd have to do about three families of washing before she could make that, because families paid one or two dollars or something like that for a week's laundry. So with the small amount of money she earned, she knew she couldn't keep me in school. That bothered her some, I think, but she took it like a lamb. Well my father just outright protested. He kept saying, 'Why does Alice want to be a teacher? None of my folks were ever teachers. Why would she ever want to be a teacher?' He never did anything to try to help or encourage me.[16]

The intervention of her Sunday school superintendent, William Russell, the only Black dentist in town, made it possible for Dunnigan to attend Kentucky State College, where she earned her two-year elementary teachers' certificate after only one year. She wanted to complete her program a year early because she needed to save money. Shortly after graduation, Dunnigan began her teaching career in a one-room rural school.

That same year, when she was 19 years old, Dunnigan married Walter Dickinson of Mt. Pisgah, Kentucky. Their union was not an easy one, as Dunnigan's level of education created a gulf between herself and her husband. As she recalled,

> I tried to make a go of it, because I guess he was a nice person, but he was a rural farmer, and of course we had different views and different values. He wanted me to give up teaching, but I was not willing to do that at the time.[17]

---

[16] Black Women's Oral History Project, p. 41.

[17] Black Women's Oral History Project, p. 13.

Dunnigan's experience in marriage was similar to the fictional character of Janie, in Zora Neale Hurston's novel, *Their Eyes Were Watching God*. Similar to Janie's first husband, Mr. Killicks, Dunnigan's husband insisted that she must help him with the farm work as the other farmers' wives did. She had to help pick cotton, cultivate tobacco, and gather corn. Dunnigan recounted:

> He told me that I ought to stay at home, as a farmer's wife should, and help with the crops. If I needed extra money I could always earn it by washing clothes for some of these good White folks.[18]

When she explained to her husband that she needed to return to West Kentucky College to get recertified, he told her to stay there, and she did. They were divorced in 1930.

In 1931, Dunnigan married Charles Dunnigan, who had been a childhood friend. She says of this marriage, "Here again was a matter of incompatibility. I was interested in intellectual things. He was not. Our friends were different. Our outlooks different. Our interests different."[19] They eventually separated in 1953, without ever divorcing. She and Charles had one child, Robert William, who eventually went on to Kentucky State and had four children of his own.

World War II had a tremendous impact on Dunnigan's life. By the time a call for government workers went out in 1942, Dunnigan was tired of teaching and of the menial jobs it was necessary for a Black teacher to take in order to eke out a living during the five months when schools were not in session. One of her summer jobs, provided by the Works Progress Administration, involved washing the tombstones at a white cemetery. At the same time, she was working four hours a day in a dairy, cleaning houses for a family, and doing washing at night for another family, earning in all only seven dollars a week.

In pursuit of a government job, Dunnigan discovered a notice on a post office wall calling for clerk-typists in Washington. She had taken typing in college and went to the postmaster to inquire about taking the examination for civil service grade two, the highest available to her in Kentucky. He said that she had to furnish her own typewriter if she

---

[18] Black Women's Oral History Project, p. 15.
[19] Black Women's Oral History Project, p. 16.

wanted to take the test. She stated in the Black Women's Oral History Project that even though she was a poor woman of the South, she had a portable typewriter that she had ordered from a magazine but wasn't accustomed to using. The typewriter was inadequate and she didn't pass the typing examination. However, she did so well on the oral exam that she was permitted to retest. She passed and subsequently entered the federal civil service as a clerk typist for the Labor Department in Washington, DC. After a year of night courses at Howard University, she reached the level of economist in the Office of Price Administration.

In 1947, Dunnigan was appointed chief of the Washington Bureau of the Associated Negro Press. She set out to get press credentials, starting with access to the press galleries of the House of Representatives and the Senate. Her request was initially denied on the grounds that she did not represent a daily paper (all papers using the services of the Associated Negro Press were weeklies). After a six-month pursuit, she succeeded and gained her accreditation about a week after the first Black man, Louis Lautier, received his. Dunnigan was the first Black woman admitted to the Capitol and the White House Press Corps. As such, she was the first Black correspondent to travel with a President of the USA, accompanying President Truman during his 1948 campaign. In 1960, she worked for Senator Lyndon Johnson, who was then campaigning for president, along with Senators Kennedy, Humphrey, and Symington. She attended the Democratic Convention in Los Angeles as a guest of Senator Johnson. Shortly after the 1960 national elections, President Kennedy issued the executive order that established the President's Commission on Equal Employment Opportunity and Vice President Johnson was made chairman. The Vice President appointed Dunnigan as education consultant for the commission. In this position, she conferred with labor and industry representatives regarding strategies for assuring equal opportunities for minorities.

Inabel Burns Lindsay, the youngest of six children, was born in St. Joseph, Missouri, on February 13, 1900, to Joseph Smith Burns and Margaret Hartshorn Burns. Margaret Hartshorn's parents were former slaves who had purchased their freedom. The Hartshorn family migrated from Virginia to Missouri during Reconstruction. Lindsay was not born into a family of educational privilege. Her mother had only an eighth grade education, but she stressed the importance of education and wanted her children to have better opportunities than she herself had enjoyed. Inabel Burns Lindsay was determined to achieve success, despite instabilities in her early life. Her parents separated when she was three, and she missed the first three years of elementary school because of vision problems. She was taught at home by her siblings with a regular school schedule. After her eye problems stabilized, she entered the fourth grade at the age of eight and was able to finish high school at the age of 15. She was encouraged to attend Howard University by her brother Ocie, who was a father figure for her.

Burns enrolled at Howard University when she was only 16 years old. Although there were institutions closer to home, the family was looking for a place that had the protected environment of a dormitory experience. Despite her youth, Lindsay led a month-long strike against the dormitory when the price of board was raised with notification to parents but not to students. The university then moved against female students living in a dormitory with a ruling that they could not eat outside the dormitory. Her campus activism aside, she graduated with honors in 1920 at the age of 19.

Geraldyn Hodges Major was born in Chicago, Illinois, on July 29, 1894. Her mother died when she was born and her mother's sister, Maude Powell Lawrence, raised her. Hodges grew up in a life of privilege, receiving many advantages to which few Black or white children were exposed. Her aunt and uncle, Maude and David Lawrence, were both professionals who provided her with dancing lessons and made accessible a social circle that included parties at the exclusive Appomattox Club. After graduating from high school at the age of 18, she entered the University of Chicago. Major had been accepted to Howard University, Fisk University, and Spelman College, but chose the University of Chicago because she received a work-study scholarship. While she was at the university, she became a charter member of the Beta Chapter of Alpha Kappa Alpha, the second chapter in the first sorority for Black college women. After graduating from the University of Chicago in 1915, Major went to teach at Lincoln Institute, a Black college in Jefferson City, Missouri. She was unhappy in this position and returned to school to pursue a teacher's certificate from Chicago Normal College, where she completed her studies in 1917.

Later that year, she married Binga Dismond, a man from Houston, Texas, whom she had met while attending the university. When he went to fight in World War I, Major attended Hampton Institute during the summer. Major was no less familiar with marital difficulties than was Dunnigan. She divorced Binga Dismond in 1933, and eventually married

Gilbert Holland during the Depression, but that marriage lasted only a short time. Her third and final marriage was to a mortician, John Major, who preceded her in death. Major's class background is reflected in her journalism. From 1928 to 1931, she was managing editor of the *Interstate Tattler*, and her articles covered society news. In 1928, she began to write the "New York Social Whirl" column for the *Baltimore Afro-American*. In March 1953, Major began working for Johnson Publishing Company in Chicago and wrote articles for *Ebony* and *Jet* magazines.

Lillian Holland Harvey was born in Holland, Virginia. She was a graduate of Lincoln Hospital's Nursing School (1939) and received a bachelor's degree from Columbia University in 1944, a master's degree in 1948, and a doctorate in 1966. Dr. Harvey arrived in Tuskegee, Alabama as a young woman in 1944, and soon became the first dean of the School of Nursing at Tuskegee Institute. During her tenure as dean (1948–1973), Harvey successfully managed the transition from a diploma program to the first baccalaureate nursing program in the state of Alabama. Harvey was instrumental in advancing opportunities for Black nurses to enter the Army Nurse Corps during World War II by maintaining a program at Tuskegee that prepared Black nurses for military service. While it was necessary to work within the segregated system that was mandated by law in the Deep South, Harvey worked endlessly toward breaking these barriers and promoting an open social system. During the early years of her career, she single-handedly undertook the task of desegregating the Alabama Nurses' Association by attending its meetings. This required an 80-mile round trip drive from Tuskegee to Montgomery. Although she had to sit in a separate section of the room, she spoke up without hesitation about the needs of nurses and nursing students.

The selection of Lorraine Hansberry for the PCSW was, perhaps, surprising because of her outspoken radical politics, which included disputes with Robert Kennedy. She was born on the South Side of Chicago on May 19, 1930, into a family of means. The Hansberrys were prominent not only in the Black community of Chicago, but also in national Black cultural and political circles. Her father, Carl Augustus Hansberry, was a successful real estate broker who had moved to Chicago from Mississippi after completing technical courses at Alcorn College. Like thousands of Southern rural Blacks, he migrated north in the early years of the twentieth century seeking better economic opportunities. Despite the economic hardships of the Great Depression, he built a real estate company that he ran as a family business, hiring other relatives who needed employment or who wanted to leave the South. A promising businessman, he made an unsuccessful bid for Congress in 1940 on the Republican ticket and contributed large sums of money to causes supported by the NAACP and the Urban League. Hansberry's mother, Nannie Perry, was a schoolteacher who later became a ward committeewoman.

The Hansberrys were at the center of Black social life in Chicago and often entertained important political figures that were visiting the city. Despite the Hansberry's comfortable middle-class economic status, they were still subject to the racial segregation and discrimination characteristic of the period, and they were active in opposing it. Carl Hansberry challenged discriminatory housing patterns in 1938 by purchasing a home in a white area. When a court order forced the family to move, Mr. Hansberry fought the case (*Hansberry v. Lee*) in the Supreme Court and won a favorable judgment. The political activism affected Lorraine to the extent that years later, in a 1964 letter to *The New York Times* she articulated her advocacy of her father's style of civil disobedience for ghetto-locked Blacks in Chicago.

A famed playwright, Lorraine Hansberry was as politically active as she was artistically creative. When the civil rights movement intensified, she publicly agreed that Blacks should defend themselves against terrorist acts. Hansberry posed a threat to the dominant culture for several reasons, and these threats intensified after her fame gave her national exposure. She was a lesbian, although never publicly; she was a Pan-Africanist; and in 1961, she donated money for the station wagon used by James Chaney, Andrew Goodman, and Michael Schwerner, who were Freedom Riders in Mississippi at the time of their murder. In 1962, Hansberry helped plan fund-raising events to support the SNCC. She expressed her disgust with the red-baiting of the McCarthy era and called for dissolving the House's Un-American Activities Committee. She criticized President John F. Kennedy's handling of the Cuban missile crisis, arguing that his actions endangered the cause of world peace. For all of these reasons, one might have reasonably expected that Hansberry would *not* be invited to serve on the commission.[20]

Indeed, Hansberry was apparently more radical than the other commission members. She was also more evolved in her feminist beliefs than most Black women of her time, and as early as 1957 she wrote a critical

[20] Thirteen (PBS) American Masters. "Lorraine Hansberry: Seeing Eyes/Feeling Heart," Original air date: January 19, 2018.

commentary of Simone de Beauvoir's *The Second Sex*, a book that had changed Hansberry's life. In May 1963, before the report of the PCSW was even published, Hansberry was asked to join a multiracial assembly that included James Baldwin, Harry Belafonte, and Lena Horne at a meeting in New York City with Attorney General Robert Kennedy to discuss the escalating protests and violence in the South. After a passionate query by Jerome Smith, a young Black Freedom Rider, as to the lack of positive leadership on the part of the US government in the South, Hansberry admonished Kennedy that he must listen to the voices of men like Smith to understand the needs of Black Americans.

Though not heard by many, playwright Lorraine Hansberry expressed racial militancy when she wrote in 1962, "The condition of our people dictates what can only be called revolutionary attitudes."[21] Countering white criticisms of "Black power" and militant opposition to racism, Hansberry declared:

> Negroes must concern themselves with every single means of struggle: legal, illegal, passive, active, violent and nonviolent. They must harass, debate, petition, give money to court struggles, sit-in struggles, sit-in, lie-down, strike, boycott, sing hymns, pray on steps – and shoot from windows when the tactics come cruising through their communities.[22]

Hansberry and peers who shared her more radical approach believed that organizing as Black feminists would be the most expedient, if not the only, way to advance their concerns. Accomplishing this goal, however, would take a decade more. In the meantime, Hansberry would articulate her concerns openly on the commission.

The Fourth Consultation proposed several relevant recommendations for enhancing the role of Black women in American society. However, despite the fact that the 24 suggestions of the PCSW were covered on the front page of *The New York Times* on October 12, 1963, none of the recommendations of the Negro Women's Consultation received media coverage, nor were they incorporated into the final summaries. Indeed,

---

[21] hooks, bell. (1990). *Yearning: Race, Gender, and Cultural Politics*. Cambridge, MA: South End Press, p. 186.

[22] hooks, bell. (1990). *Yearning: Race, Gender, and Cultural Politics*. Cambridge, MA: South End Press, p. 187.

the Black women's contributions were not mentioned at all. The fact that the Black women's suggestions were not included on the front page of *The New York Times* demonstrates that although Black women were making their way from the margins of public policy, they still were not part of the mainstream. The best way to illustrate this point is to consider that the following year, Mrs. Fannie Lou Hammer was not allowed a delegate position at the 1964 Democratic National Convention.

NOW

Yet the precedents established by the commission and the women who served on it paved the way for future organizations and efforts, both with respect to racial politics and equality and sexual-gendered politics and equality. For instance, after having worked with the commission for two years, Pauli Murray tried to bring Black women's concerns to the table of another mainstream group: the National Organization for Women (NOW). Contrary to popular belief, women of color were involved in the formation and development of NOW. In fact, this new organization's membership overlapped with that of the PCSW and the still-to-come NBFO. Three Black women—Pauli Murray, Aileen Hernandez, and Shirley Chisholm—were involved in the organization of NOW.[23] In 1966, NOW emerged out of the third annual conference of Commission on the Status of Women in Washington, DC, white women who had been involved in SNCC and other civil rights organizations were slowly being forced out and they began to focus their energies on the struggle for women's rights. As they began to look at their role as women in society, many educated, upper-middle-class white women began to recognize the relationship between sexism and racism. Many of the proponents of the NOW said they wanted "an NAACP for Women" because they felt that their issues were being pushed aside by the newly emerging Black Power movement.[24]

Pauli Murray was asked to be a founding member of NOW after Betty Friedan heard reports of her statements at the October 1965 conference of the National Council of Women in the USA. Murray had declared

[23] National Organization for Women. "History: Highlights." https://now.org/about/history/highlights/. Retrieved on May 20, 2018.

[24] From the National Organization for Women "Honoring Our Founders." Available online at http://www.now.org/history/founders.html.

that she would not shrink from the fight for equality should such a fight become necessary. In 1965, Murray wrote an important article for the *George Washington University Law Review* stating that while the brutality that African-Americans endured was far worse than that which women faced, this did not obscure the fact that the rights of both groups needed to be assured and both were human rights issues. It is important to note that Murray did not racialize the category "woman" in her article.

Along with Betty Friedan and Gloria Steinem, Fannie Lou Hamer and Shirley Chisholm attended the July 1971 National Political Caucus in Washington, DC, and spoke out in favor of more women running for political office. These women were central in NOW's development, and in their early conversations about their organization's agenda, NOW's statement of purpose incorporated many of the issues that the Black women on the Kennedy Commission had already explored. NOW's objectives centered on education, employment, legal and political rights, family life, poverty, and mass media images. There was no great focus on CR, but rather on the concrete political and legal changes needed to improve the economic situation of mainly middle- and upper-middle-class women. The NBFO was formed in 1973 partly because NOW did not deal adequately with the issue of race and the particular concern of Black working-class women.[25]

NOW Meets the Black Panther Party: The National Black Feminist Organization

The NBFO officially began on November 30, 1973, at an Eastern Regional Conference at the Cathedral of St. John the Divine in New York City. Among those present were Shirley Chisholm, Alice Walker, Eleanor Holmes Norton, Flo Kennedy, and Margaret Sloan, the NBFO's first and only president. According to Sloan, "by organizing around our needs as Black women, we are making sure that we won't be left out," which was what she felt was happening in both the Black liberation and the women's liberation movements.[26] Before and during this time, many Black women felt frustrated by the treatment they received from Black men involved in the Black Power movement. According to Pauli Murray,

[25] Yamahtta Taylor, K. (2017). *How We Get Free: Black Feminism and the Combahee River Collective.* Chicago: Haymarket Books.

[26] Sloan, p. 97.

"Black women began to sense that the struggle into which they had poured their energies – Black Liberation and the Civil Rights Movement – may not afford them rights they assumed would be theirs when the civil rights cause triumphed." Many women saw how they were being placed three paces behind their men and were expected to be content to serve as secretaries and breeders of (preferably male) revolutionaries in a movement that was supposed to be liberating for all.

The NBFO focused on issues that were not addressed by Black liberation or feminist organizations. Their initial topics for discussion were welfare rights and reform, rights of domestic workers, reproductive freedom, and the problems of unwed mothers. The NBFO formed taskforces on media, drug addiction, and women in prisons, rape, the arts, and the Black lesbian. Other task forces were formed to create an ongoing structure for the organization, to plan for a national conference, and to make connections with the press. NBFO was also concerned with healthcare issues, unemployment, childcare, and the problem of forced sterilization. The group emphasized the inclusion of all classes of women in "consciousness raising" activities.[27]

Unlike NOW, the first public statements of the NBFO emphasized issues of class and sexual orientation, a reflection of the times since the NBFO was founded seven years after NOW. The purpose of the NBFO was to be a business as well as an educational forum, with regular programs devoted to topics as diverse as female sexuality, Black women as consumers, sex role stereotyping and the Black child, and the passage of the ERA. In the organization's statement of purpose, the NBFO dealt with the response of the wider Black community to Black women's involvement in the feminist movement. The belief that these women were "sell-outs" or that there really was nothing that related to Black people within the concept of feminism was challenged. The authors explored the multiple ways in which Black women in the USA have suffered from the combined forces of racism and sexism, and exposed the myth of the Black "matriarch," the stereotypes, and the lack of positive images for Black women. They argued that their presence would lend an "enormous credibility" to the feminist movement, which unfortunately had not been valued as a "serious political and economic revolutionary

[27]Yamahtta Taylor, K. (2017). *How We Get Free: Black Feminism and the Combahee River Collective*. Chicago: Haymarket Books.

force." This coming together of feminists would strengthen the Black Power movement and encourage "all talents and creativity of Black women to emerge strong and beautiful."

With regard to women and employment, Black women had more in common with Black men than with white women. In their task force on employment, the NBFO focused on the issue of household workers, 97% of whom were female, and of those, 64% were Black. In supporting the efforts of Black domestic workers to organize for their rights, the NBFO advocated pressuring the government to enact laws to guarantee the inclusion of domestic workers under the Fair Labor Standards Act. This would mean that domestic workers would be covered by all federal laws and would be guaranteed minimum wage, sick pay, paid vacations, insurance, and the right to collective bargaining. In their report on economics and class, the women in the NBFO demonstrated their knowledge and understanding of the intersecting nature of multiple oppressions. NBFO members understood their oppression as having roots in the "classist, racist, sexist, capitalist-imperialist structures of this country." Some of their suggestions for eliminating Black women's economic distress included "income sharing, cooperative ventures, coalition politics, education and communication projects." Although the NBFO membership did not espouse socialism, some of the NBFO's ideas could be considered socialist in nature. They also recognized the class biases of some of their membership and actively encouraged Black women from every socioeconomic class to become involved. They stated, "class distinctions must be abolished and classist attitudes and policies will not be tolerated within our ranks."

The ERA was also an important issue for the NBFO. The leaders called for the ratification of the amendment by the states and encouraged their members to lobby for its passage. They endorsed the use of boycotts against a state's products to apply pressure to ratify the amendment. For Black women, the protection under the law in the workplace was more of a necessity than it was for many white women. Birth control and a woman's right to choose when and how she would bear and raise children were also important issues during this time, but they posed particular challenges for Black women. Within the Black Power movement, many of the male leaders were preaching against the use of birth control because they believed it was a "tool of the oppressor to slowly kill off the Black race." Many Black men wanted Black women to throw away their birth control pills and breed revolutionaries. Many Black women, however, felt this was just another excuse for Black men to keep women in traditional roles. For example, novelist and social critic Toni Cade argued that the pill offered women a choice as to when they feel prepared emotionally, economically, and physically to have a child, and was not a sign that the woman would not want a child in the future. bell hooks posed a more dramatic question. If birth control is truly the "trick of the man" and the Black women needed to have revolutionary babies, she asked, why are so many babies in Black orphanages? hooks called upon Black revolutionaries to adopt children until all the orphanages were empty if they wanted more Black revolutionaries.[28]

In their educational sheet on rape, the NBFO estimated that over 60% of rape victims were Black, the majority of them young girls. Rape was an important issue for the members of the NBFO, and they suggested that all states eliminate "collaboration laws," which required a witness to be present at the time of the alleged rape. The NBFO also wanted to outlaw the use of a victim's previous sexual history as evidence in rape trials. Often times, the defendant's lawyer used scare tactics to intimidate a woman who was testifying against an accused rapist; this practice discouraged other women from wanting to bring charges against their rapists. NBFO members also saw a need for a change in laws to prohibit the legal rape of wives by their husbands, for at the time non-consensual sex within marriage was not considered rape. The NBFO also planned to pressure government officials to create special police units that would be trained to deal with rape cases.

The strategy that the NBFO members used to promote all of their concerns was referred to as CR, and they explained how it had helped them explore their own heads and hearts and celebrate their strength as women. NBFO saw CR as a way to "establish a basis of trust and commitment to each other as individuals and to the organization as a whole." The goals of CR were:

1. developing love, trust and sisterhood within the group;
2. facilitating open and honest communication and positive confrontation (as opposed to negative squabbling);
3. enabling women to deal with personal prejudices;
4. raising the feminist consciousness of all Black women.

---

[28] In hooks, bell.

The NBFO developed a CR strategy that was intended to reach out to Black women and educate them about feminism. They stressed that the number of members of their organization was not as important as the quality of those members; a small and effective organization, they reasoned, is better than a large and ineffective one. The organization also stressed the need to include marginalized groups, such as lesbians and incarcerated women, as part of their target audiences. This approach was very different from that of NOW, which clearly had other priorities. The women of the NBFO valued action on a more personal and practical level, rather than on a mainstream political structural level. Perhaps the women of the NBFO thought that they lacked appropriate access to those political arenas, or perhaps they saw these changes as having a more direct effect on Black women in the USA than working within the system. Whatever their reasoning, the effect was the creation of an organization that filled a specific need. Unfortunately, the unique approach and organization of the NBFO could not be sustained. After six years, the organization disintegrated. According to Michele Wallace, the NBFO "got bogged down in an array of ideological disputes" and "action became unthinkable." Wallace also saw how "women who had initiative and spirit usually attended one meeting, were turned off by the hopelessness of ever getting anything accomplished, and never returned again." These types of problems were in no way unique to Black feminist organizing, but they did impact Black feminists' successes considerably. Black feminists continued organizing in an effort to overcome such problems. The CRC was one such effort.

THE COMBAHEE RIVER COLLECTIVE

The CRC began as the Boston chapter of the NBFO, but it broke off in 1977 to focus more exclusively on issues of sexuality and economic development. Whereas the NBFO's framework was socialist in its ideology, the CRC overtly defined itself as anti-capitalist, socialist, and revolutionary. During the six years of its existence, its members worked on a variety of issues that affected Black women, including racism in the women's movement. The CRC asserted the legitimacy of Black women's opposition to sexual exploitation and oppression and made a major contribution to the growth of Black feminism in the USA. Its widely circulated "Combahee River Collective Statement" helped to lay the foundation for feminists of color organizing in the 1980s and the 1990s. In addition to the Statement, which became a seminal document of Black feminist activists, the women of Combahee also did important work focused around media exposure of Black women's issues. One of the most important accomplishments of the CRC in this regard was their work to get the stories of the twelve Black women who were murdered in Boston moved from the sports section of *The Boston Globe* to headline news.[29]

The CRC has been printed in numerous publications, but a history of the organization and information about its members has, for the most part, been missing from the literature. In its first years, the Collective was active in projects such as support for Kenneth Edelin, a Black doctor at Boston City Hospital who was charged with manslaughter and arrested for performing a legal abortion. Collective members were also involved in the case of Ella Ellison, a Black woman who was accused of murder because she had been seen in the area where a homicide was committed. CRC members also picketed with the Third World Workers Coalition to ensure that Black laborers would be hired for the construction of a new high school in the Black community. These are just a few of the many projects in which they group participated over a five-year period.[30]

The Collective was comprised of highly educated Black lesbian feminists, six of who—Barbara Smith, Demita Frazier, Cheryl Clarke, Gloria Akasha Hull, Margo Okazawa Rey, and Sharon Page Ritchie—were interviewed for this book. Like the women who participated in the Fourth Consultation, it is important for scholars to recover the histories of contemporary Black feminists whose roles in the development of Black feminist consciousness have been central.

---

[29] Yamahtta Taylor, K. (2017). *How We Get Free: Black Feminism and the Combahee River Collective*. Chicago: Haymarket Books.

[30] Yamahtta Taylor, K. (2017). *How We Get Free: Black Feminism and the Combahee River Collective*. Chicago: Haymarket Books.

ALL OF WHO I AM IN THE SAME PLACE:
THE WOMEN OF COMBAHEE

Barbara Smith

Reentering the world of activism was something that Barbara Smith did not think she would do. Her early political work was in the civil rights movement, which she expected would lead to a social revolution. After disappointments in this first experience with political organizing, Smith did not have hope that the Black women's movement would be significantly different. As Smith recalled,

> I think that I felt my status change so much from having been raised Colored/Negro to becoming Black in the space of a short lifetime. And what those names, those labels represent is a world of difference. There is a difference between our naming ourselves and other people declaring who we were with an insulting label. When I entered college in 1965, I thought that by the time I got out of college things would be basically "fixed," you know, and since that didn't happen, I don't know if I thought we were on the verge of a revolution. It's hard to look at history with hindsight because you realize so much more than when you were actually experiencing it. I think one of the things that I was so happy about is that I had thought that I would never be involved in political work after I graduated from college because that was the height of Black Nationalism and I felt like I just wasn't permitted to be the kind of person I was in that context. I was supposed to marry someone or not marry them, who cares, but my job was to have babies for the Nation and to walk seven paces behind a man and basically be a maidservant. I didn't get involved in the women's movement for a few years after it became very visible because my perception was that it was entirely White.

After attending the NBFO meeting in New York in 1973, Smith felt she could do more in the Boston community by working from a Black feminist base. When Smith returned from the NBFO conference, she met with people from Boston and started trying to build a Boston NBFO chapter. She met Demita Frazier a few weeks later, in early 1974, and when Smith and Frazier began to meet regularly they discovered that their vision was more radical than that of the NBFO. In a 1994 interview, Demita Frazier remembered,

We wanted to talk about radical economics. Some of us were thinking that we were socialists. We thought that we needed to have an economic analysis. We were also concerned that there be a voice for Lesbians in Black women's organizations and we weren't certain where NBFO was going, even though they had been founded by women who were Lesbians. So after one of our members – and I do believe it was Barbara – went to the Socialist Feminist Organizing Conference that was held at Oberlin College in Ohio, we decided that we wanted to be a collective and not be in a hierarchy organization because it was antithetical to our beliefs about democracy and the need to share. We also felt that we had a more radical vision. And so we decided [to send] a letter saying that we were no longer going to be the National Black Feminist Organization chapter in Boston. Towards the middle of 1975, we were having serious discussions about our relationship to the National Black Feminist Organization and we made a decision [to create an independent organization] during that summer.

The organization got its new name from Barbara Smith, who had read a small book published by Left Press entitled *Harriet Tubman, Conductor on the Underground Railroad* by Earl Conrad. The Combahee River is where the abolitionist Harriet Tubman planned and led the only military campaign in US history organized by a woman. Smith wanted to name the collective after a historical event that was meaningful to Black women. There were women's groups all over the country named for Harriet Tubman, and Smith wanted to select a name that honored Tubman while offering unique symbolic value that distinguished her organization from existing groups. Smith liked the idea of naming the group for a collective action as opposed to one heroic person's feats. She chose the name of the river where 750 slaves escaped to freedom. Smith explained the symbolic meaning of the choice of the name as follows:

The boats were out there, the Yankee Union boats were out there and they [the slaves] were running, literally, to get on them, I guess, during this battle, but the thing is that it wasn't just one person who did something courageous; it was a group of people. The Combahee River is an incredible militant chapter of U.S. history, not just of Black history, but of world history. In fact, at the time when people looked at their conditions and they fought back, they took great risks to change their situation and for us to call ourselves the Combahee River Collective, that was an educational [tool] both for ourselves and for anybody who asked, "So what does that mean, I never heard of that?" It was a way of talking about ourselves being on a continuum of Black struggle, of Black women's struggle."

In the summer of 1994, Barbara Smith was filmed by the Combahee River in South Carolina. When the videographer asked Smith about the importance of the collective, she responded:

> Combahee was really so wonderful because it was the first time that I could be *all of who I was in the same place*. That I didn't have to leave my feminism outside the door to be accepted, as I would in a conservative Black political context. I didn't have to leave my lesbianism outside. I didn't have to leave my race outside, as I might in an all-White women's context where they didn't want to know all of that. So it was just really wonderful to be able to be our whole selves and to be accepted in that way. In the early 1970s to be a Black lesbian feminist meant that you were a person of total courage. It was almost frightening. I spent a lot of time wondering if I would ever be able to come out because I didn't see any way that I could be Black and a feminist and a lesbian. I wasn't thinking so much about being a feminist. I was just thinking about how could I add lesbian to being a Black woman? It was just like no place for us. That is what Combahee created, a place where we could be ourselves and where we were valued. A place without homophobia, a place without racism, a place without sexism. (emphasis added)

Sharon Page Ritchie

Sharon Page Ritchie became involved with the CRC through her connection to Margaret Sloan of the NBFO, whom she met at the University of Chicago. Ritchie grew up in a little house on the South Side of Chicago, where her father worked for the city as a building inspector and her mother was a public schoolteacher. She spoke about her early years, recalling:

> When I talk about my family, I say that I come from a long line of teachers and social workers, so education was a critically important value in my family. Literacy, reading, writing, ideas... my mother's house was nice because it was filled with books and magazines and it was always more important that we should be interested in them than that we should be perfect little housekeepers. We had an education, but we didn't have much money. My mother and my aunts were Deltas. I wasn't a Delta because I was a lesbian. However, I was a Links debutante. I wore three hairpieces and a white dress. Other girls in the cotillion were the daughters of the doctors, lawyers, and probably the undertakers, and so people like my mother always talked about the rich dentist like that was his

name. So, financially speaking, we were not in that class. There was more focus on the arts and literature and those things in my family and less so on furs.

The church is really not a very big thing to me and I really don't remember people talking about it very much. It may have been, but I don't remember. My feeling was growing up in Chicago, that sort of traditional strict Baptist church thing and the moral judgments that came out of that about how men were supposed to be and women were supposed to be, in my family that was presented as something that people of our class didn't go for. That was more of a country thing, more of a Southern thing, more of a working-class thing. So I did not think of the women who I thought of as feminists, intellectuals, or writers or any of that kind of thing to have come from a very strong religious background.

Connected to the Northeastern Collective through people she had known in Chicago, Ritchie met Demita Frazier at a Chicago Lesbian Liberation meeting when she was in her late teens. When Demita Frazier and another member, Linda Powell, moved to the East Coast, Ritchie was doing temp work, which she realized that she could do anywhere. If she moved to the Eastern seaboard, she could be close to a supportive community of friends, and that was the decision she made.

Cheryl Clarke

Cheryl Clarke was born in Washington, DC, in 1947 and grew up there. She did her undergraduate work at Howard University and then left Washington in 1969 to do graduate work at Rutgers in New Brunswick, New Jersey, where she still lives. Clarke's mother was born in North Carolina in 1916 and migrated to Washington, DC, via Detroit around 1920. Her father was born in Washington, DC, in 1913, and the only time he was ever out of Washington was in the service during World War II. Clarke characterized her family as lower-middle-class people whose forebears were laborers. Her maternal grandmother had been a domestic. Her father was a dishwasher. Her father's parents had a little bit more mobility; his mother worked for the federal government for years and retired in the late 1950s. Widowed early, Clarke's mother was the emotional bastion and sole economic support of the family; however, their large extended family provided as much help as they could. She had three children in addition to Cheryl. She recalled:

We were always told we were poor, but I always had security – my basic needs were met and I had a very sheltered upbringing. I remember at one point telling my mother that I wanted to be a nurse and she said, "I don't care what you want to be if you are going to college first." So we sort of grew up knowing that. Also, they nurtured a kind of independence in the house. My mother said, "I want you to get your education so you don't have to dependent on anybody." And that was how we were raised and sort of pushed. They gave us dance lessons, piano lessons, took us to museums. Basically it was like my mother... took charge of those kinds of things because she wanted to cultivate some kind of appetite for other than material kinds of things or at least that was in terms of how I see my upbringing.

In 1965, Clarke went to Howard, where she and Paula Giddings were classmates:

We were in the same major. Paula was the editor of the undergraduate journal and she was always a leader. She was always articulating a position. Extremely smart and extremely well liked, as she still is now. We were in our last year – well, the Spring of 1968 to the Spring of 1969, involved in a writing workshop and there were other people plus two or three faculty members who were involved where you would meet every other Sunday. And I was writing poetry then and we were reading our work to one another and it is very interesting – the results of that activity enabled us to know how to have a public voice.

Now I was not an activist when I was in college. I had other interests and was much more shy than I am now. But because of that workshop we met editors from Random House who met with us and encouraged us. We met Toni Morrison who was an editor at Random House at that time and one of my teachers. Howard exposed me to the richness of Afro-American culture, which I have particularly focused on in the literature in terms of my own intellectual development. And began really myself in literature in 1968 when I took Arthur Davis' course, Negro Literature in America, which was only offered once a year. But I watched a whole transformation of the curriculum in Howard during the time that I was there because there were many scholars at Howard who had specialized in Afro-American study who were ostracized too, people like Sterling Brown, people like E. Franklin Frazier, people like Chancellor Williams, most of them historians and sociologists.

And during that whole Black power thing, students really began to bring those people out of the woodwork. So by the time I graduated, the courses that addressed Afro-American issues came to the foreground and you know, Afro-American studies began to become a hot thing, and you could hardly get into Afro-American history courses. It became an intellectual hotbed as well as a political hotbed, and it was a real process for me to grapple with the Black nationalist issues. I have never really been a nationalist because I have always considered it impractical and negative and limited. And remember, I told you, they always nurtured independence in us so I did not want to be constrained by narrow politics. I loved Howard because of how it opened another world to me in terms of Afro-American culture.

Margo Okazawa Rey

Margo Okazawa Rey was born in Japan in 1949 to an upper-middle-class Japanese woman and a Black G. I. from working-class Chicago. Rey asserted that she obtained her class identity from her father and her cultural identity from her mother:

Women's class is very much connected to the men they are attached to. My mother's class background didn't really have an impact on how we lived our lives. So I would say I grew up working-class, lower-middle-class, but with a definite sort of Japanese cultural sensibility as well as African-American. I think my father has gotten more politicized in his old age, but when we were together, you know, he was sort of a "pull yourself up by your bootstraps" kind of guy. He was one of those people who thought that you just have to be the best person you can be.

He didn't talk about race that much and it is ironic that my mother, who is Japanese and didn't know much about American culture, instilled it but that was more of a private thing. I think the thing that is interesting about my mother is that she is a feminist, although she would never use the term. The men in her family just seemed to get everything. The boys got to do things first, like eat, take baths. Her father got to do everything first; her mother was just kind of waiting on him hand and foot. She said to herself that she was not going to let any man boss her around, which is completely counter to traditional Japanese culture.

Somehow she met my father and one of the things that she was struck by was these American men would say "ladies first" and she thought it was wonderful, but of course she didn't understand the sexist underlying stuff.

She thought America must be a wonderful place if ladies get to go first. So that sort of captured their imagination and they got together. So my early feminist leanings come from her.

Gloria Hull

Gloria Hull grew up in a three-room shotgun house in Shreveport, Louisiana. Neither of her parents finished grammar school. Her mother was a cook and a domestic. Her father was disabled, but did whatever kind of work he could pick up as a carpenter. She considered her upbringing to be working poor:

> I remember very clearly that my mother made three dollars a day. She did that so that my brother and sister and I would be able to go on trips at school, or have a white dress at graduation. Early memories that situate me class-wise were that there was no liquid money, so we kept a running tab going with the Italian grocer at the end of the block. We were paying very high prices for whatever we bought, but were able to pay him with the little bit of money that did come in. I remember that the days that we bought food were really the high point of the weekdays. Food was essential.

Hull graduated from Booker T. Washington High School in 1962 as the valedictorian of her class. She went to Southern University and then won a National Defense Education Act fellowship to the University of Illinois at Urbana to study English literature. The move was significant for her and would shape her future activism. She recalled,

> What I really wanted to do was be a journalist. The first time I got out of the South and saw a little bit of the larger world was between my junior and senior years [of college]. There was this program where Black kids from Southern colleges were brought to Northern campuses, and I spent the summer at Yale working with the New Haven Human Relations Council. I had written for the high school newspaper, the college newspaper, so I said journalism, that's really what I want to do. I had heard that Columbia was one of the best journalism schools in the country. When I was in New Haven I figured out how to get myself to New York City and I had an interview with the assistant dean at the Columbia School of Journalism. This is the summer of '65. I'm just walking around with no sense that I [should] be afraid or anything; I'm just doing this. It was a really good interview and I feel that I might have gotten somewhere with

it, but no one encouraged me. The highest aspiration anybody could see me doing or achieving was being a teacher. With the grades and the fellowship, teacher got translated into college teacher, but still a teacher. So that is how I ended up in graduate school for English.[12]

Before Hull went to graduate school she married her college sweetheart, who had graduated the year before her from Southern and had gone to pursue a Ph.D. in chemistry at Purdue University in Lafayette, Indiana. Hull's husband came from a family that was even more economically disadvantaged than hers; he had one pair of jeans that he had to wash out at night and dry in front of a space heater, iron, and put on the next morning. There were twelve children in his family. After spending one semester at Urbana, Hull gave up her fellowship and went to be with her husband at Purdue, where she became a teaching assistant. Her husband got a job at the University of Delaware when Hull was finishing her dissertation and looking for a job. About this time, Hull recounted,

> When I look back on this, I laugh about how tremendously naive I was. I mean naive in the sense of not knowing the protocol for academic professionalism. I went down there to see the chairman of the English department at the University of Delaware with my husband, with my son on my lap, dressed up in my Sunday School type chic dress, little heels. I didn't know from beans, so they offered me this position. I didn't know that I could bargain or anything. The reason he was just sitting there amazed is that a Black woman had dropped in their laps. Another little index of it is that I didn't even know how to do a professional vita. I had on it stuff like, I played piano for the Black Baptist church that I grew up in. There was no Black woman to say this is how you do it; nobody took me under her wing. It is so different now.

During three years in Delaware, Hull made connections that would change her life and inevitably link her to the CRC. She ended up working on the Feminist Reprints Committee, where she met Florence Howe and Alice Walker. Although she had done her dissertation on Byron and English dramatic poetry, she had become interested in Black women writers and African-American literature, particularly the women writers of the Harlem Renaissance. When she went to the annual meeting of the Modern Language Association in New York City in 1974, she met Barbara Smith. Having met Smith and the rest of the Boston women, she began to attend Combahee retreats, expanding her network of Black feminist contacts and thought.

Demita Frazier

Demita Frazier, who is from Chicago, brought issues of urban poverty to the Combahee discussions. Frazier arrived in Boston intending to organize Black women around feminist issues, but as she remembered, it took about a year to find others who might be interested in doing Black feminist CR:

> We each got our names from different people and we all had been involved in the National Black Feminist Organization. When we arrived it took a while, but that first meeting when we met at my house in Dorchester, Massachusetts, it was quite something because we were strangers to one another. We had gotten phone numbers and said let's try to have a meeting and talk about what we could do in terms of organizing an NBFO chapter here in Boston. We were actually saying we were feminists. We were proud of that. We were not worried about flak from anybody else. It was a moment of power because I think we all recognized very quickly in that meeting in my living room that we were at the precipice of something really important. That was literally how it started, sitting in someone's living room, having a discussion about the issues and it wasn't even the issues so much as getting to know one another and what our issues were, what brought us to think of ourselves as feminists. Where did we get these ideas? What books did we read? And then, of course, there was a sense of sharing. We were interested in so many similar things even though we came from very different places. Most of us came from an academic background. Others had been really involved in organizing from the cities that we had come from. It was quite something for us. It was really very different for me.

And so the Boston chapter of the NBFO—the precursor for Combahee—started with four Black women sitting in Frazier's living room discussing what had brought them to think of themselves as feminists. Boston in the 1970s was in turmoil over court-ordered busing to desegregate its schools. Barbara Smith described the racial tensions of the time:

> I moved to Boston in about 1972 and there were many places in Boston that to this day I have never ventured into. It was absolutely known that as a Black person you did not go to South Boston. You did not go to East Boston. You did not go to Chelsea. Those are a few of the names of neighborhoods that I remember right off the top of my head. Sometimes on the way to somewhere else, like trying to get to Dorchester, one might get lost in South Boston and on those occasions it was always like uh-oh, I really need to get out of here. It was really frightening, if indeed one got lost in

those neighborhoods trying to go from one place to another. But in general, one knew that one did not go.

For example, there was an attorney named Ted Lanzvark who was down in City Hall Plaza, which is this very modern setting. It doesn't look like colonial Boston. So he was down there for business, I am sure. And he was attacked by a group of White men and they used an American flag to beat him up. I don't know who was there on the spot with the camera, but that picture went out over the wire services all over the country, probably all over the world, to show what this country was all about and that was only about twenty years ago.

Another example was a high school student who was playing football and I don't remember what neighborhood they were playing in, if it was one of those places where one dare not venture if one was Black, but he was shot from the stands and he was paralyzed for life. So that was the kind of atmosphere that we lived in. Going into a store and being followed. When I went into a store the assumption was that I came in to rob it.

In a 1994 interview with Susan Goodwillie, Demita Frazier described the political climate of Boston in the 1970s:

I think what drew a lot of us here was the chance to really establish identities that were our own, apart from family and apart from the communities or origin that we came from. So you can picture us in 1973 and 1974 coming together as women in a city where there was so much political activity going on in Boston at that time. If you think about it, some of it wasn't progressive. Busing was just beginning at that time. The desegregation order had come down and so the busing was beginning in Boston and that was causing a lot of political forum. There was a lot of discussion about race and about class. So we arrived in that atmosphere. And for those of us who had been feminists before we came to the city and for those of us had been organizers, we were thrilled at the chance to be in a city where there seemed to be a lot of discussion. There was a feeling that you could talk about nearly anything and you could raise issues about just anything.

COMING TOGETHER: THE COMBAHEE RIVER COLLECTIVE RETREATS

We are actively committed to struggling against racial, sexual, heterosexual, and class oppression and see as our particular task the development of integrated analysis and practice based upon the fact that major systems of oppression are interlocking. The synthesis of these oppressions creates the condition of our lives. As Black women we see Black feminism as the logical political movement to combat the manifold and simultaneous oppressions that all women of color face.

The Combahee River Collective Statement

The CRC held retreats throughout the Northeast between 1977 and 1979. The first retreat was held July 8–10, 1977, in a private home at 10 Jewett Lane in South Hadley, Massachusetts. The purpose of the retreat was to assess the state of the movement, to share information about the participants' political work, and to talk about possibilities and issues for organizing Black women (May 24, 1977, letter authored by Demita Frazier, Barbara Smith, and Beverly Smith). Subsequent retreats were intended to foster unity because of members' geographic separation. The twenty Black feminists who were invited to the retreats were asked to bring copies of any written materials relevant to Black feminism—articles, pamphlets, papers, and their own creative work—to share with the group. Organizers Frazier, Smith, and Smith hoped the retreats would foster political stimulation and spiritual rejuvenation for participants. They encouraged the participants to come ready to talk, laugh, eat, dance, and have a good time. According to their recollection in interviews, this is what occurred:

> [Poet] Audre Lorde was involved in the retreats. I had just met her and I asked her to come and she was thrilled and that is really how we got to become friends because we would see each other periodically at these retreats. We would call them retreats, but in fact they were political meetings that had lots of different elements. So it was a way for people who were separated to be in the same place and do some political work with each other.

The discussion schedule for the retreat was comprised of five sections. The group met on Friday evening for a discussion about "What's Been Done, What's Happening Now, and What We Want for the Future." During this session, the group discussed political activities in which they had been involved over the past few years. On Saturday, between ten in the morning and noon, the group's topic was "Theory and Analysis." They discussed the CRC as a means of focusing the first part of the session and then moved to other topics, including the need to develop a Black feminist economic analysis, the question of violence, and lesbian separatism. After lunch, there were two sessions on organizing. In the next session, the group addressed theoretical and tactical questions: Is there a Black feminist movement? How to develop new organizing skills for Black feminist revolution? How to build new institutions? What about barriers to organizing, such as anti-feminism, repression, class, the backlash, heterosexism, racism, ageism, and sexism? Can publishing be used as a tool for organizing? How do we work out the knots that have prevented coalitions between white women and Black women? After this two-hour discussion, the group focused for another two hours on sterilization abuse, Black women's health, and battered women. For five hours on Sunday, they discussed the effects and remedies of isolation.

The second Black feminist retreat was held November 4–5, 1977, at Cassie Alfonso's home in Franklin Township, New Jersey. The items on the agenda included: (1) trust between lesbian and non-lesbian feminists; (2) socialism and a Black feminist ideology; (3) lesbian separatism and the Black liberation struggle; (4) Black feminist organization versus Black feminist movement; (5) Black feminist scholarship; (6) class conflicts among Black women; and (7) love between women—lesbian, non-lesbian, Black and white (August 25, 1977, letter written by Cheryl Clarke and Cassie Alfonso). The participants were asked to bring an object that would make a statement about themselves, such as a picture, a poem, or a journal excerpt. The retreat had five sessions that addressed a range of topics, including "the personal is political," political definitions, political realities, from analysis to action, and where do we go from here. Two bodywork/exercise sessions were also scheduled at this retreat.

The third Black feminist retreat was held March 24–26, 1978. The fourth retreat met July 21–23, 1978. After these retreats occurred, the participants were encouraged to write articles for the Third World women's issue of *Conditions*, a journal that was edited by Lorraine Bethel and Barbara Smith. The importance of publishing was emphasized in the fifth retreat, held on July 8, 1979. Participants discussed contributing articles for a lesbian herstory issue of two journals, *Heresies* and *Frontiers*. Both Beverly Smith and Barbara Smith had been approached to compile an anthology on Black feminism. Ultimately, the group's members were very active in publishing; a case in point is the anthology *But Some of Us Are Brave*, which was edited by two Combahee members.

The fifth retreat was important because the members cataloged indicators that Black feminism had grown between 1977 and 1979. Two Black feminist groups existed in Boston. Black academic women were organizing nationally in the field of history, at the Modern Language Association, and had formed *Sojourner*, a research newsletter in Third World women's studies. A group for Black women in publishing was organizing in New York. Art collaborations, like Bernice Johnson Reagon and June Jordan's performance, were happening in New York. CRISIS, a Black women's "grassroots" organization, had formed in 1979 to combat murders in Boston. Coalitions between lesbian and straight Black women mothers in Kansas City had been established. Contacts had been made with Black social service workers in New Jersey and in Minneapolis, Minnesota. The women at the fifth retreat also discussed the growth of Black feminist and lesbian culture as evidenced by the performance groups Varied Voices Tour, Sweet Honey in the Rock, and Black Earth Sisters. The group noted that white feminists had begun to take responsibility for dealing with their racism, which in turn lightened the load of Black feminists. The CRC members also attended two important poetry readings: one at the Solomon Center's Fuller Mental Health Center in Boston to hear Audre Lorde, Kate Rushin, and Fahamisha Shariat Brown, and the other at Sanders Theater at Harvard to hear Audre Lorde and Adrienne Rich.

Participants at the sixth retreat of the CRC focused on two literary events in the 1970s. They discussed articles in the May/June 1979 issue of *The Black Scholar*, collectively titled "The Black Sexism Debate," written in response to Robert Staples' "The Myth of Black Macho: A Response to Angry Black Feminists," which had been published in the previous issue. Participants also discussed the importance of writing to *Essence* to support an article in the September 1979 issue entitled "I am a Lesbian," by Chirlane McCray. McCray was a Combahee member and the importance of the article was that at this time *Essence* had a policy on publishing articles and fiction about lesbians. The group was hoping that their positive letters would counteract the homophobic letters that they expected *Essence* to receive.

The seventh retreat was held in Washington, DC, on February 16–18, 1980. Smith reflected upon the significance of the Combahee retreats:

The retreats were multidimensional, multimedia events. They were so many different things. Of course, it was a time to talk politics. It was a time to have parties. It was a time to flirt, for some. It was a time to have these incredible meals. We used to bring literature and things that we had read, articles, we would bring enough copies for everyone. We would have stuff laid out on the table. Now, having been a publisher for 13 years for the only press of women of color in this country, I think how a part of that was bringing Xerox copies because that was all we had then if we wanted to read about ourselves in any fashion or read things that were relevant to us.

What I really see is Black feminism as a building block. I think that we always felt a kinship, sisterhood and solidarity with not just women of color, but with people of color, generally. That is articulated in the statement and certainly in the kinds of things that we move on to work on and do political work on, but it is like building blocks. Our major felt contradiction is/was, as Black women, this will be the White women's movement. So if we were going to build something it was going to be the opposite of what existed, in other words, Black, which was who we were.

The retreats were wonderful. They sort of came about as a brainstorm. We realized we wanted to meet with more Black feminists. In Boston, we had a very large group, but we knew that there was organizing going on in New York and in New Jersey and in Chicago and very similar places. So we put a call out and called our friends and basically that is what we did. We called everybody we knew who we thought might be interested in spending a weekend talking politics, playing cards, eating good food, and spending time together to give you the support and also to give ourselves a sense of a broader community. So I don't remember what the year was. It might have been 1976, 1977... 1976, we organized our first Black feminist retreat. And we didn't advertise, we just did word of mouth. And we met with 25 or 30 women at the first one, sleeping over on a weekend in Western Massachusetts in South Hadley, Massachusetts. It was wonderful. First of all, at that point, we had been organizing for a couple of years and while we were feeling isolated, we did feel hungry for more. We wanted different perspectives. We were just ourselves. We wanted to hear from other people. The thrill of having people arriving, car load after car load of women who knew each other, but some of us didn't know we were being brought together by five different women. We were just thrilled. There were so many colors, so many faces, so many bodies, from all over and a chance to hear what was going on in different cities. This standing around and looking at us all standing on that lawn and realizing we are all women who are taking this big risk because it was risky to be a feminist in the Black community.

We realized it was risky and there we were, all these risk takers, all these ground breakers. It was very powerful for us and it was wonderful also because we had the opportunity at that first meeting to go around and talk about, from sort of an autobiographical perspective, how we all came to be feminists and we got to tell our stories, fascinating places. Very interesting. One thing that I think we all had in common was again, we were all, it seemed like almost all of us were women who never quite fit any sort of stereotype about wherever we were. We weren't appropriate little girls, necessarily. And if we were appropriate little girls, we weren't very appropriate teenagers. We were girls who were rebellious and if we weren't rebellious in act, we were definitely rebellious in thought. We were girls who early on either had been sexually abused or physically assaulted and never wanted that to happen to us again. So we were bringing a sort of reality politics, like you know I don't want this to happen to me or my children. There must be a way to talk about this.

COMMUNITY ACTIVISM

All of the Combahee women were involved in other civil rights and women's issues groups and there was a lot of interconnection among the groups and their issues. When they first got together in the CRC, there was no battered women's shelter in Boston or the surrounding area. Within several years, the women could count among their accomplishments the establishment of Transition House and the organization of take back the night marches. The work that the Combahee members had done had resulted in significant positive political and social outcomes; for the first time in Boston history, rape cases were not treating victims as criminals. A woman could bring a rape charge before the court and not be viewed as a perpetrator. Clearly, the work of the Combahee women had broad implications, affecting not only Black women, but whites and other ethnic women, too. As insider members of the Black community, Black women of the CRC had credibility in raising feminist issues that white women could not have pursued effectively. In publications and presentations, CRC members asserted that if Black women were free, then everyone would be free, because all the systems of oppression that affect Black women and women of color affect everyone else also.

When the collective got involved with the case of L. L. Ellison, a Black woman who defended herself against a sexual assault by a guard at Framingham State Prison by murdering him, it brought them into a circle of people who were fighting the death penalty in the state. This interaction helped Combahee forge a coalition with other community activists, and it brought them into another sector of the Black community they might not have reached otherwise. They worked with women's church groups, including the auxiliaries of a couple of Baptist churches. They were asked to speak about Black feminist politics and implications for Black women. According to Barbara Smith, Combahee was very successful, because even though it caused a lot of upheaval, the members brought the question to the table:

> One meeting that we went to [was] in a church where we showed up. We used to show up for these gigs. We would show up ready to create our discussion. Talk about consciousness raising and the importance of looking into the issues of violence against Black women. And also, an analysis about what it meant for us to take one step back and what it meant to support Black men. Did we have to necessarily walk behind Black men to be supportive of Black men and therefore supportive of our whole community? So things got very hot and heavy at this meeting. We were being told 'What made you think you represent all Black women? You don't represent me, necessarily.' It wasn't a hostile group, but people were feeling what does this mean. How can you say this represents, how can you say that you are representing us? An older Black woman, she must have been in her sixties or seventies, said, "Well, from what I can understand, what they are saying sounds right to me, so they represent me." And that was, again, one of those moments when we've got affirmation from someone who you would respect because you were taught to respect older Black people as a child. You were just taught to respect your elders and it was so affirming to have her say that. And it sort of really put other women... it sort of gave other women the permission to say that they could understand and support the issues.
>
> The simple truth is because she didn't have anything to lose. She is an older woman who has had a whole lifetime of experience. And I see it in my own mother now. You just don't have to lie anymore after you get past a certain age as a woman, and she was just very clear. She worked in people's houses cleaning them, and primarily White people, and she talked about having to fend off the husband or the older son when she was a young woman doing that work and what it meant for her. She lost many jobs and she understood sexual politics. So that was why she was important. It is so funny. If you knew the people involved, you would understand that it was never an issue. We were lesbians. We were not going to be repressed or oppressed in a group that we were organizing for it. We had a

couple of women who were bisexual in the group and they were fine with us. At least I can say they were fine with me. Because the women who were integral to organizing Combahee were lesbians; it was just done, it was just as it was. We were the women who came together and we made it a part of our politics that we thought that we were open to all women, Lesbians, straight women and bisexual women. So at that time, as far as we were concerned, it wasn't an issue. People always act as if homophobia is something the Black community invented. We all know that that is not true. We didn't find that women were completely closed to the idea of being in a room with a group of lesbians talking about feminist politics. We just were a group of women trying to come together to talk about what it meant to be Black and female and Lesbians were on the spectrum. So that is just how it was.

I don't ever remember us going anywhere and people saying things like, "Here come the bull daggers" or "Here come those dykes." We didn't have that problem. It also may have been because in the venues that we found ourselves, we took ourselves to, we were involved with progressive people and progressive organizations. It is different when you are going out to do a speaking engagement, to talk about Black feminist organizing, because inevitably we would always say, as an organization, we support and respect the right for women to make the decisions about themselves, their sexuality, their lives, whatever. And so we always stated that and if we got.... it would create some interesting discussions, but it was not as if we went someplace and got stoned or we went to a meeting in a church and had people threaten to nail us to the cross and set us on fire. It just didn't happen that way.

What we had there was also a certain amount of respect that you get as a political activist. I found this to be true when you are working with people of color. Because we were really focusing on the issues and these were life and death, bread and butter issues. And we just acted as if it were perfectly alright for us to be who we were and be respected for who we were. So we didn't have problems as a group going into situations like that which is not to say, as individuals we didn't have problems in the community. But I never did.

The women of the CRC created a theory that was more polyvocal than the theories espoused by the Kennedy Commission women and the NBFO. The theory that they were able to provide is a useful tool to analyze the position of Black women in the 1990s. As Smith recalled,

I think we came up with the term "identity politics." I never really saw it anywhere else and I would suggest that people, if they really want to find the origin of the term, that they try to find it in any place earlier than in the Combahee River Collective statement. I don't remember seeing it anywhere else. But what we meant by identity politics was a politics that grew out of our objective material experiences as Black women. This was the kind of politics that had never been done or practiced before to our knowledge, although we began to find out that there were Black feminists in the early part of this century and also, perhaps, in the latter part of the nineteenth century. But it had never been quite formulated in the way that we were trying to formulate it, particularly because we were talking about homophobia, lesbian identity, as well.

So there were basically politics that worked for us. There were politics that took everything into account as opposed to saying leave your feminism, your gender, your sexual orientation, you leave that outside. You can be Black in here, but you can't be a lesbian, you can't be a feminist; or you can be a feminist in here, but you can't be Black. That's really what we meant. We meant politics that came out of the various identities that we had that really worked for us. It gave us a way to move, a way to make change. It was not the reductive version that theorists now really criticize. It was not being simplistic in saying I am Black and you are not. That wasn't what we were doing.

It was remarkable that without a clear model, without a huge amount of applause from the stands or whatever, that we took this on. We took on the contradictions of being in the U.S. and living in U.S. society under this system. We took on race, class, sexual orientation, and gender. And we said, instead of being bowled over by it and destroyed by it, we are going to make it into something vital and inspiring. I have to say that I really did know what we were doing when we were doing it. I think that because I have such a grounding in Black history and in Black culture, I was quite aware that we were doing something new.

One of the things that I used to feel was the lack of role models for myself. I used to feel like if only Lorraine [Hansberry] hadn't died so early then there would be someone who is older than me who is trying to carve out the territory. Audre [Lorde] was important to me in that way. Being able to look over to and up to someone who had been here more years than I, who shared the same kind of vision in politics, but I was very aware that we were doing something new because I knew enough about history and about political organizing to know that we were doing something that was never attempted before. But that doesn't mean that I felt competent at every moment. It was absolutely daunting work. It was depressing. It was frightening. It was exhausting. Yes, I think that metaphor of a river that begins in a dark swamp and small spaces and opens out I think that is quite apt. I was excited because I assumed that the 80s would be similar in their degree of growth and energy as the 70s had been. But as it turned out, I was not right about that.

The 1980s turned out to be the Reagan years, and political organizing became increasingly difficult. Public sentiment moved to the right, and the economic situation got even worse for those who were supposed to have benefited from trickle-down economics. Nevertheless, when 12 Black women were murdered in Boston in 1979, the Black feminist agenda would go into full effect. The only research that has been done to date about the activism of the CRC occurred in response to the collective's action in response to this crime. In Jamie Grant's unpublished article, "Who Is Killing Us?," the author explained that between January 28 and May 30, 1979, 13 women, 12 Black and one white, were murdered within a two mile radius in Boston. All but one of the victims was found in predominantly Black neighborhoods in the contiguous districts of Roxbury, Dorchester, and the South End. Many of the women were strangled, with bare hands or a scarf or cord, and some were stabbed; two were buried after they were killed, and two were dismembered. Several of the women had been raped.

Boston, which was notorious for its poor treatment of Blacks with the busing situation, a Black attorney stabbed with an American flag, and an attack on a Black high school football player, reflected the social climate in its major newspaper, *The Boston Globe*. The January 30, 1979, edition of the *Globe* noted the discovery of the bodies of the first two murder victims, then unidentified, on page 30 beside the racing forms. The murders merited only a four paragraph description with the headline "Two bodies found in a trash bag." On January 31, the murder of Gwendolyn Yvette Stinson was noted on page 13 under the headline, "Dorchester girl found dead." Caren Prater's death, on February 6, finally warranted a small block on the front page, followed by a confusing article about community outrage and police resources. On February 7, on page 8 of its Metro report, the *Globe* covered a community meeting with Mayor White at the Lee School in Dorchester, which more than 700 people attended.

The *Globe* took no responsibility for its complicity in the lack of public attention to the murders. When the *Globe* did focus attention on the crimes, it was to attack the Black community's response. Except for a small February 17 article on the murders, the *Globe* remained silent about the crisis until February 21, when Daryl Ann Hargett was found dead in her apartment. Even then, *The Globe's* journalistic treatment of the fifth death of a Black woman within 30 days fell short of what such a situation warranted. Hargett, whose first name was misspelled, appeared on the front page in a small text box in the lower left-hand corner of the front page. In contrast to *The Globe, The Bay State Banner*, the Black community weekly, ran full coverage of the crimes from the first of February and reported on the Black community's response. *The Banner* continued detailed, front page coverage throughout the year.

On April 1, following the deaths of six Black women, 1500 people took to the streets to mourn the loss of their sisters, daughters, mothers, and friends. The memorial march commenced in Boston's South End at the Harriet Tubman House and paused first at the Wellington Street apartment of Daryl Ann Hargett, the fifth victim, who was found strangled on the floor of her bedroom. The Combahee women reflected upon the tension in the political and cultural environment that pervaded Boston at the time:

> By that time in April, six women had been murdered and there was a memorial march in the South End about the murders. It was a protest march. It was also trying to commemorate them and there was a rally at the Stride-Rite factory field and you heard things that had already been said, but the message came across loud and clear from the almost entirely Black male speakers that what Black women needed to do was stay in the house. That's the way you saved yourself from being murdered. You stayed in the house and/or you found a man to protect you. If you were going to leave the house, you had to find a man to go with you to take care of you.
>
> And also, the murders were being viewed at time as being completely racial murders. It was all women and some of the women had been sexually assaulted, but they were still seen as racial murders. There were a lot of feminist lesbians at that rally so there were at least some people there that when they heard this message that these were just racial murders, our ears perked up, stood up, whatever and we were thinking, no, no, I don't think so because there was something called violence against women that we were all too familiar with and we just felt... so it was just such a difficult afternoon because at one level, we were grieving because Black women were being killed, we felt like we were at risk. We knew we were, in fact. We were scared. It was a very frightening time to be a Black woman in Boston. So there was that kind of collective shared grieving and then there was this real feeling of real fury.

It was just infuriating because we knew that it was not a coincidence that everybody who had been murdered was female and as it turned out, by the time it was over, 12 Black women had been murdered. When the marchers reached the Stride Rite factory on Lenox Street in Roxbury, where the bodies of the first two women were found, Lorraine Bethel who eventually co-edited "Conditions Five" with Barbara Smith was there. Smith remembers Lorraine saying, "This is just horrible, we've got to do something."

Smith's anger and frustration at the rally speakers' failure to acknowledge sexism as a factor in the deaths of the women propelled her into action. She returned to her apartment in Roxbury and began developing a pamphlet that would speak to the fears of Black women in Boston. She remembered,

I said, I think we really need to do a pamphlet. We need to do something. So I started writing a pamphlet that night and I thought of the title, "Six Black Women, Why Did They Die?" and I wrote it up. I always write everything longhand to begin with and then I type it. I had a little Smith-Corona electric portable at that time. And by the next morning, it was basically done. I called other people in the Collective. The Collective was never huge so I am not talking about calling 20 people. But I called other people in the group and I read it to them. This was before faxes and all that madness. I read it to them and then I also called up Urban Planning Aid in Boston and went down there and got assistance with laying out the pamphlet, using my actual typing from my own typewriter at home.

Basically, what we wanted to say and did say in the pamphlet is that we had to look at these murders as both racist and sexist crimes and that we really needed to talk about violence against women in the Black community. We needed to talk about those women who did not have men as a buffer. Almost no woman has a man as a buffer between them and violence because it doesn't make any difference if you are married or heterosexual, whatever, all kinds of women are at risk for attack in different kinds of circumstances. And in fact, most women are attacked by the men they know. So obviously, having a man isn't going to protect you from violence. But we really wanted to, first of all, get out that sexual political analysis about these murders. We wanted to do some consciousness-raising about what the murders meant. We also wanted to give women hope. So the pamphlet had the statement, the analysis, the political analysis, and it said that it had been prepared by the Combahee River Collective. That was a big risk for us, a big leap to identify ourselves in something that we knew was going to be widely distributed. It also had a list of things that you can do to pro-tect yourself. In other words, self-defense methods. I remember consult-ing with people like some of the violence against women organizations to really check out to make sure that the things that we were suggesting were usable and good and then also, we had a list of organizations that were doing work on violence against women in Boston.

We got great support from the community churches. We got a lot of support from very diverse groups of people, but I must say, the larger White feminist community was incredibly supportive. It was a real oppor-tunity to do some coalition building and we were able to mobilize hun-dreds and hundreds of people to come out and to speak out to talk about the issue. We were able to bring together very diverse groups of people around the issue of violence against women. And we never felt that it had lost the focus on the fact that the women were Black. One thing we did say though is that these are women, these are Black women who were being murdered. They could have been you. It could have been any of us.

Throughout the interviews, all six founding members of the CRC cited numerous reasons for the eventual disintegration of the organ-ization. What seemed to come to the surface after much investigation were accusations that the group was less egalitarian than it claimed to be. Several of the interviewees alluded to the fact that although hierar-chies were not supposed to exist, indeed they did. There was also men-tion of love relations that went awry, leaving at least one member of the Collective not wanting to attend retreats. Having given this issue much thought, it seems that the Collective was most cohesive and active when the issue of the murders in Boston was occurring. Having an event to respond to and organize around represented a cause where the group could concentrate its energies, which distracted them from the in-fight-ing that existed over power struggles and broken hearts. Also, according to Margo Okazawa Rey, who had attended graduate school at Harvard, this was a time in many of their twenty-something lives when geograph-ical dispersion was bound to happen. By the early 1980s, several of the members had left the Boston area to begin the next phase of their lives.

Most of the women continued the work of the collective through aca-demia. Rey and Hull are examples of two members who ended up in California teaching race, class, and gender theory at San Francisco State University and The University of California-Santa Cruz, respectively.

Sharon Page Ritchie plans to join the California University system to study clothing design. Cheryl Clarke is working on her dissertation about contemporary Black women poets at Rutgers University, where she is an administrator and advocate for the gay/lesbian/bisexual students on campus. Barbara Smith is working on a gay and lesbian studies anthology and resides in New York, and Demita Frazier has returned to Chicago to practice law. Although they no longer operate as a collective, the women of CRC left a legacy for Black feminists of the twenty-first century to study, to learn from, and to continue.

CHAPTER 5

Doubting the Democrats: Current Disenchantment and Political Futures

From the 1960s on, African-Americans have been one of the Democratic Party's most important political constituencies. Black voters have offered nearly unwavering support to Democratic candidates. For the Democrats, it has been easy to maintain this relationship by taking credit for good deeds, and blaming the Republicans for trying to reverse the gains of the 1960s during the 1980s. The Republicans have never completely accepted the Democratic Party's hold over the Black electorate, but they have never made a concerted effort until the opening of the twenty-first century. Recent Republican campaigns and even national conventions have been carefully orchestrated to appeal to Black voters, and several Black women and men hold high-level Cabinet positions, Condoleezza Rice being one of them.

Two of the three African-Americans who addressed the 2000 Republican National Convention were also two of the biggest names in George W. Bush's administration: Condoleezza Rice and Colin Powell. Powell is, of course, the more familiar of the two names to most Americans, having served as the Chairman of the Joint Chiefs of Staff during George Bush Sr.'s administration, gaining name and face recognition during the Gulf War, and acquiring a highly visible international presence as Secretary of State. Yet both Rice and Powell presented certain challenges to the kinds of narratives that had, until their tenure, characterized Black Americans' involvement in political life. On the one hand, Colin Powell was largely able to surmount the race

© The Author(s) 2019   137
D. Harris, *Black Feminist Politics from Kennedy to Trump*,
https://doi.org/10.1007/978-3-319-95456-1_5

factor altogether. Consider, for example that former Secretary of Defense Caspar Weinberger was quoted as saying, "The fact of the matter is that with Colin I never think of whether he's Black or white...." What stands at the center of Weinberger's sentiment is that Black Americans have permitted white Americans to define Blackness for far too long. If Black racial identity is constructed in a manner that allowed the group's members to have positive attributes related to character, Colin Powell could be simultaneously impressive and Black, a privilege that most Black Americans are denied.

While Colin Powell was able to transcend race in his public post, in which perceptions were foisted upon him and not projected by him, he did not make the effort to do so in his memoir. In *My American Journey*, Colin Powell asserts his Blackness, a side of Colin Powell that most white and Black Americans had not seen. In his memoir, General Powell does not just wear a uniform; he wears the proverbial mask that Paul Lawrence Dunbar mentions in his poetry. In the imagery of African folk literature, Powell can be understood as a trickster; here you have a Black man who spent 35 years manipulating the dominant culture's inability to racialize competence, and now will sell them a book that actually supports affirmative action, denounces the Willie Horton campaign, celebrates the Buffalo soldiers, and tells of his initial concern that his son married a white woman. All of this, of course, is enveloped within a red, white, and blue jacket cover. To avoid these subjects in his public speaking, but to address them in writing is nothing short of brilliant; Powell is "banking" on the old adage that if you want to keep something secret, put it in a book.

Similar to Martin Luther King, Jr., Powell was held up by white America as an icon for the ability of all people to achieve the American Dream. Before King died, he denounced the Vietnam War and began to embrace self-defense in a manner not very different from Malcolm X. For some reason, however, even though these actions are recent enough for anyone 40 or older to remember, our nation suffers from social amnesia. Our country has successfully appropriated a resistant figure like Dr. King, whose views changed dramatically in the last four years of his life, as proof that Blacks would overcome. I have never attended an event where a white person quoted one of Dr. King's speeches written after 1963. When Dr. King expressed his rage as a Black man in America, his popularity diminished quickly. The same will hold true for General Powell if anyone bothers to read all 613 pages of his book.

Powell wrote, "My Blackness has been a source of pride, strength, and inspiration, and so has my being an American. I started out believing in an America where anyone, given equal opportunity, can succeed through hard work and faith. I still believe in that America." Equal opportunity is the key phrase in this manifesto, and the four-star general never tried to claim that equality exists. Embedded within this hyper-patriotic text, a dialectic strategy in itself, are stories of resistance, stories that are largely predicated on aspects of racial identity. Powell recalled his pride when his daughter Linda performed a segment of Ntozake Shange's controversial play, *for colored girls who have considered suicide/when the rainbow is enuf*, against the direct orders of her high school administration. Powell also acknowledged the fact that, as a Jamaican, he has a fundamentally different relationship to America than many African-Americans. Finally, Powell attempted to use race as a way to reaffirm his identity as a Black man and to establish a link and sense of identity with readers, quipping, "When Blacks go off in a corner for their kind of music or dancing, I'm tempted to say to my white friends, 'Don't panic, we're just having fun.'" Powell stopped short, however, of articulating the most audacious ambition for a Black man, staying within bounds "appropriate" for his race. On the 609th page, he assures his reader that he would not run for the highest office in the land because he did not want to be seen as the "Great Black Hope," providing a role model for African-Americans or a symbol to whites of racism overcome.

Although Powell refused to be a pawn in America's race game, his background in military conservatism created the conditions that influenced his somewhat tenuous relationship with the Black community. In direct conflict with the Congressional Black Caucus, Powell opposed lifting the ban on gays in the armed forces. The General also spoke out against the Million Man March on national television on the day of the event. Unlike some prominent Black men, like Johnnie Cochran, who boycotted the March because of its exclusion of Black women, Powell did not address the destructive issue of gender divisiveness. While many national leaders were able to separate the messenger from the message, Powell publicly drew an analogy between Louis Farrakhan's anti-Semitism and Mark Fuhrman's racism. On a day that was set aside for Black economic empowerment, Powell empowered himself: He held a signing and sold his book. Powell's book signing and promotion remind us that his economic allegiances tied him to the power elite, not to the historically downtrodden.

Powell is a Black man, but in the tradition of H. Ross Perot he tried to convince us that he is a common man, and nothing could be further from the truth. As a self-proclaimed "fiscal conservative with a social conscience," Powell articulated no vision for the 50% of Black children who grow up in poverty. While the responsibilities of his position did not require insight or involvement in such matters, Powell demonstrated a preoccupying lack of knowledge about broad-based issues affecting the community with which he would have liked his reader to believe he was aligned. During his September 15, 1995, interview with Barbara Walters, Powell admitted that he did not know very much about the welfare system. The former Chairman of the Joint Chiefs of Staff had no insight into this problem, and why should he? Colin Powell had moved far from his humble South Bronx beginnings, and as he told *The New Yorker*, "...I just figured out what the white guys were doing," and, presumably, appropriated and imitated their strategies. Powell's message to Black America seems to be, "Give white America what they want and then get them to purchase it from you." With his book, Powell produced a commodity. If the astute reader happens to catch on that Powell isn't just like them but darker, Powell could choose not to notice that the consumer is white, just that their money is green. The General figured out what most Black people know but haven't actualized: The true American journey is to the bank.

As the foreign policy advisor during the Bush campaign, Condoleezza Rice was a new face to voters. Powell and Rice were very significant figures during the Republican convention, as they and Oklahoma congressman J. C. Watts were given prime-time slots to address the delegates. As part of the strategy of appealing to African-American voters, Powell and Rice had very different roles, with Powell playing the conscience of the Republican Party and Rice playing its cheerleader. In his speech, Powell charged the party to remember those moments in history when it had injured Black Americans. Without making a direct statement about racism, per se, Powell addressed many of the political issues that have continually allied Black Americans with the Democrats, including affirmative action, welfare, universal health care, education, and criminal justice. Very early in his speech, Powell stated:

The issue of race still casts a shadow over our society, despite the impressive progress we have made over the last 40 years to overcome the legacy of our troubled past. So, with all the success we have enjoyed and with all the wealth we have created, we have much more work to do and a long way to go to bring the promise of America to every American.[1]

Powell went on to explain:

The party must follow Governor Bush's lead and reach out to minority communities and particularly the African-American community--and not just during an election year campaign. It must be a sustained effort. It must be every day. It must be for real. The party must listen to and speak with all leaders of the Black community, regardless of political affiliation or philosophy.

We must understand the cynicism that exists in the Black community. The kind of cynicism that is created when, for example, some in our party miss no opportunity to loudly condemn affirmative action that helped a few thousand Black kids get an education, but hardly a whimper is heard from them over affirmative action for lobbyists who load our federal tax codes with preferences for special interests.[2]

Taken out of context, this bit of rhetoric could be easily mistaken for a sound bite from the Democratic national convention, or even from a more progressive organization like the Black Radical Congress. Powell's defense of affirmative action was unprecedented. His final statement about affirmative action for special interests could very easily be read as an attack on the types of tax incentives and federal aid offered to corporations: a form of welfare that, as many liberals and leftists have pointed out, is far more expensive than AFDC ever was. In addition, by using the term "special interests" to characterize people, groups, and organizations who are *not* Black Americans, Powell moved away from lines of Republican discourse that cast African-Americans as another special interest group begging for special rights that are not granted to other Americans.

---

[1] http://www.washingtonpost.com/wp-srv/onpolitics/elections/cpowelltext073100.htm.

[2] Ibid.

As the conscience of the party, Powell's speech was the sharpest critique that the Republicans were willing to receive during their own convention. It was a well-orchestrated finale to George W. Bush's speech before the NAACP, incorporating Bush's rhetoric about the Republican Party again assuming responsibility as the party of Lincoln. Powell's speech was targeted to the Black working-class and poor, the people whom William Julius Wilson describes as "the truly disadvantaged." Powell's appeal to the Republican Party was meant to be overheard by those Black Americans whose economic status is still over determined by their racial identity and who may require federal assistance in order to sustain their lives and the lives of their families. More than anything else, Powell appealed to African-Americans' sense of themselves as a heterogeneous social group in the USA that has suffered and continues to suffer from the material and psychological impact of racism. He called for Black Americans, en masse, to look to the Republican Party for leadership in the new century.

Condoleezza Rice's appointment to the important post of National Security Advisor was a significant part of the Bush administration's strategy to provide the kind of leadership Black Americans were looking for. Angela D. Dillard's work *Guess Who's Coming to Dinner Now? Multicultural Conservatism in America*[3] demonstrates that even though fewer than 10% of African-Americans voted for George W. Bush, the ones who did would wield power. Dillard wrote, "In pursuing the historical and contemporary expressions of Black conservatism, I began to find intriguing intersections and parallels among Latino, homosexual, and women conservatives...."[4] Dillard added:

> Along with their mainstream allies, they [conservatives] have worked to repeal affirmative action and other race and gender conscious policies; to dismantle the welfare state for the sake of the poor; to discredit bilingual education; to stem the tide of special rights of homosexuals; and to counter such supposedly radical and therefore dangerous academic trends as queer theory, afrocentrism, Chicano studies, feminism and anything else judged to under gird identity politics: a politics engendered by conceiving of individuals as members of oppressed and victimized groups.[5]

[3]Dillard, A. D. (2001). *Guess Who's Coming to Dinner Now?: Multicultural Conservatism in America.* New York: New York University Press.

[4]Dillard, A. D. (2001). *Guess Who's Coming to Dinner Now?: Multicultural Conservatism in America.* New York: New York University Press, p. 2.

[5]Dillard, A. D. (2001). *Guess Who's Coming to Dinner Now?: Multicultural Conservatism in America.* New York: New York University Press, p. 3.

Although Dillard does not mention Condoleezza Rice anywhere in her 182-page book, the former Stanford provost fits Dillard's categorization of the classic "multicultural conservative."

Rice, the second Black American to speak at the convention, had a different message from that of Powell, but one that was equally essential to the Republicans' appeal to African-American voters. As foreign policy advisor, Rice's primary purpose as a speaker was to underscore Bush's ability to lead the USA in matters related to national and international security. But as *The New York Times* noted the day after Rice gave her speech, her presence at the podium only served to underscore Bush's regularly stated commitment to place "minorities" in key administrative positions. The significance of Rice's speech, however, was even more covert than the *Times* noted. Where Colin Powell played the conscience of the Republican Party and appealed to Black Americans' sense of community and racial identity, Rice took a deliberately opposite approach. Instead of speaking to group identity, Rice spoke to her own particularity, to her individuality, by citing her personal reasons for being involved with the Republican Party. Unlike Powell's speech, which was designed to appeal to the Black working-class and poor, attracting a broader base to support Bush and his party, Rice's speech was designed to appeal to the new Black middle class by appealing to a sense of individual identity, apart from the so-called Black masses. A Democrat in her youth, Rice offered the following remarks about her decision to join the Republican Party:

> The first Republican I knew was my father, and he is still the Republican I most admire. He joined our party because the Democrats in Jim Crow Alabama of 1952 would not register him to vote. The Republicans did. My father has never forgotten that day, and neither have I.
>
> I joined for different reasons. I found a party that sees me as an individual, not as part of a group. I found a party that puts family first. I found a party that has love of liberty at its core. And I found a party that believes that peace begins with strength.[6]

Rice's speech was peppered with frequent references to individuality, as well as references to her own family's history—a history that was deliberately decontextualized and vague, so as to cast the achievements of her family members as individual successes, removed from history or

[6]http://www.washingtonpost.com/wp-srv/onpolitics/elections/ricetext080100.htm.

community. The story of Rice's family was woven throughout the speech in a remarkably skillful manner, also playing upon a gendered narrative in which the woman was located within the context of her family history. While Rice bolstered George W. Bush's limited expertise in matters related to foreign policy, she was simultaneously painting her own American dream: the dream where hard work, determination, and patriotism pay off in the end. In Rice's own words:

> In America, with education and hard work, it really does not matter where you came from — it matters where you are going. But that truth cannot be sustained if it is not renewed in each generation as it was with my grandfather.[7]

Rice went on in her speech to offer her "Granddaddy Rice" as a shining example of a good new Republican. Granddaddy Rice was a poor farmer in rural Alabama, and in 1918 he decided he wanted to go to college. Seventy-two years later, his granddaughter offered these thoughts on the matter:

> After the first year, he ran out of cotton and needed a way to pay for college. Praise be — God gave him one. Grandfather asked how the other boys were staying in school. "They have what's called a scholarship," he was told, "and if you wanted to be a Presbyterian minister, then you could have one, too." Granddaddy Rice said, "That's just what I had in mind." And my family has been Presbyterian and college-educated ever since. This is not just my grandfather's story — it is an American story.

Rice's presence on the dais of the convention was used to reflect back upon her family's history, as a silent testimony to the power of the American dream. Her grandfather was a sharecropper who went to Stillman College. His granddaughter was the provost at Stanford. Granddaddy Rice found his true calling as a Presbyterian minister. Condoleezza Rice may have found her true calling preaching for George W. Bush. In reflecting on this history, however, the aim is to illustrate the "individual" achievements that brought Granddaddy Rice and his family from rural Alabama to Capitol Hill. With its "anyone can make it in America" giddiness, Rice's story simultaneously moved the Black middle

---

[7] http://www.washingtonpost.com/wp-srv/onpolitics/elections/ricetext080100.htm.

class further away from the Black working class and poor by tying "hard working, determined Blacks" into the immigration narrative of white America, and silently pathologizing working-class and impoverished Blacks.

It remains to be seen whether these types of tactics will begin to change the voting patterns within Black America. Some analysts have argued that a turn to conservatism could provide a whole new set of options for Black Americans. For myself, I stand with the late great Judge A. Leon Higginbotham, the noted Black American jurist. In an open letter to Clarence Thomas after his controversial Supreme Court appointment, Higginbotham addressed Thomas's "Black conservatism" by remarking, "[O]ther than their own self-advancement, I am at a loss to understand what it is that the so-called Black conservatives are so anxious to conserve." Higginbotham's observations have no less relevance today than they did after Thomas's confirmation. In the year 2000, Black Americans *did not* have anything more to conserve than they did in 1992, and there was nothing that Colin Powell, Condoleezza Rice, or George W. Bush did to provide compelling evidence that they would change their trajectory.

STAYING OUT OF THE BUSHES: BARBARA LEE AND CYNTHIA MCKINNEY

On November 7, 2000, Al Gore thought that he had lost the presidency, but he wasn't sure. After originally conceding the election, he retracted his concession and demanded a recount in what became the closest presidential election in American history. Vice President Al Gore led the popular vote by a narrow margin. In the 2000 election, the NAACP launched the biggest voter drive in its 91-year history, spending more than $10 million to encourage what civil rights leaders believe was the biggest Black voter turnout in decades. Voting records confirmed that Black voters in Florida and around the country turned out in record numbers. Yet after the election, many complained that Florida election officials removed large numbers of minorities from state voting rolls, wrongly classifying them as convicted felons. Florida electoral officials were also accused of using police to intimidate voters in some areas. The Reverend Jesse Jackson cited the reports of students from historically Black colleges in Florida, who said they went to the polls carrying voter identification cards and were told that they were not on the voter rolls. After the Florida recount (overseen by Governor Jeb Bush, the Republican candidate's brother), the Supreme Court's 7-2 opinion concluded that the recounts would violate the Constitutional guarantees of equal protection under the law, since the counts were being conducted under different standards in different counties. Reverend Jesse Jackson compared the decision to the infamous nineteenth-century rulings upholding slavery and later, segregation. Pennsylvania Representative Chakah Fattah called the decision "out of step with a century of American progress" toward voting rights. Under the direction of Dr. Mary Frances Berry, the US Commission on Civil Rights undertook an investigation into allegations by Floridians of voting irregularities, but this did not change the outcome: Bush's accession to the presidency.

Ten months after assuming his position in the Oval Office, George Bush was faced with the bombing of the World Trade Center and the Pentagon on September 11, 2001. Most Americans outside of Oakland, California didn't know much about California's Ninth District US Representative, Barbara Lee. However, on September 15, 2001, the Senate passed a use-of-force resolution and the House overwhelmingly approved it by a 420-1 margin. Congresswoman Barbara Lee (D-CA) was the lone dissenting voice. Lee's resistance to Bush's domination provided a new model of Black female political leadership.

When it comes to military action, Congresswoman Lee has a history of dissent. In 1999, she was the only member of the House to vote against a resolution of support for US troops in Yugoslavia. In 1998, she opposed the Clinton administration's bombing of Iraq. Ironically, voting "no" after terrorists attacked the USA generated death threats for this pacifist. Congresswoman Lee explained her vote in the following statement:

WHY I OPPOSED THE RESOLUTION TO AUTHORIZE FORCE

Barbara Lee

On September 11, terrorists attacked the United States in an unprecedented and brutal manner, killing thousands of innocent people, including the passengers and crews of four aircraft. Like everyone throughout our country, I am repulsed and angered by these attacks and believe all appropriate steps must be taken to bring the perpetrators to justice.

We must prevent any future such attacks. That is the highest obligation of our federal, state and local governments. On this, we are united as a nation. Any nation, group or individual that fails to comprehend this or believes that we will tolerate such illegal and uncivilized attacks is grossly mistaken.

Last week, filled with grief and sorrow for those killed and injured and with anger at those who had done this, I confronted the solemn responsibility of voting to authorize the nation to go to war. Some believe this resolution was only symbolic, designed to show national resolve. But I could not ignore that it provided explicit authority, under the War Powers Resolution and the Constitution, to go to war.

It was a blank check to the president to attack anyone involved in the September 11 events—anywhere, in any country, without regard to our nation's long-term foreign policy, economic and national security interests, and without time limit. In granting these overly broad powers, the Congress failed its responsibility to understand the dimensions of its declaration. I could not support such a grant of war-making authority to the president; I believe it would put more innocent lives at risk.

The president has the constitutional authority to protect the nation from further attack and he has mobilized the armed forces to do just that. The Congress should have waited for the facts to be presented and then acted with fuller knowledge of the consequences of our action.

I have heard from thousands of my constituents in the wake of this vote. Many—a majority—have counseled restraint and caution, demanding that we ascertain the facts and ensure that violence does not beget violence. They understand the boundless consequences of proceeding hastily to war, and I thank them for their support.

Others believe that I should have voted for the resolution—either for symbolic or geopolitical reasons, or because they truly believe a military option is unavoidable. However, I am not convinced that voting for the resolution preserves and protects U.S. interests. We must develop our intelligence and bring those who did this to justice. We must mobilize and maintain an international coalition against terrorism. Finally, we have a chance to demonstrate to the world that great powers can choose to fight on the fronts of their choosing, and that we can choose to avoid needless military action when other avenues to redress our rightful grievances and to protect our nation are available to us.

We must respond, but the character of that response will determine for us and for our children the world that they will inherit. I do not dispute the president's intent to rid the world of terrorism—but we have many means to reach that goal, and measures that spawn further acts of terror or that do not address the sources of hatred do not increase our security.

Secretary of State Colin Powell himself eloquently pointed out the many ways to get at the root of this problem—economic, diplomatic, legal and political, as well as military. A rush to launch precipitous military counterattacks runs too great a risk that more innocent men, women, [and] children will be killed. I could not vote for a resolution that I believe could lead to such an outcome (*San Francisco Chronicle*, September 23, 2001).

This attitude inspired Alice Walker's tribute to Barbara Lee in *Sent by Earth: A Message from the Grandmother Spirit After the Attacks on the World Trade Center and Pentagon*. Alice Walker's affirmation of Barbara Lee received less hostility than Michelle Wallace's *Black Macho and the Myth of the Superwoman* of the 1970s primarily because, in the midst of national tragedy, it received less attention. In Kim Springer's 1999 dissertation, "Our Politics Was Black Women," Springer attributed Black feminist organizational decline to three factors: (1) insufficient monetary resources, (2) activist burnout, and (3) ideological disputes. I agree with Springer's assessment that Black feminist organizations encountered issues of Black self-determination, racial authenticity, and source and control dilemmas. Springer concluded that the political opportunity structure that yielded so many positive results for the civil rights movement closed in the 1980s, leaving Black feminist organizations to either fold or wait in abeyance for new opportunities for gains against racist, sexist, heterosexist, and classist discrimination. Springer's dissertation leaves off in 1980. The question this book leaves us asking is, "*Were* their new opportunities for gains, and why didn't Black feminist politics survive for the next 20 years?"

When I wrote this book, I set out to answer two questions: (1) "What did feminist identified Black women do to gain 'political power' between 1961 and 2001 in America?", and (2) "Why didn't they succeed?" This book has shown that Black women have tried to gain centrality by their participation in Presidential Commissions, Black feminist organizations, theatrical productions, film adaptations of literature, beauty pageants, electoral politics, and Presidential appointments. I am working with the

assumption that "success" means that, among other more general constructs, (1) the feminist identified Black women in the Congressional
Black Caucus who voted against Clarence Thomas's appointment would
have spoken on behalf of Anita Hill; (2) Senator Carol Moseley Braun
would have won reelection; (3) Lani Gunier would have had a hearing; (4) Dr. Joycelyn Elders would have maintained her post; and (5)
Congresswoman Barbara Lee wouldn't have stood alone in her opposition to the war resolution.

Collective Black feminism has met the resistance of the American public in general, and their most obvious allies—Black men, white women,
and the Democratic Party in particular. The individual gains and achievements of Condoleezza Rice demonstrate that in the twenty-first century, Black female political prominence *is* possible... as long as it is not
feminist.

The first edition of this book was written during the summer of
2008, before the presidential election. Of course, what would unfold
after the book's initial publication offered far more material for analysis
about Black feminists' role and agency in American political life. There
was, for example, Oprah Winfrey's endorsement of Obama, and her
increasing influence over the political sphere. As Patricia Williams wrote
in *The Nation* in 2007, the "Double O's" (Obama and Oprah), were
"an arresting team [and] brilliant speakers, easy with large audiences,"
with a "particular form of raced celebrity [that] enshrines the notion of
American mobility."

The "Double O" mania, which was certainly acknowledged by people other than Williams, tended to overshadow two Black women who
should not have been overlooked: Barack's wife, Michelle, and Green
Party presidential nominee, Cynthia McKinney. Despite Barack Obama's
worldwide popularity, many did not take to his brown-skinned, working-
class, South Side Chicago wife. Those attributes were more visible than
the fact that she was also a Princeton alum, and graduated Harvard Law
School before the Senator did, and was actually his boss when he was
still a student. Her unusual brand of candor also raised eyebrows, especially in the white establishment of conservative politics. When she told a
Milwaukee crowd in February 2008 that, "For the first time in my adult
lifetime, I am really proud of my country, and not just because Barack
has done well, but because I think people are hungry for change," conservative talk show host Bill O'Reilly, took a call from one of his lis-
teners, who addressed Michelle Obama's apparent gaffe from earlier in

the week ("for the first time in my adult lifetime, I'm really proud of my country"). The caller, who identified herself as Maryanne, claimed to have insight into the character of Michelle Obama, saying that she is "very angry" and "militant."

In response, O'Reilly came to Obama's defense with this bizarre rant:

> You know, I have a lot of sympathy for Michelle Obama, for Bill Clinton, for all of these people. Bill Clinton, I have sympathy for him, because they're thrown into a hopper where everybody is waiting for them to make a mistake, so that they can just go and bludgeon them...That's wrong. And **I don't want to go on a lynching party against Michelle Obama** unless there's evidence, hard facts, that say this is how the woman really feels. If that's how she really feels — that America is a bad country or a flawed nation, whatever — then that's legit....

Although O'Reilly later apologized for his "lynching party" comment, several months later he continued to depict Michelle Obama as "angry."

From the September 16 edition of Fox News' *The O'Reilly Factor*:

> *O'REILLY*: In the "Obama Chronicles" segment tonight: the controversial wife of the Democratic candidate, Michelle Obama. "Chronicle" facts: Mrs. Obama was born on January 17, 1964, in Chicago. Her father worked for the city. He died from MS in 1991. Her mother worked as a secretary. She still lives on the south side of Chicago. She has one sibling, her brother, who coaches the Oregon State University basketball team. She graduated from Princeton and has a law degree from Harvard. She married Barack Obama in 1992. They have two young girls.
>
> Joining us now from Washington, Michelle Oddis, a columnist for HumanEvents.com, and here in the studio, Rebecca Johnson, who wrote a profile of Mrs. Obama for *Vogue* magazine.
>
> You spent some time with her. How much time?
>
> *REBECCA JOHNSON (Vogue* magazine contributing editor): A few hours.
>
> *O'REILLY*: Just a few hours with her?
>
> *JOHNSON*: Hmm-mm. Half a day.
>
> *O'REILLY*: How did you find her in person? Was she engaging?
>
> *JOHNSON*: I found her lovely, actually, very bright, very thoughtful and, you know, an impressive person, intelligent. She was great. I was impressed.

O'REILLY: Now, I have a lot of people who call me on the radio and say she looks angry. And I have to say there's some validity to that. She looks like an angry woman. Did you ask her about that?

JOHNSON: Don't they say that about you, too?

O'REILLY: Yeah, but I'm not running for—I'm not going to be the first lady.

JOHNSON: But she's—

O'REILLY: I hope not, anyway. The perception is that she's angry in some quarters. Valid?

JOHNSON: Well—they say she looks angry because of maybe of the cast of her eyebrows or something like that. But, no, I don't find her to be angry. I think what happens is that we expect women to be cheerful and happy all the time in that kind of television personality kind of way. And she's not like that. She's a thoughtful person. She's not going to—

O'REILLY: Warm and fuzzy?

JOHNSON: No.

O'REILLY: Not warm and fuzzy?

JOHNSON: No.

O'REILLY: Even to you, who she's trying to win over as an author of the piece?

JOHNSON: You know, she was not trying to win me over in any way.

O'REILLY: Really?

JOHNSON: No, not at all.

O'REILLY: Because it's interesting, because most people—talking to somebody who's going to write about them—want to win you over. She didn't want to win you over?

JOHNSON: No, not at all.

O'REILLY: Why not?

JOHNSON: And it's interesting, because I actually—I've also interviewed Sarah Palin, and she was very friendly and very—

O'REILLY: Tried to win you over.

JOHNSON: Yeah. But Michelle wasn't trying to win me over with a kind of a false chumminess. She is somebody who speaks her mind, and stands on her own. And whether I liked her or not, I don't think was particularly important to her, no.

O'REILLY: OK, interesting.

In the fall of 2008, we did not know who the next President of the USA would be. I made a safe prediction that it would not be Cynthia McKinney. In her July 12, 2008, Green Party nominee acceptance speech she said:

Thank you all for being here and standing with me today.

In 1851, in Akron, Ohio a former slave woman, abolitionist, and woman's rights activist by the name of Sojourner Truth gave a speech now known as "Ain't I a Woman" Sojourner Truth began her remarks, "Well children, where there is so much racket, there must be something out of kilter." She then went on to say that even though she was a woman, no one had ever helped her out of carriages or lifted her over ditches or given her a seat of honor in any place. Instead, she acknowledged, that as a former slave and as a black woman, she had had to bear the lash as well as any man; and that she had borne "thirteen children, and seen most all sold off to slavery, and when I cried out with my mother's grief, none but Jesus heard me! And Ain't I a woman?" Finally, Sojourner Truth says, "If the first woman God ever made was strong enough to turn the world upside down all alone, these women together ought to be able to turn it back, and get it right side up again!"

As it was in 1851, so too was it in 2008. There was so much racket that we, too, knew something was out of kilter. In 1851, the racket was about a woman's right to vote. In 1848, just a few years before Sojourner uttered those now famous words, "Ain't I a Woman?" suffragists met in Seneca Falls, New York and issued a declaration. That declaration began:

> We hold these truths to be self-evident: that all men and women are created equal; that they are endowed by their Creator with certain inalienable rights; that among these are life, liberty, and the pursuit of happiness; that to secure these rights governments are instituted, deriving their just powers from the consent of the governed. Whenever any form of government becomes destructive of these ends, it is the right of those who suffer from it to refuse allegiance to it, and to insist upon the institution of a new government … But when a long train of abuses and usurpations, pursuing invariably the same object evinces a design to reduce them under absolute despotism, it is their duty to throw off such government, and to provide new guards for their future security. Such has been the patient sufferance of the women under this government, and such is now the necessity which constrains them to demand the equal station to which they are entitled.[8]

---

[8] https://www.nps.gov/articles/sojourner-truth.htm.

Two hundred sixty women and forty men gathered in Seneca Falls, New York and declared their independence from the politics of their present and embarked upon a struggle to create a politics for the future. That bold move by a handful of people in one relatively small room laid the groundwork and is the precedent for what we do today. The Seneca Falls Declaration represented a clean break from the past: Freedom, at last, from mental slavery. The Seneca Falls Declaration and the Akron, Ohio meeting inaugurated 72 years of struggle that ended with the passage of the 19th Amendment in August of 1920, granting women the right to vote. And 88 years later, with the Green Party as its conductor, the History Train is rolling down the tracks.

To paraphrase a member of the Combahee River Collective, when it came to the Democratic Party, Hilary Clinton was white, Barack Obama was a man, but Cynthia McKinney was brave.

CHAPTER 6

The State of Black Women in Politics Under the First Black President

History was made in November 2008. Record-breaking numbers of voters lined up to vote the first African-American President into office, with Barack Obama handily beating Arizona Republican Senator John McCain and winning 52% of the electoral vote, a clear mandate for change.[1] African-Americans made up 13% of the electorate, a two percent increase from the 2006 elections,[2] and approximately 95% of black voters cast their ballots in favor of Obama.[3] Within that 13%, black women had the highest voter turnout rate among all racial, gender, and ethnic groups.[4]

As the election results were posted, the media and the president-elect himself made grand proclamations about the significance of the election, as well as what it portended for the country's future. *New York Times* writer Adam Nagourney described voters' election of Obama as "sweeping away the last racial barrier in American politics," continuing with a quote from Obama's victory speech in Grant Park, Chicago:

---

[1] Johnson, Alex . (2008, November 5). "Barack Obama Elected 44th President." MSNBC. com. http://www.msnbc.msn.com/id/27531033/. Retrieved on August 24, 2010.

[2] Nagourney, Adam . (2008, November 4). "Obama Elected President as Racial Barrier Falls." *The New York Times.* http://www.nytimes.com/2008/11/05/us/politics/05elect. html. Retrieved on August 24, 2010.

[3] Lopez, Mark Hugo, & Taylor, Paul. (2009, April 30). "Dissecting the 2008 Electorate: Most Diverse in U.S. History." Pew Research Center. http://pewresearch.org/pubs/1209/racial-ethnic-voters-presidential-election. Retrieved on September 1, 2010.

[4] Lopez and Taylor.

© The Author(s) 2019
D. Harris, *Black Feminist Politics from Kennedy to Trump,*
https://doi.org/10.1007/978-3-319-95456-1_6

If there is anyone out there who still doubts that America is a place where all things are possible, who still wonders if the dream of our founders is alive in our time, who still questions the power of our democracy, tonight is your answer.... It's been a long time coming, but tonight, because of what we did on this date in this election at this defining moment, change has come to America.[5]

It would be nice to think that Obama's election was the positive end-note of over four hundred years of slavery, Jim Crow laws, and institutionalized racism. That the promise stated by our founders, "all men are created equal," had finally been realized. And there was a certain quintessence once a black family moved into the White House, a national monument primarily constructed with the use of slave labor. For a nation weary of its own racist history, the Obama administration was a historic marker that many, especially those on the Right, could point to and say, "See, it's over."

But on closer examination, particularly with regard to the status of Black women in the political sphere, the early years of the Obama administration were a dismal replay of the mistakes made by the much-lauded Clinton (the "first black president") administration. Such a statement isn't intended to dismiss President Obama's many accomplishments. He constituted the most diverse Cabinet in history, captained the successful passage of a health care reform bill, and negotiated the military withdrawal from Iraq, all significant achievements. Nevertheless, President Obama and his administration continued to shy away from conversations about race. Many political commentators went so far as to say that America had entered a "post-racial" phase, with President Obama being the first "post-racial" President.

Black women begged to differ. While the Obama presidency began positively, with several positions within the administration offered to Black women during the initial wave of change, there were two early incidents comparable to Bill Clinton's betrayals of Lani Guinier and Dr. Joycelyn Elders. President Obama failed to stand up for press secretary Desiree Rogers; then, he left Shirley Sherrod (formerly of the USDA), to fend for herself in a crucial and very public incident in which his support could have changed the course of events. And remarkably, given the opportunity to appoint two Supreme Court Justices, not a single qualified Black woman moved from the nominee list to face-to-face interviews with the President in the nomination and review processes.

[5] Nagourney.

These are just some examples that speak to why Obama was often a source of disappointment for Black women. Yes, there were numerous African-American women in his administration, but few of them were assigned to positions with true power. And for those chosen few, the new president seemed unwilling to defend them, even in the face of misconstrued or erroneous reports. It appeared that the price of having the first African-American President was that he could not, or would not, address issues of race beyond the vaguest allusions that construed slavery as just another immigrant story. Over the course of his administration, it became increasingly difficult to believe that change had come to America in a meaningful way, especially for Black women.

THE OBAMA WOMEN

The administration began with such promise. With the election of Obama came the appointment of the most diverse cabinet in history.[6] According to Sam Ali, writing for *Diversity Inc.com*, 30% of Obama's cabinet appointments were women and 39% were Black, Latino, and Asian. Among these appointments were many black women, including senior advisor Valerie Jarrett (a Chicago colleague of the Obamas, who served as a top advisor on Obama's campaign and then as co-chair of his transition team); US ambassador to the United Nations, Susan Rice (Rice was Assistant Secretary of State for African Affairs during Clinton's second term); social secretary Desiree Rogers (another Obama Chicago colleague); and Lisa P. Jackson, Administrator of the Environmental Protection Agency (former commissioner of the New Jersey Department of Environmental Protection). Several of these women were the first black or biracial women in their positions: Jackson, Melody Barnes (Director of the Domestic Policy Council), Mona Sutphen (Deputy Chief of Staff for Policy), and Margaret (Peggy) Hamburg (Food and Drug Administration Commissioner).[7] Krissah Thompson, writing for *The Washington Post*, said African-American women occupied about seven of three dozen senior positions in Obama's early administration and that the women who were

[6]Ali, Sam . (2009, November 4). "Obama Vs. Bush: Scorecard on Cabinet Diversity." DiversityInc.com. http://www.diversityinc.com/content/1757/article/6319/. August 13, 2010.

[7]Thompson, Krissah . (2009, March 18). "The Ties That Align: Administration's Black Women Form a Strong Sisterhood." *The Washington Post.* http://www.washingtonpost. com/wp-dyn/content/article/2009/03/17/AR2009031703744.html. Retrieved on August 15, 2010.

new to the Washington, DC, environment found a supportive network extended by their predecessors. Those women included Donna Brazile, political strategist and the first African-American woman to direct a political campaign (Al Gore's in 2000), and Cheryl Mills, who was the first black woman deputy White House council, during Clinton's administration. Such a support network was—and remains—important in an arena that is still largely white and male.

In addition to the appointment of a number of black women to his administration and staff, during his first months in office, Obama took several actions that showed solidarity and support for women. The first bill he signed into law was the Lilly Ledbetter Fair Pay Act, which made it easier for workers to sue their employers after discovering discriminatory payment practices, rather than having to report incidents within six months of the first occurrence. The bill changed the initial Supreme Court ruling of *Ledbetter v. Goodyear*, which denied Lilly Ledbetter the right to sue her employer of nearly 20 years after discovering men in her same position received more money than she, because she reported the discrimination more than 180 days after its first occurrence. Obama's signing of the bill allowed workers who discover pay discrimination to sue within six months of learning of the discrimination, regardless of when it began.[8]

Less than two months later, on March 11, President Obama signed an executive order to create the White House Council on Women and Girls, headed by Valerie Jarrett, with Tina Tchen, Director of the White House Office of Public Engagement, serving as executive director. The Council consisted of heads of every Cabinet and Cabinet-level agency, and its purpose, according to Obama, was "to ensure that each of the agencies in which they're charged takes into account the needs of women and girls in the policies they draft, the programs they create, the legislation they support."[9] The White House Web site dedicated a section to the Council, where Tchen, Jarrett, and others posted regular updates about the effects of administration's policies and actions on women. Obama declared August 26, 2010, "Women's Equality Day," in commemoration of the ratification of the 19th amendment, which granted women

[8] Montopoli, Brian. (2009, January 29). "Obama Signs Equal Pay Bill." *CBSnews.com.* http://www.cbsnews.com/8301-503544_162-4762222-503544.html. Retrieved on August 25, 2010.

[9] Sweet, Lynn . (2009, March 11). "Obama Signs Order Creating Council on Women and Girls." *Chicago Sun Times.* http://blogs.suntimes.com/sweet/2009/03/obama_signed_order_creating_co.html. Retrieved on August 13, 2010.

the right to vote. In his proclamation, Obama reminded Americans of his administrations' commitment to "...advancing women's equality in all areas of our society and around the world."[10] These efforts—the bill, the Council, the proclamation—and the diversity of his administration, at least showed that Obama kept women, Black women included, in mind. But upon closer inspection, and as time passed, these acts appeared to be merely token gestures made to appease those who bought into the hope and change promised by the Obama campaign.

In November 2009, *Essence.com* posted a "Power List" of 20 black women in Obama's administration (including some left the administration). The slideshow presented photographs and blurbs of the "big names," like Jackson, Hamburg, and Jarrett, but the 20 black "Obama women" also included members of the First Lady's staff (Kristen Jarvis, Special Assistant for Scheduling and Travel Aide, and Dana Lewis, Special Assistant and Personal Aide); the Director of White House Events and Protocol, Micaela Fernandez; and Daniella Gibbs Leger, Director of White House Message Events.

While the work these women did should not be underestimated, Travel Aide to the First Lady and Ambassador to the UN or Surgeon General are very different positions. If looking exclusively at Black women in the Cabinet or in Cabinet-level positions, the tally of 20 black women in the Obama administration shrank to two: Lisa P. Jackson and Susan Rice. Furthermore, in the selection of Surgeon General, the black woman who ultimately accepted that position was not the President's first choice. Regina Benjamin was only offered the job after Obama's first choice, CNN's chief medical correspondent Sanjay Gupta, turned it down. So while we saw a diverse staff, there was still a telling lack of Black women at the head of the administration and in positions of true power.

In a September 2009 article for *More.com*, Teresa Wilz, senior culture editor at *The Root*, discussed this absence of Black women in upper management and executive positions, despite the numbers of highly qualified Black women available to serve in such capacities. Regarding the women selected to work in Obama's Cabinet and the White House, Wilz said,

---

[10] Obama, Barack. (2010, August 26). "Presidential Proclamation—Women's Equality Day, 2010." *WhiteHouse.gov*. http://www.whitehouse.gov/the-press-office/2010/08/26/presidential-proclamation-womens-equality-day-2010. Retrieved on September 6, 2010.

"Let me be clear: Not many individuals, black, white, brown or other, achieve that level of power, whether at the White House or at Xerox. And yet there are hundreds of thousands of us, highly qualified and highly educated, available to be tapped."[11] Of the associate and bachelor's degrees awarded to Black students, women earn approximately two-thirds, according to the National Center for Education Statistics,[12] and between 1996 and 2007, the number of black women getting master's degrees grew by 130%, while white women's increase was only 38%.[13]

Krissah Thompson also pointed out the shortage of black women in visible positions of power, citing the Bureau of Labor's statistic that more than 2.6 million black women were in management and professional jobs, yet "women and minorities still lack representation in proportion to their numbers on the federal level. In Congress, only 90 members are women, 42 are African-American, 28 are Latino and nine are Asian."[14] And, from Wilz again:

> According to Catalyst, a New York–based research firm that studies women in business, African-American women hold only five percent of all managerial, professional and related positions; white women hold 41 percent. Women of color are similarly scarce on corporate boards. And until Ursula Burns was tapped… to head Xerox, there were no black female CEOs of Fortune 500 companies.[15]

Wilz pointed to the long-held belief in the Black community that education was the only way to excel as the reason behind this pool of highly educated and qualified Black women. She blamed their underrepresentation in upper-level positions both on a lack of enforcement of company diversity policies, and on quotas: "…whenever one of us does manage to break through, her very presence may provide an excuse for keeping other black women out," she wrote.[16] Frequently, once a company hires one Black woman, the feeling is that one is enough, and there is no need to hire another.

[11] Wilz, Teresa . (2009, October). "'Obama Effect' for Black Women?" More.com. http://www.more.com/2050/8161-an-obama-effect-for-black. Retrieved on August 14, 2010.

[12] Thompson, 3.

[13] Wilz, 1.

[14] Thompson, 3.

[15] Wilz, 2.

[16] Wilz, 2.

Finally, she wrote that Black women are rarely hired for or encouraged to pursue positions that put them on an executive track, like sales or profit-related positions. Instead, companies hire them into static positions like community outreach or training jobs. Looking to the Obama administration, we saw this trend perpetuated with the appointment of black women to primarily non-Cabinet-level positions. And for the few appointed to positions of power, when it came time to defend these Black women, the efforts made by the Obama administration were too little (in the case of Desiree Rogers, the former social secretary), or too late (for Shirley Sherrod).

Tellingly, the administration did stand up for Supreme Court nominee Elena Kagan, despite concerns regarding her own lack of diversity in hiring practices and apparent racial insensitivity.

Appointing Kagan, Overlooking Black Women

Early in his administration, President Obama had the opportunity to appoint two justices to the Supreme Court, replacing Justices David H. Souter and John Paul Stevens. In May 2009, he selected Sonia Sotomayor, a Hispanic woman who Clinton appointed to the 2nd US Circuit Court of Appeals, to take the place of Souter. In May 2010, he announced Elena Kagan, Solicitor General and former Harvard Law School dean, as his choice to replace Stevens. While the appointment of the first Hispanic to the court was a notable and historic accomplishment toward diversifying the Court, it was disappointing that not a single qualified Black woman made it past the initial nominee list. This oversight on Obama's part emphasized Wilz's point on the lack of Black women in upper-level positions, despite the number of qualified candidates, as did Kagan's own hiring history while dean at Harvard Law School between 2003 and 2009.

Prior to the announcement of Kagan's nomination, civil rights groups, bloggers, and Black female attorneys expressed concern about both Kagan's hiring record and her failure to take action against racism within the law school. In a *Salon.com* piece, four law professors from different schools examined Kagan's record, praising her for the number of faculty members she hired. Yet,

> [o]f these 32 tenured and tenure-track academic hires, only one was a minority. Of these 32, only seven were women.... When Kagan was dean of Harvard Law School, four-out-of-every five hires to its faculty

were white men. She did not hire a single African American, Latino, or Native American tenured or tenure track academic law professor. She hired 25 men, all of whom were white, and seven women, six of whom were white and one Asian American. Just 3 percent of her hires were non-white....[17]

After Duke University's Guy-Uriel Charles, one of the *Salon.com* authors, wrote a blog post expressing the group's concern, the White House released talking points in Kagan's defense. As indicated in the professors' essay, the White House defense did not contest the numbers the essay cites. Instead, it presented the number of visiting professor offers Kagan made, with percentages of how many of these offers were made to minorities and women. Numbers on tenure-track offers made to minorities and women were not included. The authors also pointed out that at Yale Law School, the dean (who served at approximately the same time as Kagan, from 2004 to 2009), while hiring only 10 professors compared to Kagan's 32, "...still managed to hire nearly as many women (five of 10 at 50%), and just as many minorities (one of 10 at 10%) as Dean Kagan."[18]

In addition to the clear lack of diversity in Kagan's hiring record, there was criticism of Kagan's reaction to a Harvard Law School parody, a skit performed by students and professors in which they "roast" other students. In a guest post on the blog *Feministe*, Diane Lucas, a Harvard graduate and now an attorney in New York, wrote about the parody that took place while she was at the school in 2006 during the time Kagan was dean. She described how the parody portrayed at least four women of color in an offensive manner:

> One of my friends who is a very articulate, intelligent, black woman, was made to sound like a Shanaynay-like character from the show, Martin (I love Shanaynay — who doesn't? But, really?!). Another woman, who is Cuban-American was depicted as having very large breasts, which were

[17] Charles, Guy-Uriel, Chander, Anupam, Fuentes-Rohwer, Luis, & Onwuachi-Willig, Angela. (2010, May 7). "The White House's Kagan Talking Points Are Wrong." http://www.salon.com/news/opinion/2010/05/07/law_professors_kagan_white_house>. Retrieved on August 27, 2010.

[18] Charles.

actually balloons that were violently popped during the play. They portrayed another woman, who is Dominican-American and speaks fluent English, as barely speaking a word of English. Another black woman was depicted as being sexually promiscuous with classmates and professors.[19]

Lucas says when students brought their concerns to Kagan, she refused to make a statement or issue an apology for the play. After pressure from students, two other professors organized a meeting to discuss the parody, but the school's effort to create a conversation on race ended there, despite students asking Kagan to implement diversity sessions. Kagan's disregard for legitimate concerns about racism in her school clearly demonstrated a lack of sensitivity and awareness to the experience of minority women, and her inability to find an African-American professor for tenure (but 25 white men) during her time at Harvard further suggested an indifference to the creation of any real diversity in the faculty or the experience of Harvard Law students.

When it became apparent that Obama would move forward with Kagan's nomination, many parties protested. They questioned not only Kagan's diversity record, but also the dearth of Black women considered for the nomination. On May 9, 2010, 28 women from the Black Women's Roundtable network of the National Coalition on Black Civic Participation (NCBCP) sent President Obama a letter, voicing their unease regarding Kagan's possible nomination. In the letter, they reminded the president of the role African-American women played in the 2008 election and stated their concern over Kagan's "...lack of a clearly identifiable record on the protection of our nation's civil rights laws."[20] The letter continued:

> Especially disconcerting is the perceived lack of real consideration of any of the extremely qualified African American women as potential nominees. While we were very pleased to witness the placement of the Honorable Leah Ward Sears and Judge Ann Claire Williams on the reported lists of potential nominees, there did not appear to be any serious consideration

[19]Lucas, D. (2010, April 30). "The Racist Breeding Grounds of Harvard Law School." Feministe.com. http://www.feministe.us/blog/archives/2010/04/30/the-racist-breeding-grounds-of-harvard-law-school/. Retrieved on August 17, 2010.

[20]Edney, H. T. (2010, May 10). "Despite Widespread Appeals, Obama Fails to Nominate Black Woman to Supreme Court." *TheSkanner.com*. http://www.theskanner.com/article/view/id/12154. Retrieved on August 13, 2010.

of their candidacy, once again.... Mr. President, the nominations and appointments you make today will be far-reaching, particularly for the Supreme Court. As we continue to promote the legacy of our late founding leader and Co-Convener, Dr. Dorothy I. Height, we will always seek to highlight the concerns of Black women, our families and our communities. Thus, as Dr. Height stated in our previous meeting with your Administration, we believe it is time for African American women to be represented in all sectors of government – including the Supreme Court of the United States, which in its 221 year history has not had a Black woman nominated to serve on our highest court in the land.[21]

The letter mentioned Justice Stevens' emphasis on the protection of civil rights, saying he should have been replaced with someone who held similar views. The letter was signed by Melanie Campbell (CEO of the NCBCP and convener of the Black Women's Roundtable, "an intergenerational civic engagement network"[22]) and 27 others. The letter came too late. The President announced Elena Kagan as his nomination the next day.

Two days later, NAACP leaders and other legal groups met with Senior Advisor Valerie Jarrett to discuss their concern about Kagan's nomination. After the meeting, the Reverend Al Sharpton said Jarrett described how civil rights groups could be involved in supporting future solicitor general and district and appellate judge nominees.[23] On his blog, CNN political analyst Roland Martin linked the lack of serious consideration of a Black female candidate and the role Black women voters played in Obama's election to the discontent expressed at Kagan's nomination. He pointed to the lack of prominent African-Americans at Kagan's nomination unveiling (only Harvard professor Charles Ogletree, who taught the Obamas and worked with Kagan, and Wade Henderson, Leadership Conference on Civil and Human Rights president, were present) and the "lukewarm" press statements on the nomination announcement from the NAACP Legal Defense and Education

---

[21] Edney.

[22] "Who We Are." *The National Coalition on Black Civic Participation*, 2010. http://ncbcp.org/programs/bwr/. Retrieved on August 13, 2010.

[23] Thompson, K., & Harris, H. (2010, May 12). "White House Seeks to Defend Kagan's Diversity Record." *The Washington Post.* http://www.washingtonpost.com/wp-dyn/content/article/2010/05/11/AR2010051103390.html. Retrieved on September 1, 2010.

Fund and the National Urban League as further evidence of African-Americans' general frustration with the Obama administration's refusal to address race.[24]

This was all for good reason. There were a number of qualified African-American women for President Obama to consider for nomination, in addition to the two who made the list of potential nominees, former Georgia Chief Justice Leah Ward Sears, and Judge Ann Claire Williams, the first African-American judge in the Seventh Circuit Court of Appeals, nominated by Ronald Reagan. Sonia Nelson, founder and chair of the board of iask, Inc (I Am My Sister's Keeper, an organization dedicated to supporting and encouraging professional Black women) provided a short list of a few women she thought should make the list:

> ...Marian Wright Edelman, longtime president of the Children's Defense Fund and the first black woman admitted to practice in the state of Mississippi in the 1960s; Judge Janice Rogers Brown, who sits on the U.S. Court of Appeals, D.C. Circuit, and who Obama supported while he was a senator; Harvard Law professor Lani Guinier, who, despite the controversy when she was nominated by President Bill Clinton to be an assistant U.S. attorney general, is an excellent legal scholar; and Elaine R. Jones, formerly of the NAACP Legal Defense Fund, who has three decades of experience as a litigator and civil rights activist.[25]

It is no wonder then that black women were frustrated with the President—especially so since Kagan's nomination and tapping fell between two egregious instances of Obama neglecting to defend prominent Black women: Desiree Rogers, who resigned after the White House party crasher fiasco, and the firing of Shirley Sherrod, USDA's Director of Rural Development for Georgia.

[24] Martin, R. (2010, May 14). "The Delicate Dance Between Obama and Black Leaders." RolandSMartin.com. http://www.rolandsmartin.com/blog/index.php/2010/05/14/the-delicate-dance-between-black-leaders-and-obama/. Retrieved on September 1, 2010.

[25] Nelson, S. (2010, May 12). "A Supreme Snub by Obama." *The Root.* http://www.theroot.com/views/supreme-snub-obama?page=0,0. Retrieved on September 1, 2010.

DESIREE ROGERS

An original "Obama woman," appointed as White House social secretary in November 2008, Desiree Rogers was a New Orleans native, Harvard graduate, and a personal friend of Michelle Obama. The two met through Rogers' ex-husband, John Rogers, Jr., who played basketball at Princeton with Craig Robinson, Michelle Obama's brother. Rogers served as the director of the Illinois State Lottery, acted as the first Black president of Peoples Gas and North Shore Gas in Chicago, and ran a social networking site at AllState Financial before accepting the position with the White House. She successfully promoted what she called the "Obama brand"[26] for a year, making the White House seem like a fun, welcoming place by planning events like an Easter Egg Roll on the White House lawn, inviting local children to trick-or-treat at the White House, organizing a concert featuring Stevie Wonder, and hosting dinners with dance floors and music provided by bands like Earth, Wind, and Fire. She drew criticism for her expensive fashion choices, as well as for attending events like New York Fashion Week, but it was uninvited guests at a White House dinner that resulted in a media fiasco ending with Rogers' resignation.

On November 24, 2009, the Obamas held their first state dinner in honor of Indian Prime Minister Manmohan Singh and his wife, Gursharan Kaur. During the event, Virginia socialite couple Tareq and Michaele Salahi slipped past security, even though their names appeared on no guest lists. The couple joined the party, posing for photographs with Vice President Joe Biden and even shaking the President's hand. The security breach led to a Secret Service investigation and heavy criticism of Rogers. According to *The New York Times*, in planning the party, Rogers consulted and followed records from two of Laura Bush's dinners, stationing someone at the East Portico of the White House to ensure guests were on the Secret Service list; at this dinner, however, no one was placed at an outer checkpoint as had been done in the past.[27]

[26]Chozick, A. (2009, May). "Desiree Rogers' Brand Obama." *WSJ Magazine*. http://magazine.wsj.com/features/the-big-interview/desiree-rogers/. Retrieved on August 16, 2010.

[27]Baker, P. (2010, March 11). "Obama Social Secretary Ran into Sharp Elbows." *The New York Times*. http://www.nytimes.com/2010/03/12/us/politics/12rogers.html. Retrieved on August 16, 2010.

In the investigation that followed the dinner, the House Homeland Security committee invited Rogers to testify on the Tareqs' security breach, even threatening a subpoena when the White House refused to make her available, stating their internal report would be sufficient. The White House also argued that permitting Rogers to testify would infringe upon the separation of powers. Senior Advisor Valerie Jarrett, on ABC News, said the White House felt its staff should be able to engage with the President without having to report to Congress,[28] and during a White House briefing, Robert Gibbs, Obama's press secretary, in response to a question regarding Rogers' planning, said, "The first family is quite pleased with her performance."[29] When Rogers' resignation was announced at the end of February, she asserted that she felt her work in creating a "people's house" was complete that it seemed like a good time to examine her prospects in the corporate world (she was hired as CEO of the Johnson Publishing Company, which publishes *Ebony* and *Jet*, about six months after announcing her resignation) and that "the incident at the State Dinner was not a deciding factor... but it did show me a side of the job and of Washington that I had not seen before."[30] The Obamas, for their part, released a statement saying,

> We are enormously grateful to Desiree Rogers for the terrific job she's done as the White House Social Secretary. When she took this position, we asked Desiree to help make sure that the White House truly is the People's House, and she did that by welcoming scores of everyday Americans through its doors, from wounded warriors to local school- children to NASCAR drivers. She organized hundreds of fun and creative events during her time here, and we will miss her. We thank her again for her service and wish her all the best in her future endeavors.[31]

[28] Burns, A. (2009, December 3). "White House to Desiree Rogers Critics: Back Off." Politico.com. http://www.politico.com/news/stories/1209/30193.html. Retrieved on August 16, 2010.

[29] Gay Stolberg, S., & Lorber, J. (2009, December 2). "White House Blocks Testimony on Party Crashers." The Caucus: The Politics and Government Blog of the Times. *NYTimes.com*. http://thecaucus.blogs.nytimes.com/2009/12/02/white-house-revises-rules-for-major-events/. Retrieved on August 16, 2010.

[30] Sweet, L. (2010, February 26). "White House Social Secretary Desiree Rogers to Step Down." *Chicago Sun Times*. http://blogs.suntimes.com/sweet/2010/02/white_house_social_secretary_d.html. Retrieved on August 16, 2010.

[31] Sweet.

Despite this statement from the first couple and Rogers' given reasons for her departure, it is difficult to believe that the White House dinner party did not play a greater role in her resignation, especially considering news of her resignation began leaking before she planned to make it known,[32] and the speed in which her replacement, Julianna Smoot, was announced (Rogers' resignation was announced on February 26, and Smoot was confirmed as her replacement later the same day).

Writing for *The New York Times*, Peter Baker said that trouble for Rogers began before the uninvited couple crashed the White House dinner. She met with Senior Advisor David Axelrod after her May 2009 appearance in *WSJ Magazine*. Axelrod reprimanded her both for referring to the President as a brand and for her lavish dress and jewelry in the spread during an economic recession. Baker says "her profile was deliberately lowered,"[33] with the White House canceling a photo shoot featuring Rogers in an Oscar de la Renta gown and the First Lady's new chief of staff paying closer attention to Rogers' public appearances. After the White House security breach and the following public scrutiny of Rogers, she felt that no one in the White House did much to defend her or correct the record, said Baker, quoting unnamed sources. He continued:

> After the Salahi incident, these associates said Ms. Rogers was barred by the White House from testifying before Congress or giving interviews or even answering written questions. She was told she could not attend the Kennedy Center Honors, a major annual Washington event. And even her decision to finally resign leaked before she could secure a new job.[34]

Despite Rogers' and the Obamas' parting statements regarding the social secretary's resignation, the White House's refusal to allow Rogers to testify about the events that lead to the security breach, the leaking of Rogers' resignation news, and the swiftness with which she was replaced suggested that her departure was not solely about making her next career step, as she insinuated in interviews. Considering her success in planning White House activities—in 2009, she organized 309 events, while there

---

[32] Kantor, J. (2010, February 26). "White House Social Secretary Resigns." The Caucus: The Politics and Government Blog of the Times. *NYTimes.com*. http://thecaucus.blogs. nytimes.com/2010/02/26/white-house-social-secretary-resigns/. Retrieved on August 16, 2010.

[33] Baker, 2.

[34] Baker, 1.

were only 231 events during Bush's final year[35]—and the friendship she had with the Obamas, the lack of defense from the President and Mrs. Obama was both surprising and disappointing. Yet upon comparing the Desiree Rogers incident with Obama's overall record on African-American women within his administration, and race in general, the surprise is diminished. In fact, the reaction just seems standard.

Shirley Sherrod

On March 27, 2010, Shirley Sherrod, USDA's Georgia Director of Rural Development, gave a 40-minute speech at a NAACP event. During the speech, she shared her background with the audience, including the murder of her father in 1965 by two white men who were never indicted. She continued by relating an anecdote from her time working as the director of a nonprofit that aided black farmers. She spoke frankly about how Roger Spooner, a white farmer, came to her for assistance and at first she was unenthusiastic about helping him, directing him to a white lawyer so it would at least appear that she tried to help him. She then went on to explain that when the lawyer ultimately failed to assist Spooner, she called everyone she could think of to find someone who could help her with the case (this took place over the course of two years). Sherrod said working with Spooner taught her an important lesson and made her realize that class played as much a role as—if not more than—race in discrimination. She commented:

> Well, working with him made me see that it's really about those who have versus those who don't, you know. And they could be black, and they could be white; they could be Hispanic. And it made me realize then that I needed to work to help poor people -- those who don't have access the way others have.[36]

Four months later on July 18, conservative blogger Andrew Breitbart posted a 2-minute and 38-second clip of Sherrod's speech on his Web site, *BigGovernment.com*. Breitbart (also responsible for the edited videos that resulted in the anti-poverty group Acorn's loss of government

---

[35] Baker, 2.

[36] Sherrod, S. (2020, March 27). "Address at the Georgia NAACP 20th Annual Freedom Fund Banquet." *American Rhetoric.com*. http://www.americanrhetoric.com/speeches/shirleysherrodnaacpfreedom.htm. Retrieved on August 18, 2010.

funding) edited his Sherrod tape so it sounded as though Sherrod ended her aid to Spooner when she sent him to the white lawyer, because she wasn't going to do all she could do for a white man. He also misrepresented the story as taking place while Sherrod was in her position at USDA. Breitbart used this doctored video, taken out of context, as proof that the NAACP—who had recently criticized the Tea Party, an extreme right wing movement, for racism among its followers—was itself a racist organization who approved of their guest speaker's unfair treatment of a white man.

Breitbart posted his video at 11:18 AM on July 19, 2010.[37] In the following hours, FOX News ran the video, posting it online and calling for Sherrod's immediate resignation. Conservative talk show host Bill O'Reilly taped his show that afternoon, discussing the "news" revealed in the video. By the time it aired that evening, Sherrod had resigned after receiving three phone calls in her car from Cheryl Cook, deputy undersecretary at USDA. Sherrod said on the third call, Cook asked her to pull over and submit her resignation via her Blackberry, because Sherrod was going to be on Glenn Beck that evening.[38] Even the NAACP didn't pause to ask questions about the source of the video. That evening, President Ben Jealous said on the online social forum, Twitter, "Racism is about abuse of power. Sherrod had it at USDA. She abused a white farmer because of his race. NAACP is appalled."[39]

By the next day, it became apparent that Sherrod had been wronged. In an interview with CNN, she explained that the story she told in the video took place 24 years ago and that she had worked with the Spooners to save their farm. When asked why she didn't tell the USDA this when they called her, she said, "I did... but they, for some reason, the stuff that Fox and the Tea Party does is scaring the administration."[40] That evening, Democratic strategist Donna Brazile said on CNN that she had listened to the entire tape and that it had been taken out of context. By Wednesday afternoon, Secretary of Agriculture Tom

---

[37] "Timeline of Breitbart's Sherrod Smear." Media Matters for America, July 22, 2010. http://mediamatters.org/research/201007220004. Retrieved on August 18, 2010.

[38] *Media Matters for America.*

[39] *Media Matters for America.*

[40] *Media Matters for America.*

Vilsack apologized, admitting that he had acted too quickly in ordering Sherrod's resignation. He asked her to return to USDA in a new position, but she demurred, saying she did not want to be entirely responsible for solving the department's race problems. (Vilsack later offered her a different, outreach position at the USDA, but she again declined, saying the events that led to her resignation left "a sour taste."[41]) The NAACP also issued a statement, saying that it had been "snookered by Fox News and Tea Party Activist Andrew Breitbart."[42] President Obama called Sherrod on July 22, 2010, to personally apologize. President Obama said that he thought Vilsack was being sincere both in his apology and his job offer. In interviews, Sherrod had expressed her belief that she deserved a call from Obama, but did not think he owed her an apology. She remarked:

> I'd like to talk to him a little bit about the experiences of people like me, people at the grass-roots level, people who live out there in rural America, people who live in the South.... I know he does not have that kind of experience. Let me help him a little bit with how we think, how we live, and the things that are happening.[43]

What Sherrod said here emphasized a key issue that came into play in her forced resignation: Obama and his staff either lacked the experience and point of view of African-Americans, or the courage to consider that experience and say anything about it. In an op-ed column, Maureen Dowd suggested that anyone with knowledge of the civil rights movement would have recognized the name "Sherrod"; the Reverend Charles Sherrod was a civil rights leader who co-founded the Student Nonviolent Coordinating Committee. He is Shirley Sherrod's husband. Dowd quoted South Carolina Congressman James Clyburn, who said he didn't think a single black person had been consulted before the decision to fire

[41] Thompson, K. (2010, August 24). "Shirley Sherrod Turns Down USDA Job After Video Controversy." *The Washington Post.* http://www.washingtonpost.com/wp-dyn/content/article/2010/08/24/AR2010082406493.html?sid=ST201007210658. Retrieved on September 6, 2010.

[42] *Media Matters for America.*

[43] Gay Stolberg, S., Dewan, S., & Stelter, B. (2010, July 21). "With Apology, Fired Official Is Offered a New Job." *The New York Times.* http://www.nytimes.com/2010/07/22/us/politics/22sherrod.html. Retrieved on August 18, 2010.

Sherrod was made, and Congresswoman Eleanor Holmes Norton, who said, "The president needs some advisers or friends who have a greater sense of the pulse of the African-American community, or who at least have been around the mulberry bush."[44]

Sherrod's forced resignation brought to mind Lani Guinier's and Dr. Joycelyn Elders' snubs by the Clinton administration. Sadly, years later, little had changed, even under America's first Black president. Granted, Obama was not directly responsible for Sherrod's expulsion. He only spoke with Sherrod on Thursday, two days after the full story was revealed, because he could not reach her Wednesday evening. Nevertheless, by missing several opportunities to fill his administration with a balanced group of people who could provide key insight in real time, Obama suffered the appearance of being out of touch with his core constituency in political skirmishes that should have been child's play to any Democratic President, like why it might be unwise to so hastily dismiss someone based on a video publicized by a man who had previously used falsified evidence to support a right wing agenda. So who in Washington *did* come to Sherrod's defense? Donna Brazile—a black woman. Perhaps if a few more black women were in decisive positions within the Obama administration, Shirley Sherrod could have been spared the shoddy treatment she received, and the only embarrassed parties would have been the pundits at FOX News.

Following his campaign, Obama tried to avoid any discussion about race, creating the space for the right to not so subtly play on the country's racist sentiments (who can forget Rush Limbaugh playing *Barack the Magic Negro?*). Bob Herbert wrote in a column about the Sherrod incident, "...President Obama seems reluctant to even utter the word black."[45] CNN political analyst Roland Martin discussed the Obama administration's avoidance of race conversations in his blog post on Kagan's nomination, saying "...[Obama's] White House has been especially scared of touching anything dealing with race" because the

[44]Dowd, M. (2010, July 24). "You'll Never Believe What This White House Is Missing." *The New York Times.* http://www.nytimes.com/2010/07/25/opinion/25dowd.html?_r=1. Retrieved on August 18, 2010.

[45]Herbert, B. (2010, July 23). "Thrown to the Wolves." *The New York Times.* http://www.nytimes.com/2010/07/24/opinion/24herbert.html. Retrieved on August 18, 2010.

President can't be perceived to favor African-Americans.[46] The fear is obvious when we look at how quickly Sherrod was pushed out of her job as a result of the accusations of racism from the conservative media. Said author and professor Ricky L. Jones, "If anything, [Obama's] horribly detached, 'I'm above it all' approach to race emboldens the mean-spirited xenophobes who long for the 'purity' of antebellum America."[47] Again, the Sherrod case proves this point—were conservatives not so aware of the Obama administration's reluctance to address race, would Breitbart have made such an impudent move? In her column, Dowd said,

> The president appears completely comfortable in his own skin, but it seems he feels that he and Michelle are such a huge change for the nation to absorb that he can be overly cautious about pushing for other societal changes for blacks and gays. At some level, he acts like the election was enough; he shouldn't have to deal with race further. But he does.[48]

The President proved Dowd's point when he commented on Sherrod's forced resignation in a speech he gave at the National Urban League Centennial Conference on July 29, 2010. He agreed that people should have frank discussions about "...the divides that still exist—the discrimination that's still out there, the prejudices that still hold us back....",[49] but he says these discussions should happen "...not on cable TV, not just through a bunch of academic symposia or fancy commissions or panels, not through political posturing, but around kitchen tables, and water coolers, and church basements, and in our schools, and with our kids all across the country." At water coolers and kitchen tables? So apparently Americans should talk about race, and the President may do so as well, but not on TV or any other public forum. And when it comes to healing the 400+-year racial divide, and addressing the increasingly racist fever demonstrated by the extreme right, leadership, particularly by this country's first African-American President, was not required.

[46] Martin, R. (2010, May 14). "The Delicate Dance Between Obama and Black Leaders." RolandSMatin.com. http://www.rolandsmartin.com/blog/index.php/2010/05/14/the-delicate-dance-between-black-leaders-and-obama/. Retrieved on September 1, 2010.

[47] Jones, R. L. (2010, August 18). "What Changes If Republicans Win?" *Leo Weekly*, 10.

[48] Dowd.

[49] "Remarks by the President on Education Reform at the National Urban League Centennial Conference." White House.gov, July 29, 2010. http://www.whitehouse.gov/the-press-office/remarks-president-education-reform-national-urban-league-centennial-conference. Retrieved on August 18, 2010.

The White House may not have wanted Obama to be seen as favoring African-Americans, but he neglected them at his political peril, because it was African-Americans, and especially African-American women, who helped to elect Obama to the White House. There was no doubt that we wanted him to succeed. Even after the unfair treatment Sherrod received from the administration, she said, "We love him. We want him to be successful because we feel he thinks in some ways like we do."[50] Black leaders trod softly in their criticism of Obama, fearing condemnation from their supporters and the White House, said Martin, but with Kagan's appointment and then Sherrod's dismissal, the feelings of love and the hesitation to criticize the President were felt to be subsiding. The Black Women's Roundtable voiced their disappointment with Obama for once again overlooking qualified Black women in his Supreme Court nomination choice. Sherrod, while professing her wish for the President's success, voiced her opinion on his lack of understanding of the experience of Black women ("people like me").[51] If Obama is not ready to address his "Black Woman problem,"[52] as freelance journalist Jeff Winbush called it, by showing them some of the love they've given him, the least he could do is acknowledge the racism that clearly still exists in America, even under a Black President, and demonstrate leadership on the issue of racism at the national level.

PRESIDENTIAL ACCOUNTABILITY COMMISSION AND LOOKING AHEAD

In 2008, at its State of the Black World Conference in New Orleans, the Institute of the Black World twenty-first Century (IBW) announced a new initiative: the Shirley Chisholm Presidential Accountability Commission (SCPAC), named in honor of the first black woman elected to Congress and the first black woman to seek the Democratic nomination for president. The Commission's members were charged with the task of grading presidential administrations on how their practices and policies

---

[50] Cosby, F. (2010, July 23). "Obama Calls Shirley Sherrod, Apologizes for Firing." BlackAmericaWeb.com.   http://www.blackamericaweb.com/?q=articles/news/moving_america_news/20472/1. Retrieved on August 18, 2010.

[51] Stolberg.

[52] Winbush, J. (2010, July 22). "Barack's Black Woman Problem." *The Domino Theory.* http://jeffwinbush.com/2010/07/22/baracks-black-woman-problem/. Retrieved on August 13, 2010.

affect African-Americans. The Commission was comprised of 11 members, including Syracuse University professor Dr. Boyce Watkins and Dr. Julianne Malveaux, president of Bennett College for Women. Said Richard Adams, Chairman of the Board of IBW and convener of the Commission:

> The Shirley Chisholm Accountability Commission was not organized to react to President Barack Obama. As we indicated when the idea of the Commission was announced at the State of the Black World Conference, we need a mechanism that can monitor progress on the Black Agenda, no matter who occupies the White House. We finally have a structure that can fulfill that function in Black America.[53]

Of course, because of timing, the Obama administration was the first to receive a grade from the Commission. In October 2009, talking to *Essence.com*, Dr. Malveaux shared a story of Franklin D. Roosevelt telling civil rights leader A. Philip Randolph and other black leaders concerned about jobs for African-Americans to "raise enough hell" so that Roosevelt had no choice but to address their needs.[54] She related the anecdote to the Commission and Obama: "He's our brother, and he gets it, but we're not his only constituency. He's not the President of Black America. We have to make him do right. He's not going to do right just 'cause. We've got to make him."[55]

In full disclosure, I was also a member of the Commission. It was our hope that the work of the Commission and letters like that of the Black Women's Roundtable would begin the hell-raising that needed to be done in order to get President Obama's attention, force him to address race, and compel him to create policies that clearly assist African-Americans. On June 18, 2010, the inaugural meeting of the Commission was held, featuring a discussion titled "Black America: The Economic State of Emergency," in which the problem of joblessness and

---

[53] Anderson, F. (2010, July 18). "Shirley Chisholm Presidential Accountability Commission Launched." Anderson@Large. http://andersonatlarge.typepad.com/andersonlarge/2010/06/shirley-chisholm-presidential-accountability-commission.html. Retrieved on September 2, 2010.

[54] "Dr. Julianne Malveaux on President Obama." *Essence.com*, October 15, 2009. http://www.essence.com/news/obama_watch/hope_and_accountability_dr_julianne_malv.php. Retrieved on September 2, 2010.

[55] *Essence.com*.

unemployment in African-American communities was addressed. It was an issue that, sadly, had not been covered by any major media outlet, or championed by any presidential appointee, or even mentioned by the President himself.

WHO ARE THE "WE" IN "WE ARE THE ONES WE'VE BEEN WAITING FOR"?

In his 2008 inaugural speech, Obama said, "We are the ones we've been waiting for. We are the change that we seek." But ironically for African-Americans, and Black women in particular, the administration was not as inclusive of the "we" that *we* had assumed it would be. Instead, in America's first black President, we had someone who was paralyzed at the very mention of race, someone who was more concerned about appearing impartial than providing leadership to a still racially divided nation, and someone who was unable to even defend himself in the face of egregious racist slurs, preferring to be "above it all" while letting his political opponents slay his popularity by tapping into the latent xenophobic and racist fears that have long plagued this country. His appointment of Sonia Sotomayor suggested a serious effort at diversifying the government, and immediately following his election, Obama's appointment of numerous Black women to staff and cabinet positions within his administration seemed like the first rewards for the support African-American women gave him. Eleanor Holmes Norton, in speaking of Valerie Jarrett's authority, euphorically stated, "I'm not sure there's ever been a black woman who has enjoyed as much of the president's confidence as Valerie Jarrett. She has not been compartmentalized and is used in a variety of ways that I think is a first. The Obama women are a sign of how far we've come."[56] But Obama's lukewarm and slow responses to the resignation of his press secretary and Sherrod's firing, and the exclusion of Black female candidates for Supreme Court consideration, suggested the importance of those early appointments was quickly forgotten.

Perhaps Teresa Wilz's idea of trickle-down improvement was shared by Obama. She suggested that the mere sight of these successful Black women in Obama's cabinet would make the notion of an educated,

---

[56]Thompson. "The Ties That Align: Administration's Black Women Form a Strong Sisterhood," 1.

African-American woman less unusual, more mainstream. Based on Obama's aversion to talking about race, it seemed that he was also hoping for the trickle-down effect, but Malveaux was right—we needed to force the conversation then. Shirley Sherrod, Desiree Rogers, Leah Ward Sears, and all the other Black women who supported Obama in his campaign were ignored at the peril of his political future.

But What About Loretta Lynch?

There was one other Black woman who held a high Cabinet post in the Obama administration, and that came toward the end of his presidency. Loretta Lynch, a Harvard-educated attorney, was familiar to Obama and came to the appointment with a curried pedigree. Having served as US Attorney for the Eastern District of New York, a highly visible position in the judiciary, from 1999 to 2001 (during the Clinton era) and again from 2010 to 2015, as well as the board of the Federal Reserve Bank of New York, Lynch was highly skilled, well-respected, and well-connected.

Obama nominated Lynch for position of US Attorney General in early November 2014, a bid to fill the seat that was being left vacant by outgoing Attorney General, Eric Holder, who was also African-American. Lynch was confirmed by the House and Senate and was sworn into the position of Attorney General in late April 2015. She became the first Black woman to ever fulfill the role and only the second Black person and second woman to fulfill the position. When he forwarded her name for the nomination, President Obama praised her effusively, summing up her experience and qualifications, both professional and personal, as follows:

> It's pretty hard to be more qualified for this job than Loretta. Throughout her 30-year career, she has distinguished herself as tough, as fair, an independent lawyer who has twice headed one of the most prominent U.S. Attorney's offices in the country. She has spent years in the trenches as a prosecutor, aggressively fighting terrorism, financial fraud, cybercrime, all while vigorously defending civil rights.
>
> A graduate of Harvard College and Harvard Law School, Loretta rose from Assistant U.S. Attorney in the Eastern District of New York to Chief of the Long Island Office, Chief Assistant U.S. Attorney, and U.S. Attorney. She successfully prosecuted the terrorists who plotted the bomb – plotted to bomb the Federal Reserve Bank and the New York City subway. She has boldly gone after public corruption, bringing charges against public officials in both parties. She's helped secure billions in settlements

from some of the world's biggest banks accused of fraud, and jailed some of New York's most violent and notorious mobsters and gang members.

One of her proudest achievements was the civil rights prosecution of the officers involved in the brutal assault of the Haitian immigrant Abner Louima. Loretta might be the only lawyer in America who battles mobsters and drug lords and terrorists, and still has the reputation for being a charming "people person."

That's probably because Loretta doesn't look to make headlines, she looks to make a difference. She's not about splash, she is about substance. I could not be more confident that Loretta will bring her signature intelligence and passion and commitment to our key priorities, including important reforms in our criminal justice system.[57]

After her swearing in, Lynch was immediately confronted with a series of high-profile matters in which race played a significant, central role. There was the 2015 shooting at the Mother Emanuel Church in Charleston, South Carolina, where a white supremacist's gun rampage left nine Black church members dead. Lynch moved to charge shooter Dylann Roof with a hate crime, later announcing that the Department of Justice would pursue the death penalty for Roof.[58] Other race-related cases that she would address during her relatively brief tenure as Attorney General were the police-related deaths of Laquan McDonald and Eric Garner.

Together, Obama and Lynch were criticized by the right for championing what they viewed as overly liberal views and policies—even before Lynch took office. Unsurprisingly, these criticisms themselves were largely framed through the lens of race. The *National Review*, in an editorial calling upon Republicans to vote against Lynch's nomination as a "rebuke" to Obama, epitomized such arguments by contending that Lynch had "been the beneficiary of a glut of identity politics" at the dangerous intersection of gender and race. "[S]upporters [of Lynch] have

---

[57] Obama, B. (2014, November 9). Remarks by the President at the Nomination of Loretta Lynch for Attorney General. https://obamawhitehouse.archives.gov/the-press-office/2014/11/09/remarks-president-nomination-loretta-lynch-attorney-general. Retrieved on May 22, 2018.

[58] Department of Justice. (2016). https://www.justice.gov/usao-sc/pr/statement-attorney-general-loretta-e-lynch-case-united-states-v-dylann-roof. Retrieved on May 22, 2018.

hardly finished attacking opponents as racist before labeling them sexist as well," the magazine's editorial board wrote.[59] In a separate editorial on the same subject, the editors continued, "As an African-American woman, Lynch represents a gloriously double-barrelled opportunity to accuse Republicans of sub-rosa hatreds."[60]

Lynch did not meet a similar fate as those confronted by other Black women in the Obama administration, and that may be due in large part to the fact that she served a short term, one that was ended by the fact that Obama's own term as president was ending. At the same time, however, Lynch's tenure was not unmarked by scandal. Former FBI director James Comey cast doubt on Lynch's independence and impartiality with respect to her investigation and handling of her department's investigations into the Hillary Clinton email debacle (which, readers will recall, was itself largely promulgated by Comey). The doubt cast on Lynch by Comey persisted even after she and President Obama left office, particularly in the lead-up to the 2018 release of Comey's memoir, *A Higher Loyalty*.[61] For his part, in the face of such criticisms, Obama was largely silent, allowing Lynch to defend herself, alone.

BLACK LIVES MATTER AND THE PRICE OF THE TICKET

You could fill the wing of a library with all of the books written about President Barack Obama. In Frederick C. Harris' *The Price of the Ticket: Barack Obama and the Rise and Decline of Black Politics*, he argues that the election of Obama exacted a heavy cost on Black politics. Published in 2012—the same year that Trayvon Martin was killed—Harris' book contends that Obama's race-neutral approach to governing and policy-making, along with the Black elites' refusal to pressure the president to address community interests, incurred a political price for Black Americans. Melanie Y. Price's *The Race Whisperer: Barack Obama and the Political Uses of Race*, is the response to Frederick C. Harris' call in *The Price of the Ticket*.

[59] https://www.nationalreview.com/2015/04/defeat-loretta-lynch/.

[60] https://www.nationalreview.com/2015/03/dont-confirm-loretta-lynch-rich-lowry/.

[61] https://www.cnn.com/2018/04/15/politics/loretta-lynch-james-comey-criticism/index.html.

Price's work was lucid and compelling. She contextualized Barack Obama as uniquely situated to tap into multiple racial appeals. He was able to make authentic and politically useful connections to multiple groups, including whiteness, without actually being white. She explained that a significant portion of this ability stemmed from his capacity to tailor his biography to establish powerful connections with many groups. His multiracial background, his experiences living abroad, his Ivy League education, and his organizing skills all provided source material for bold and genuine claims to membership across and among identities and categories. In this way, he was able to tap into narratives of Blackness, whiteness, migration, and other identities with a good amount of credibility. Price's book examined how he was able to do this, and the resulting implications for our understanding of Barack Obama's racial legacy and the future of Black politics.

I rely on Harris and Price because I don't think you can address the policy agenda of Black Lives Matter without considering the fact that the most resistant Black activist movement since the Panther Party came on the scene during the second term of our first Black President. Price reminded us that there had been Black presidential candidates before—Chisholm in '72, Jackson in '84 and '88, and Sharpton in '04. As a young adult in the '80s, I can't imagine why my generation didn't organize Black Lives Matter during the Reagan administration. We should have, but we didn't.

The policy agenda for Black Lives Matter has been relevant for as long as we have had Black lives. I did not expect the election of Barack Obama, either time, to give Black people political power. But the fact that we must still "demand" that all people have the right to vote, despite it being the twenty-first century, is ironic at best. Black Lives Matter is needed now more than ever because of backlash against Obama and the war against us. Knowing America the way that I do, some people will be afraid of the Black Lives Matter platform. As an academic, I know that we have seen this platform before. In 1963, the NAACP, Urban League, Southern Christian Leadership Conference, the Student Nonviolent Coordinating Committee, and the Congress on Racial Equality came together with a set of goals:

- Passage of meaningful civil rights legislation;
- Immediate elimination of school segregation;
- A program of public works, including job training, for the unemployed;

- A Federal law prohibiting discrimination in public or private hiring;
- A $2-an-hour minimum wage nationwide;
- Withholding Federal funds from programs that tolerate discrimination;
- Enforcement of the 14th Amendment to the Constitution by reducing congressional representation from States that disenfranchise citizens;
- A broadened Fair Labor Standards Act to currently excluded employment areas;
- Authority for the Attorney General to institute injunctive suits when constitutional rights are violated.

This was the platform for the March on Washington, one of the most celebrated events in our nation's history. So why are we so afraid of Black Lives Matter and their six-point platform today?

I would argue that many Americans, of many racial backgrounds, saw the election of a Black President as an opportunity for Black satisfaction, or rather, complacency. Since a Black man had reached the highest office in the nation, it obviously meant that racism was over. Nothing could be further from the truth.

> Price wrote,
> ...[a]s America's first Black president prepares to leave the White House, we have learned many lessons about race and politics. If Black politics remains a group-based endeavor that is led, in part, by Black elected officials, then Black elected officials have to talk about the way certain public policies continue have a disproportionate impact on Black communities. That is an explicit racial discussion that threatens to upset dominant perceptions and norms and potentially spurns white voters. Understanding how to simultaneously support Black candidates who run for office at the state and national level and a Black political agenda that ameliorates racial inequality is the most important challenge to emerge in the Obama era. (p. 156)

That challenge has only become more urgent in the post-Obama era. I propose that the ticket that could save us is, in fact, the platform of Black Lives Matter. It's a ticket we can't afford not to buy. Otherwise, the price that we'll continue to pay is the war on Black people; lack of reparations; lack of investment in Black communities, unaddressed economic injustice; continued political disenfranchisement; and lack of community control. Black Lives Matter in the post-Obama age just might be the fire this time.

CHAPTER 7

Your President Is (a) White (Supremacist): Post Obama and Black Feminist Politics

For the majority of Black Americans—and, it must be said, for plenty of other Americans of color and for many white Americans, too—the transition of presidential power that occurred on January 20, 2017, was a devastating sociopolitical, cultural, and historic moment. It wasn't simply the fact that America's first Black President was leaving office after two terms, the end of an era that, for all its flaws, was still historically, socially, and politically significant. President Obama was leaving the Oval Office, handing over its literal and metaphorical keys to a man who would come to be nicknamed—and not unfairly—by many individuals, organizations, political analysts, and even media outlets as the white-supremacist-in-chief.[1]

Millions of Americans struggled to square the juxtaposition, which was the most extreme swing of the pendulum imaginable. The day of the inauguration provided endless opportunities for political commentary and armchair speculation in response to the question, "How did we get here?" There were the basic facts: America's beloved first (Black) couple, sophisticated, savvy, and smart, were ceding their posts to a white

---

[1] See, for example, Community Party USA (http://www.cpusa.org/article/donald-trump-white-supremacist-in-chief/), Presente.org (http://presente.org), and *Washington Monthly* (https://washingtonmonthly.com/2017/08/19/babysitting-the-white-supremacist-in-chief/_) for just a few among innumerable examples.

© The Author(s) 2019
D. Harris, *Black Feminist Politics from Kennedy to Trump*,
https://doi.org/10.1007/978-3-319-95456-1_7

couple whose common bond was a love of over-the-top tawdry,[2] a lack of self-restraint and social decorum,[3] and a rejection of all things intellectual.[4] Then, there were the particular facts of the specific day itself, moments that quickly converted into viral memes. There was Trump, bounding out of a car, leaving his wife behind.[5] She wasn't an afterthought—she simply wasn't a thought at all. That moment was followed by the world's most awkward gift exchange between the outgoing and incoming First Ladies.[6] There was the ominous hellfire and brimstone inauguration speech given by the new president, one in which he managed to reference and link inner cities, gangs, and "American carnage," building up to a call to rediscover patriotism. "[W]hether we are black, or brown, or white, we all bleed the same red blood of patriots," Trump intoned, adding, "When you open your heart to patriotism, there is no room for prejudice."[7] After the swearing in, there was the new president's patently false contention that his inauguration was attended by more than 1.5 million people,[8] a "fact" that was easily corrected by the most cursory of glances at photographs from his inauguration and the preceding two inaugurations of President Obama. Then, within hours, vital pages on the White House Web site began disappearing, including one about LGBT rights[9] and a Spanish-language version[10] of the site.

From the inauguration onward, the assaults on decency, diplomacy, and facts haven't just been daily. They have been ongoing, all day, every day. They start at the moment Trump wakes up and starts tweeting

---

[2] https://www.forbes.com/sites/chasewithorn/2017/05/03/donald-trump-has-been-lying-about-the-size-of-his-penthouse/.

[3] https://historynewsnetwork.org/article/166806.

[4] https://newrepublic.com/minutes/133566/donald-trump-doesnt-read-books.

[5] https://www.cnn.com/2018/01/31/politics/michelle-obama-ellen-degeneres-melania-trump-inauguration-gift/index.html.

[6] https://www.cnn.com/2018/01/31/politics/michelle-obama-ellen-degeneres-melania-trump-inauguration-gift/index.html.

[7] https://www.politico.com/story/2017/01/full-text-donald-trump-inauguration-speech-transcript-233907.

[8] https://www.nytimes.com/2017/01/21/us/politics/trump-white-house-briefing-inauguration-crowd-size.html.

[9] https://www.washingtonpost.com/local/2017/live-updates/politics/live-coverage-of-trumps-inauguration/lgbt-rights-page-disappears-from-white-house-website/?utm_term=.346eaf0aaff2.

[10] https://qz.com/1204953/the-white-houses-spanish-language-site-is-still-missing/.

foreign policy blunders, conspiracy theories, and vacuous "thoughts and prayers" about the latest school shooting, to the moment he goes to bed, still tweeting. They have been difficult to keep up with, though many major media outlets have tried. *The Washington Post* has kept a running tab of lies and false claims Trump has uttered since taking office (3001 and counting as of May 2018).[11] Meanwhile, *The New York Times* has maintained a "definitive list" of Trump's racist speech and behavior during the same period, and extending back to his public life, pre-presidency.[12]

Liberal and progressive white Americans wake up daily, read the newspaper or listen to the news, and sigh heavily, wringing their hands and shaking their heads. They wonder to themselves, and then ask on social media, "How did this happen? How did we get here?" They look, wrote psychoanalyst Lynne Layton, for silver linings, a defensive reaction that was particularly common and acute immediately following the election and inauguration, saying that perhaps it's best that the "long...hidden or denied shadow [of American racism and xenophobia] was now out in the open."[13] These are, she says, "perverse and pleasurable lies" that allow white liberals to "turn away from the pain of acknowledging the damaging effects of white narcissism."[14] Further, she warns, this "pleasure in a fantasied white liberal goodness" is as potentially harmful as Trump himself.

But for African-Americans, the answer to the question—"How did we get here?"—was all too easy to identify and articulate. There was no shocked bewilderment, for there was no transition to "here." The "here" had always been there, at least for Black Americans. As psychoanalyst Layton observed, "Trump is perhaps both mentally ill and evil, but, more important, *he is an incarnation of something that has always existed on U.S. soil*" (emphasis added). Layton's recognition of this fact made her personally chagrined. As a white progressive, she had believed herself

---

[11] https://www.washingtonpost.com/news/fact-checker/wp/2018/05/01/president-trump-has-made-3001-false-or-misleading-claims-so-far/?noredirect=on&utm_term=.9ad4178962d2.

[12] https://www.nytimes.com/interactive/2018/01/15/opinion/leonhardt-trump-racist.html.

[13] https://www.tandfonline.com/doi/pdf/10.1080/1551806X.2018.1396122?needAccess=true.

[14] Ibid., p. 19.

to be woke. The election, inauguration, and first year of the Trump presidency, however, made her realize that "I, like many others, took way too much solace from Obama's presidency." Black Americans, meanwhile, may have wanted—even expected—more from Obama's presidency, but they were largely wary of such solace narratives. They knew there was no such thing as a "post-racial America."[15] They knew, too, as Eduardo Bonilla-Silva and David Dietrich wrote so presciently in *The ANNALS of the American Academy of Political and Social Science* in 2011 that "the tentacles of color-blind racism will reach even deeper into the crevices of the American polity" as a result of the post-racial narrative.

Any white Americans who still believed in the post-racial narrative were disabused of it immediately as Trump swept into office. In addition to a not-so-shocking dearth of people of color in his administration (Ben Carson being an exception), Trump tapped advisors and Cabinet members who were known white supremacists, including Steve Bannon, co-founder of the alt-right Web site Breitbart, who served as Trump's chief strategist, and Jeff Sessions, the former Alabama senator and US Attorney for the Southern District of Alabama who was appointed to become US Attorney General, succeeding Loretta Lynch, the first Black woman to hold that position. Bannon and Sessions were hardly the only white supremacists in the administration, and they were surrounded, too, by coterie of casual, passive racists, those who simply don't think of people of color at all, even when crafting, enacting, or enforcing policies that will enlarge or constrict their opportunities and possibilities.

This point is an important one. For all of the active, virulent racism, it is the casual racism, embodied most visibly in the failure to install any qualified people of color in positions of power and influence, is what may have even more impact, both in the short-term and long-term, both on African-American communities across the country and in American life and its institutions generally. At a political and cultural moment when people of color need visibility and the ability to exercise their voice and agency more than ever, the formal opportunities for them to do so within the president's administration simply do not exist. And while there *are* Black representatives and senators at the federal level who are contesting Trump's every racist move, most notably Representatives John Lewis and

[15] https://doi.org/10.1177/0002716210389702.

Maxine Waters, who will be discussed at greater length in the conclusion of this book, the claiming of agency and the raising of voices are occurring more powerfully and productively *outside* of Washington and through two primary channels, each of which will be examined in turn in this chapter. The two primary forums where Black feminists are exercising their power and influence are in grassroots organizing through Black Lives Matter and nonprofit advocacy and organizing groups like Color of Change and in campaigns and elections for state and municipal offices.

GRASSROOTS ORGANIZING AND BLACK FEMINISTS IN THE TRUMP ERA

By now, anyone interested in and concerned about Black cultural and political life—about Black people's very survival—in America knows the origin story of Black Lives Matter. They know that it emerged in 2013, created by Patrisse Cullors, Alicia Garza, and Opal Tometi as a response to the acquittal of George Zimmerman, the murderer of Trayvon Martin.[16] They know that it rapidly gained momentum and adherents as more and more Black men and women were being killed by police, as more and more people of color were being flagged as threats to public safety by white people who found them "suspicious" and called the police with little or no reason. Cullors, Garza, and Tometi were well aware of the history of earlier civil rights groups and movements, aware, above all, that there was a pervasive, persistent pattern of men relying upon women's labor, while never acknowledging it, much less centering it or their needs or wishes. To that end, Cullors, Garza, and Tometi were exceptionally deliberate when it came to clarifying how leadership in Black Lives Matter would be centered. They wrote:

> As organizers who work with everyday people, BLM members see and understand significant gaps in movement spaces and leadership. Black liberation movements in this country have created room, space, and leadership mostly for Black heterosexual, cisgender men—leaving women, queer and transgender people, and others either out of the movement or in the background to move the work forward with little or no recognition. As a network, we have always recognized the need to center the leadership of women and queer and trans people. To maximize our movement muscle,

[16]https://blacklivesmatter.com/about/herstory/.

and to be intentional about not replicating harmful practices that excluded so many in past movements for liberation, we made a commitment to placing those at the margins closer to the center.[17]

Cullors, Garza, and Tometi were clear that #BlackLivesMatter meant *all* Black lives. But, they pointed out, they are especially committed to "highlight[ing] the egregious ways in which Black women, specifically Black trans women, are violated."[18] The movement caught fire, fast, with BLM contingents and their supporters showing up en masse in response to the 2014 police shooting of Michael Brown in Ferguson, Missouri. From there, the movement's roots were firmly established and a global network of BLM chapters with an "adaptive, decentralized" structure began springing up with a tripartite goal: (1) to "end state-sanctioned violence against Black people," (2) "to support the development of new Black leaders," and (3) "to create a network where Black people feel empowered to determine our destinies in our communities."[19]

Those goals seem innocuous enough for people who care about quality and the creation of a nonviolent society; however, it soon became clear that the movement founded by three Black feminists who were committed to intersectionality was threatening to the white establishment. Though it came as little or no surprise to people who participate regularly in protests and are familiar with the scenario of local police units filming protesters, in November 2017, it came to light that Black Lives Matter had been—and continued to be—scrutinized by the FBI and the Department of Homeland Security.[20] The federal entities believed that Black Lives Matter was a militant group, describing it as a "black supremacist extremist" organization.[21] An alternate term, "Black Identity Extremists" was used to describe individuals who were formally affiliated with or participated in Black Lives Matter actions.[22] Meanwhile, around the same time, white supremacists held a rally in Charlottesville, Virginia, during which their actions killed three people and injured

[17] https://blacklivesmatter.com/about/herstory/.

[18] Ibid.

[19] Ibid.

[20] https://www.aljazeera.com/news/2017/11/documents-show-monitoring-black-lives-matter-171128110538134.html.

[21] Ibid.

[22] Ibid.

dozens more.[23] The white supremacy rally was downplayed as such by President Trump and did not appear to elicit the same degree of concern as nonviolent Black Lives Matter actions on the part of the FBI and other law enforcement entities. As Brandi Collins, campaign director for the advocacy group Color of Change, pointed out, "The subtext... is stunning. It tells us who the government is training to view as threats and the rightful targets of ongoing surveillance and which groups will be offered protection." The groups offered protection, of course, were white supremacists actively engaged in harmful behavior that resulted in fatalities. The groups pegged as literal terrorists, as Patrisse Cullors wrote in her recently released memoir, *When They Call You a Terrorist: A Black Lives Matter Memoir*, were those Black feminist-led, Black feminist-centered groups that were engaged in civil, First Amendment-protected activities demanding that, indeed, Black Lives Matter.

While Black Lives Matter became, and remains, the most visible and robust (and, to government agencies' minds, the most threatening) means for Black feminists to engage in political action and discourse that moves the needle on policy outside the formal Washington, DC, halls of power, it is not the only group having an impact that centers Black feminist thought and ideology. Another powerful organization in that vein is Color of Change, a 501(c)3 nonprofit whose goal is to "amplify Black America's political voice by building an online movement for racial justice." Like MoveOn and UltraViolet, Color of Change mobilizes members to sign online petitions, pressuring politicians, corporations, media outlets, and other entities to change practices and narratives that are harmful to people of color. Launched in 2005, before Black Lives Matter, the organization has become increasingly prominent since the 2016 election, touching practically every aspect of American life and culture, from the criminal justice and carceral systems, to Hollywood entertainment and corporate greed. A majority of Color of Change's permanent team is comprised of Black women, who work on local and national initiatives aimed at calling out and changing racist practices.

The fundamental assumption and belief undergirding Black Lives Matter and Color of Change, as well as other groups and efforts not mentioned here, are that grassroots action can have a significant impact, and that women—Black women, specifically—are central to that action.

---

[23] http://nymag.com/daily/intelligencer/2017/08/state-of-emergency-in-va-after-white-nationalist-rally.html.

But their centrality is not invisible or unacknowledged. Instead, it is driving and shaping the very conversation, identifying and cementing action priorities, and determining the scope and nature of action and desired outcomes. It is not asking for permission, but rather, setting the parameters for engagement and inclusion, refusing to accept an incidental, footnoted acknowledgement of effort and intention. This is a marked shift, for example, from the Black feminist of the Black Panther Party era. As Melissa Brown writes in "Black Women as Agents of Change in the Obama Presidency," Black feminism in the post-Obama era means embracing the concept of embodied intersectionality to achieve "grassroots organizing and civic engagement" while harnessing the power of technology to reach formerly disenfranchised people, especially queer women, and to give them opportunities for direct activist engagement.[24] Further, Brown notes that decentralized leadership, a form of leadership which neither positions nor privileges a single or small group of individuals as idealized figureheads, is essential to this model of Black feminist engagement in our current political and social climate. The essential premise of this approach to Black feminism in the Trump era? Every person is needed, and every person has the agency and resources to be involved in feminist responses to current conditions.

Black Feminists Running for Office

Black Lives Matter and Color of Change may be the two most prominent means for "ordinary" Black feminists to engage in political action, but the traditional pathways to power remain alluring to a number of people. In the wake of Trump's election to office and his blatant, unashamed moves to stack his administration with white supremacists and casual racists, there has been a groundswell movement of "ordinary" women running for elected office.[25] The offices they are pursuing vary. Certainly, there are many federal-level posts in electoral contention, with twice as many women running for Congress in 2018 as ran in 2016.[26]

[24] Brown, M. (2017). "Black Women as Agents of Change in the Obama Presidency." In *How the Obama Presidency Changed the Political Landscape*, eds. Larry J. Walker, Erik Brooks, & Ramon B. Goings. Santa Barbara, CA: ABC-CLIO.

[25] https://www.npr.org/2018/02/20/585542531/more-than-twice-as-many-women-are-running-for-congress-in-2018-compared-to-2016.

[26] Ibid.

But it's outside the Beltway where things are getting really interesting, especially in the Southern states, where Black women and, in particular, Black feminists, have long been at the extreme margins of social and political life.

According to *The Observer*, "nationwide, nearly 600 Black women are running for elected office...."[27] It is a number that has been described as unprecedented. US Senator Kamala Harris, in the foreword of "The Chisholm Effect: Black Women in American Politics 2018," wrote "Black women are central to a strategy for potential progressive gains in 2018," and she added that she was excited and proud to see so many Black women running for office.[28] The room for growth, she noted, was immense, given the fact that while Black women constitute 7.3% of the US population, they represent less than 1% of statewide elected officials, and zero governorships in the entire history of the nation.

As this book goes to press, American voters are witnessing a thrilling moment. Not only have women generally shown up en masse to run for elected office. Black women, in particular, have thrown their proverbial hats in the ring. As of this writing, the group Black Women in Politics has documented 375 Black women running for elected office across the USA.[29] One of the most fascinating and important elections is that of Stacey Abrams, a Democratic State Representative in Georgia. Abrams is running for governor of Georgia. As this book goes to press, Abrams has clinched the nomination of the Democratic party for that position, and continues to actively campaign for the election, which will occur on November 6, 2018. If elected, she will be the first Black woman governor in the history of the USA.[30] The groundswell of Black feminists running for office—and their increasing viability for winning—has given rise to organizations like Higher Heights, which "was founded by Black women for Black women's political growth and equity, [with] a winning plan for building collective political power and expanding Black women elected leadership in 2018, 2020 and beyond."[31] Centering Black

---

[27] http://observer.com/2018/05/black-women-politicians-new-york-united-states/.

[28] http://www.cawp.rutgers.edu/sites/default/files/resources/chisholm_effect_black_women_in_politics.pdf.

[29] https://blackwomeninpolitics.com/.

[30] https://fivethirtyeight.com/features/can-stacey-abrams-really-turn-georgia-blue/.

[31] http://www.higherheightsforamerica.org/about_higher_heights.

feminists, Higher Heights not only supports Black women candidates; it provides Black women and woman-identified voters with information and tools they need to make informed decisions.

THE FUTURE IS FEMALE…BLACK FEMALE

While the Trump presidency and his gang of white supremacist cronies are inevitable downers and necessitate our ongoing concern, attention, and activism, the locus of our attention should be focused primarily on these groups and efforts: Black Lives Matter, Color of Change, and the fierce and fearless Black feminists, especially in Southern states, (Stacey Abrams) who are running for electoral office. The future is female—Black female—and in a moment when this administration would upend everyone's liberties, it is crucial that we both protect and assert this fact continuously, without ceasing.

CHAPTER 8

Conclusion: Reclaiming Our Time—Black Feminist Politics in the Trump Era

The Trump presidency, still, incredibly, in its infancy as this edition of the book goes to press, puts into stark relief the barriers that still stand between Black women and specifically, Black feminists, and their full participation and power in the American political process. The examples of Trump's overt and barely concealed racism are too numerous to document in detail; indeed, they are daily threats and active assaults on people of color and immigrants, generally, and on Black women in particular. Trump has had moments where he has professed his love for Black people—or, as *New Republic* writer Juliet Kleber has written, "his version of the "I have black friends" spiel,"[1] most notably pointing to his appointments of Omarosa Manigault and Ben Carson to positions within his administration as "proof" of his "color blind" politics. Anyone who proffers even the most cursory analysis of his policies and actions, however, understands that Trump and his administration represent a constant, unyielding act of sustained white supremacy.

Despite the racist onslaught that is our daily news and life in the age of Trump, Black feminists are, once again, taking up the mantle of leadership and asserting that they must be central to the narrative and practice of the ongoing American political experiment. The most visible of these figures is 79-year-old Representative Maxine Waters (D-CA), who has been unrelenting in her criticism of the Trump administration and in

---

[1] Kleber, Juliet. (2017). "Minutes: News & Notes." *The New Republic*. https://newrepublic.com/minutes/140337/donald-trump-just-gave-version-i-black-friends-spiel.

© The Author(s) 2019
D. Harris, *Black Feminist Politics from Kennedy to Trump*,
https://doi.org/10.1007/978-3-319-95456-1_8

her insistence that the president must take accountability for his words and actions. As adept a Twitter user as Trump, if not more so, Waters has used the social media platform, as well as other tools and resources, to continuously assert that Trump should be impeached, and that he and the members of his administration are beholden to the law they seem so determined to flout.

Waters' visibility increased exponentially when, in a July 2017 Congressional hearing, she challenged Treasury Secretary Steven Mnuchin, who was testifying before the committee about the state of the international finance system. Waters, the committee's ranking Democrat, asked why his office had not responded to a letter from her regarding President Trump's financial ties to Russia. Mnuchin tried to sidestep the question with platitudes and compliments, apparently attempting to run out the clock on her questioning. The strategy didn't work. Waters shut down his rambling and redirected him to her question again and again with the phrase "Reclaiming my time," a stone-faced invocation of House procedural rules. The Internet rejoiced, turning Waters' "Reclaiming my time" into a widely shared meme.

In a year studded with absurd examples of men interrupting their female colleagues, a dignified woman's firm insistence on being heard and getting straight to business was a welcome and empowering surprise. After all, most of the news-making male–female interactions of the moment were notable for the male counterpart believing (wrongly) that his opinion should take precedence over anyone else's—whether the woman in question was a prominent representative in the House or Senate, a distinguished board member at a company-wide meeting or even a renowned theoretical physicist at a science convention. For many women and people of color, the phrase "reclaiming my time" felt particularly poignant, with the idea of reclamation specifically speaking to both the present and the past. Society has been wasting not only their time but also their voices, agency, and potential—for years. Waters' quashing of Mnuchin's attempted misdirection used long-established rules to her advantage. She *knew* the rules, and she wasn't afraid to use or enforce them, even in the most hostile administration this country has seen in years. That allowed "Reclaiming my time" to be read by many as a powerful overturning of a system usually used to keep Waters and those like her "in their place." Rather than continuing to cede the floor to others, "reclaiming my time" signaled that it was the moment for Waters— and maybe all of us—to take our power back. Waters' "Reclaiming my time" moment, and all of her efforts to center people who are so often pushed to the margins, earned her a TIME magazine nod as one of the 100 most influential people of 2018.[2]

Despite the deserved acclaim Waters has received, it is worth pointing out that the country should not invest its full hopes and expectations in one representative. It is unfair for the Democratic Party and for liberals and progressives generally to keep hanging its hope on Black messianic figures, whom it hopes can bring new relevance to a struggling movement. In addition to Waters, there is the figure of Senator Kamala Harris, the first Black woman to hold a Senate position since Carol Moseley-Braun in the 1990s. Harris's policy positions on free college, single payer health care, an increased minimum wage, and criminal justice reform are solidly to the left. Still, Black women are not saviors. It's not right to expect us to fix what white Americans are so committed to breaking. The embrace and analysis of Waters and Harris, then, should not be centered solely on their anti-Trump stance, but about the emotional and political labor that Black women are expected to do to save America's soul.

Since the Nixon era looms large in this moment when the Trump administration is beset by scandal, it bears noting that this era was the same moment when Black women became the official conscience of the American republic. On July 25, 1974, Congresswoman Barbara D. Jordan, the first Black woman elected to the House of Representatives from Texas, gave one of the most important speeches of the Nixon impeachment crisis. She began by reminding her colleagues,

> Earlier today, we heard the beginning of the Preamble to the Constitution of the United States, 'We, the people.' It is a very eloquent beginning. But when the document was completed on the seventeenth of September 1787, I was not included in that 'We, the people.' I felt somehow for many years that George Washington and Alexander Hamilton just left me out by mistake. But through the process of amendment, interpretation and court decision I have finally been included in 'We, the people.'

Then, after urging the House to impeach Nixon, she said, "My faith in the Constitution is whole, it is complete, it is total. I am not going to sit here and be an idle spectator to the diminution, the subversion, the destruction of the Constitution."

[2]http://time.com/collection/most-influential-people-2018/5217567/maxine-waters/.

Today, Barbara Jordan's remarks and her loyalty to the promise of
the US Constitution and her belief in change within the existing system
would be perceived as a naïve centrism about the ability and willing-
ness of the US body politic to self-correct and become more inclusive
over time. But in that moment, she came to act as the conscience of the
nation, calling it back to its stated democratic principles. She went on to
be a keynote speaker at the 1976 Democratic National Convention. And
in 1992, in the aftermath of the L.A. race riots, when Democrats sought
to regain control of the presidency, she was again asked to come rally the
party to unite behind Bill Clinton.

When Barack Obama, himself a former constitutional law professor
emerged on the scene in 2004, reminding the country of its best self,
he was using the playbook of Barbara Jordan. In the current moment,
Representative Maxine Waters, who is decidedly more phlegmatic than
Jordan, has been slotted into this role. Whether Jordan calling for
Nixon's impeachment, Waters holding Steve Mnuchin's feet to the fire,
or Harris grilling Trump appointees during congressional hearings, Black
women are always seen as the keepers of our democratic integrity. And
then those on the far-left use this same labor that we do to save democracy to argue that we are too deeply invested in the establishment.

In fact, the left has a Black-woman problem. In May 2017, a group
of Black women wrote an open letter to DNC Chairman Tom Perez
requesting that he meet with Black women politicians and policy makers.
The letter noted that the 115th Congress has "20 Black women—the
largest number in history" and reminded Perez that in 2008 and 2012,
Black women were the party's most loyal voting bloc. The DNC refused
to even give Black women an official response to the letter. The DNC is
engaging in the kind of moral dishonesty that is rooted in a devaluing
of Black women's clear and consistent contributions to the stability and
health of the party.

In 2016, Black women, the ones who have been called to take the
scraps handed to us by the nation and painstakingly build communities,
families, and institutions, did the work of showing up. But continuing
to bear the cross of the Democratic Party is not our work. In the age of
Trump, with two hundred years of tradition, Black women are reclaiming our time.

Appendix A

Interview Questions

The common questions I asked all the women were:

Q. Where were you born?

Q. How central was sexual orientation to the organization's agenda?

Q. How would you describe your class background?

Q. What political movements were you involved with?

Q. What was your relationship to the church?

Q. Where did you get your education?

Q. How did you negotiate the issue of violence against women with the image of Black men?

Q. What did it mean to you to support Black men?

Q. What political movements were you involved with?

I asked the Kennedy women specifically:

Q. How were you chosen to be a part of the commission? Why did you accept?

Q. Were you a supporter of John F. Kennedy as president?

Q. What kind of leadership did Eleanor Roosevelt provide before she died?

Q. What did your parents do for a living?

Q. What kind of neighborhood did you grow up in?

Q. Do you think that the Black women on the commission shared similar class backgrounds?

© The Editor(s) (if applicable) and The Author(s) 2019
D. Harris, *Black Feminist Politics from Kennedy to Trump*,
https://doi.org/10.1007/978-3-319-95456-1

Q. Were there large age disparities on the commission?

Q. What did you set to accomplish as a member of the commission? Did they have any specific expectations?

Q. I have looked at the minutes from the April 19, 1963, meeting of the Fourth Consultation. According to the minutes, you expressed concern about the effect of the matriarchal family in the Black community. Why was this so important to you?

Q. When you talked about female-headed households, was it always in negative terms, or did some people consider it a viable option?

Q. The commission's final report did not support the ERA. What were the discussions among Black women like? What were your feelings on the matter?

Q. Why did you think (some members think) it was important to have legislation passed for federal programs for children? Did you know of any programs that existed?

Q. Several members of the commission expressed concern about the treatment of Black girls in integrated public high schools. Why was this?

Q. Black women's relationship to the labor force seemed to be one of the biggest concerns of the commission. In what ways did Black women's work affect the Black family?

Q. Do you remember how public assistance legislation was discussed at this time?

Q. In the 1970s, what did you think of the National Black Feminist Organization?

Q. Did you consider yourself a feminist at the time?

Q. Was there any discussion of Black lesbians on the commission?

Q. Where did Black lesbians fit into Black women's activism?

Q. Was the commission successful?

I asked the National Black Feminist Organization women:

Q. Did your organization critique capitalism?

Q. Why do you think the group failed?

Videographer Susan Goodwillie interviewed Barbara Smith and Demita Frazier in 1994. I asked the women of the Combahee River Collective questions similar to those used in Goodwillie's videotaped interviews:

Q. Did the conversations around sexuality in the '70s focus on homophobia in both Black and white communities?

Q. What kind of organizing were you doing in women's groups (reproductive rights, forced sterilization, women in prison)?

Q. What happened at the Socialist Feminist Conference in 1975?

Q. Why did you break off from the NBFO?

Q. What was the aesthetic of the group?

Q. What was the role of food at the retreats?

Q. What exactly was Black feminist consciousness raising?

Q. Were the women at the retreats of similar class backgrounds?

Q. How did you find out about the retreats? Were you involved, and how were they conducted?

APPENDIX B

Executive Order 10980 Establishing the President's Commission on the Status of Women[1]

WHEREAS prejudices and outmoded customs act as barriers to the full realization of women's basic rights which should be respected and fostered as part of our Nation's commitment to human dignity, freedom, and democracy; and

WHEREAS measures that contribute to family security and strengthen home life will advance the general welfare; and

WHEREAS it is in the national interest to promote the economy, security, and national defense through the most efficient and effective utilization of the skills of all persons, and

WHEREAS in every period of national emergency women have served with distinction in widely varied capacities but thereafter have been subject to treatment as a marginal group whose skills have been inadequately utilized; and

WHEREAS women should be assured the opportunity to develop their capacities and fulfill their aspirations on a continuing basis irrespective of national exigencies, and

---

[1] John F. Kennedy. "Executive Order 10980—Establishing the President's Commission on the Status of Women." December 14, 1961. Online by Gerhard Peters and John T. Woolley, *The American Presidency Project*. http://www.presidency.ucsb.edu/ws/?pid=58918.

© The Editor(s) (if applicable) and The Author(s) 2019
D. Harris, *Black Feminist Politics from Kennedy to Trump*,
https://doi.org/10.1007/978-3-319-95456-1

WHEREAS a Governmental Commission should be charged with the responsibility for developing recommendations for overcoming discriminations in government and private employment on the basis of sex and for developing recommendations for services which will enable women to continue their role as wives and mothers while making a maximum contribution to the world around them:

NOW, THEREFORE, by virtue of the authority vested in me as President of the United States by the Constitution and statutes of the United States, it is ordered as follows:

Part I—Establishment of the President's Commission on the Status of Women

SEC. 101. There is hereby established the President's Commission on the Status of Women, referred to herein as the "Commission". The Commission shall terminate not later than October 1, 1963.

SEC. 102. The Commission shall be composed of twenty members appointed by the President from among persons with a competency in the area of public affairs and women's activities. In addition, the Secretary of Labor, the Attorney General, the Secretary of Health, Education and-Welfare, the Secretary of Commerce, the Secretary of Agriculture and the Chairman of the Civil Service Commission shall also serve as members of the Commission. The President shall designate from among the membership a Chairman, a Vice-Chairman, and an Executive Vice-Chairman.

SEC. 103. In conformity with the Act of May 3, 1945 (59 Stat. 134, 31 U.S.C. 691), necessary facilitating assistance, including the provision of suitable office space by the Department of Labor, shall be furnished the Commission by the Federal agencies whose chief officials are members thereof. An Executive Secretary shall be detailed by the Secretary of Labor to serve the Commission.

SEC. 104. The Commission shall meet at the call of the Chairman.

SEC. 105. The Commission is authorized to use the services of consultants and experts as may be found necessary and as may be otherwise authorized by law.

PART II—DUTIES OF THE PRESIDENT'S COMMISSION ON THE STATUS OF WOMEN

SEC. 201. The Commission shall review progress and make recommendations as needed for constructive action in the following areas:

a. Employment policies and practices, including those on wages, under Federal contracts.
b. Federal social insurance and tax laws as they affect the net earnings and other income of women.
c. Federal and State labor laws dealing with such matters as hours, night work, and wages, to determine whether they are accomplishing the purposes for which they were established and whether they should be adapted to changing technological, economic, and social conditions.
d. Differences in legal treatment of men and women in regard to political and civil rights, property rights, and family relations.
e. New and expanded services that may be required for women as wives, mothers, and workers, including education, counseling, training, home services, and arrangements for care of children during the working day.
f. The employment policies and practices of the Government of the United States, with reference to additional affirmative steps which should be taken through legislation, executive or administrative action to assure nondiscrimination on the basis of sex and to enhance constructive employment opportunities for women.

SEC. 202. The Commission shall submit a final report of its recommendations to the President by October 1, 1963.

SEC. 203. All executive departments and agencies of the Federal Government are directed to cooperate with the Commission in the performance of its duties.

PART III—REMUNERATION AND EXPENSES

SEC. 301. Members of the Commission, except those receiving other compensation from the United States, shall receive such compensation as the President shall hereafter fix in a manner to be hereafter determined.

JOHN F. KENNEDY
THE WHITE HOUSE,
December 14, 1961

Appendix C

Members of the President's Commission and Its Committees and Consultations

Mrs. Eleanor Roosevelt, *Chairman*

Mrs. Esther Peterson, *Executive Vice Chairman*, Assistant Secretary of Labor

Dr. Richard A. Lester, *Vice Chairman*, Chairman, Department of Economics, Princeton University

Honorable Robert F. Kennedy, Attorney General of the United States

Honorable Orville L. Freeman, Secretary of Agriculture

Honorable Luther H. Hodges, Secretary of Commerce

Honorable Arthur J. Goldberg, Secretary of Labor

Honorable Abraham Ribicoff, Secretary of Health, Education, and Welfare

Honorable Anthony J. Celebrezze, Secretary of Health, Education, and Welfare

Honorable W. Willard Wirtz, Secretary of Labor

Honorable George D. Aiken, U.S. Senate

Honorable Edith Green, U.S. House of Representatives

Honorable Jessica M. Weis, U.S. House of Representatives

John W. Macy, Jr., Chairman of the Civil Service Commission

Mrs. Macon Boddy, Henrietta, Texas

Dr. Mary I. Bunting, President, Radcliffe College

© The Editor(s) (if applicable) and The Author(s) 2019
D. Harris, *Black Feminist Politics from Kennedy to Trump*,
https://doi.org/10.1007/978-3-319-95456-1

Mrs. Mary E. Callahan, member, Executive Board, International Union of Electrical, Radio, and Machine Workers

Dr. Henry David, President, New School for Social Research

Miss Dorothy Height, President, National Council of Negro Women, Inc.

Miss Margaret Hickey, Public Affairs Editor, *Ladies Home Journal*

Miss Viola Hymes, President, National Council for Jewish Women, Inc.

Miss Margaret J. Mealey, Executive Director, National Council of Catholic Women

Mr. Norman Nicholson, Administrative Assistant, Kaiser Industries Corp. Oakland, California

Miss Marguerite Rawalt, Attorney; Past president of the Federal Bar Association, National Association of Women Lawyers, National Federation for Business and Professional Women's Clubs, Inc.

Mr. William F. Schnitzler, Secretary-Treasurer of the AFL-CIO

Dr. Caroline F. Ware, Vienna, Virginia

Dr. Cynthia C. Wedel, Assistant General Secretary for National Council of the Churches of Christ in the U.S.A.

COMMITTEE ON CIVIL AND POLITICAL RIGHTS

Honorable Edith Green, Chairman and Commission Member

Miss Marguerite Rawalt, C-Chairman and Commission Member

Mrs. Harper Andrews, Former President, Illinois League of Voters, Kewanee, Illinois

Mrs. Angela Bambace, Organizer, International Ladies' Garment Workers' Union

James B. Carey, President, International Union of Electrical, Radio and Machine Workers

Miss Gladys Everett, Attorney, Portland, Oregon

Mrs. Sophia Yarnall Jacobs, President, National Council of Women of the United States, Inc.

John M. Kernochan, Director, Legislative Drafting Research Fund, Columbia University

Miss Pauli Murray, Senior Fellow, Law School, Yale University

Mrs. E. Lee Ozbirn, President, National Federation of Business and Professional Women's Clubs, Inc.

Miss Katherine Peden, President, National Federation of Business and Professional Women's Clubs, Inc.

Mrs. Harriet F. Pilpel, Attorney, Greenbaum, Wolff, Ernst, New York
Frank E. Sander, Professor of Law, Law School of Harvard University
Miss Mary Eastwood, Technical Secretary

COMMITTEEE ON EDUCATION

Dr. Mary I. Bunting, Chairman and Commission Member
Miss Edna P. Amidon, Director, Home Economic Education Branch, U.S. Office of Education
Mrs. Algie E. Ballif, Former President, Utah School Board Association
Mrs. John D. Briscoe, Board of Directors, League of Women Voters of the United States
Mrs. Opal D. David, Former Director, Commission on the Education of Women, American Council on Education
Dr. Elizabeth M. Drews, Professor, College of Education, Michigan State University
Dr. Seymour M. Farber, Assistant Dean for Continuing Education in Health Sciences, University of California, San Francisco Medical Center
Mrs. Raymond Harvey, Dean, School of Nursing, Tuskegee Institute
Mrs. Agnes E. Meyer, Washington, DC.
Dr. Kenneth E. Oberholtzer, Superintendent, Denver Public Schools
Dr. Esther Raushenbush, Director, Center of Continuing Education, Sarah Lawrence College
Lawrence Rogin, Director of Education, AFL-CIO
Miss Helen B. Schleman, Dean of Women, Purdue University
Dr. Virginia L. Senders, Lecturer, Former Coordinator of Minnesota Plan, Lincoln, Massachusetts
Dr. Pauline Tompkins, General Director, American Association of University Women
Mrs. Antonia H. Chayes, Technical Secretary

COMMITTEE ON HOME AND COMMUNITY

Dr. Cynthia C. Wedel, Chairman and Commission Member
Mrs. Marguerite H. Coleman, Supervisor of Special Placement Services, New York State Division of Employment
Dr. Rosa L. Gragg, President, National Association of Colored Women's Clubs, Inc.

Mrs. Randolph Guggenheimer, President, National Committee for Day Care of Children, Inc.

Mrs. Viola Hymes, Commission Member

Mrs. Emerson Hynes, Arlington, Virginia

Maurice Lazarus, President, Wm. Filene's Son's Co., Boston

Mrs. Martha Reynolds, United Community Services, AFL-CIO, Grand Rapids, Michigan

Charles I. Schottland, Dean of Faculty, Brandeis University

Miss Ella V. Stonsby, Dean of College of Nursing, Rutgers University

Dr. Caroline F. Ware, Commissioner Member

Dr. Esther M. Westervelt, Instructor, Guidance and Personnel Administration, Teachers College, Columbia University

Miss Ella C. Ketchin and Mrs. Margaret M Morris, Technical Secretaries

COMMITTEE ON PRIVATE EMPLOYMENT

Dr. Richard A. Lester, Chairman and Commission Member

Jacob Clayman, Administrative Director, Industrial Union Department, AFL-CIO

Miss Caroline Davis, Director, Women's Department, United Automobile, Aerospace and Agricultural Implement Workers of America

Miss Muriel Ferris, Legislative Assistant to Honorable Philip A. Hart, U.S. Senate

Charles W. Gasque, Jr., Assistant Commissioner for Procurement Policy, General Services Administration

Miss Dorothy Height, Commission Member

Joseph D. Keenan, Secretary, International Brotherhood of Electrical Workers

Norman E. Nicholson, Commission Member

Frank Pace, Jr., General Dynamics Corp., New York

Mrs. Ogden Reid, Former President, Board Chairman, *New York Herald Tribune*

John A. Roosevelt, Bache and Co., New York

Samuel Silver, Industrial Relations Adviser, Office of Assistant Secretary of Defense for Manpower, U.S. Department of Defense

Sam A. Morgenstein, Technical Secretary

COMMITTEE ON PROTECTIVE LABOR LEGISLATION

Miss Margaret J. Mealey, Chairman and Commission Member

Mrs. Margaret F. Ackroyd, Chief, Division of Women and Children, Rhode Island State Department of Labor

Dr. Doris Boyle, Professor of Economics, Loyola College, Baltimore, Maryland

Mrs. Mary E. Callahan, Commission Member

Dr. Henry David, Commission Member

Mrs. Bessie Hillman, Vice President, Amalgamated Clothing Workers of America

Mrs. Paul McClellan Jones, Vice President, National Board, Young Women's Christian Association of the U.S.A.

Mrs. Mary Dublin Keyserling, Associate Director, Conference on Economic Progress

Carl A. McPeak, Special Representative on State Legislation, AFL-CIO

Clarence R. Thornbrough, Commissioner, Arkansas State Department of Labor

S. A. Weslowski, Assistant to the President, Brookshire Knitting Mills, Inc. Manchester, NH.

Miss Ella C. Ketchin, Technical Secretary

COMMITTEE ON SOCIAL INSURANCE AND TAXES

Honorable Maurine Neuberger, Chairman and Commission Member

Honorable Jessica M. Weiss, Associate Chairman and Commission Member

Dr. Eveline M. Burns, Professor of Social Work, New York School of Social Work, Columbia University

Mrs. Margaret B. Dolan, Chairman, Department of Public Health Nursing, University of North Carolina

Dean Fedele F. Fauri, School of Social Work, University of Michigan

Dr. Richard B. Goode, Brookings Institution

Miss Fannie Hardy, Executive Assistant, Arkansas State Insurance Commissioner

Miss Nina Miglionico, Attorney, Birmingham, Alabama

J. Wade Miller, Vice President, W.R. Grace & Co., Cambridge, Massachusetts

Dr. Raymond Munts, Assistant Director, Social Security Department, AFL-CIO

Mrs. Richard B. Persinger, Chairman, National Public Affairs Committee, Young Women's Christian Association of the U.S.A.

Dr. Merrill G. Murray, Technical Secretary

First Consultation: Private Employment Opportunities

Eileen Ahern
Continental Can Co.

Charles B. Bailey
Brotherhood of Railway and Steamship Clerks, Freight Handlers, Express and Station Employees

Tony M. Baldauf
U.S. Department of Agriculture
Ethel Beall
Boston University

Mrs. Robert Bishop
Wellesley College

Louise Q. Blodgett
National Consumers League

Irving Bluestone
United Automobile, Aerospace and Agricultural Implement Workers of America

Bernard Boutin
General Services Administration

H. T. Brooks
General Dynamic Corp.

E. B. Bruner
American Telephone and Telegraph Co.

William G. Bullard
Kelly Girls, Service, Inc.

David Burke
U.S. Department of Commerce

Mary E. Callahan
Commission Member
International Union of Electrical, Radio and Machine Workers

Dorothy Carlson
Office of Emergency Planning

R. P. Carlson
The Martin Co.

Jacob Clayman
Member, Commission's Committee on Private Employment, AFL-CIO

Marguerite H. Coleman
New York State Division of Employment

John M. Convery
National Association of Manufacturers

Wesley W. Cook
Textile Workers Union of America

Mrs. C. E. Cortner
Girl Scouts of America

J. Curtis Counts
Douglas Aircraft Co., Inc.

Lucinda Daniel
National Council of Negro Women, Inc.

Marie Daniels
Rhode Island Department of Employment Security

Henry David
Commission Member
New School for Social Research

Caroline Davis
Member, Commission's Committee on Private Employment United
    Automobile, Aerospace and Agricultural Implement Workers of America

Mary M. Dewey
Connecticut Department of Labor

Anne C. Draper
AFL-CIO

Lloyd Dunkle
General Services Administration

Alice Dunnigan
President's Committee on Equal Employment Opportunity

Charles E. Engelbrecht
Insurance Workers International Union

Leslie Essom
U.S. Department of Commerce

Gerald B. Fadden
Philco Corp.

Walter R. Farrell
Kaiser Industries Corp.

Muriel Ferris
Member, Commission's Committee on Private Employment
Office of Senator Philip A. Hart

M. Irene Frost
Trenton Trust Co.

G. Roy Fugal
General Electric Co.

Charles W. Gasque, Jr.
Member, Commission's Committee on Private Employment
General Services Administration

Sherman L. Gillespie
Hughes Aircraft Co.

Ann Gould
U.S. Department of Commerce

Rosa L. Gragg
National Association of Colored Women's Clubs, Inc.

Stephen Habbe
National Industrial Conference Board

Evelyn Harrison
U.S. Civil Service Commission

Doris Hartman
New Jersey Division of Employment Security

Miriam Healey
Girl Scouts of the United States of America

Dorothy Height
Commission Member
National Council of Negro Women, Inc.

S. P. Herbert
General Precision Equipment Corp.

Fred Z. Hetzel
U.S. Employment Service for the District of Columbia

Jack Hurt
U.S. Department of Labor

Mrs. Sophia Yarnall Jacobs
National Council of Women of the United States, Inc.

Cenoria D. Johnson
National Urban League

Elizabeth S. Johnson
Pennsylvania Department of Labor and Industry

Gloria Johnson
International Union of Electrical, Radio and Machine Workers

Lowell F. Johnson
American Home Products Corp.

Mrs. Paul McClellan Jones
Young Women's Christian Association of the U.S.A.

Dan A. Kimball
Aerojet-General Corp.

Paul A. King
Scholastic Magazines, Inc.

Elizabeth J. Kuck
International Harvester Co.

Maurice Lazarus
Wm. Filene's Sons Co.

Sarah Leichter
United Hatters, Cap and Millinery Workers International Union

Richard A. Lester
Vice Chairman of the Commission, Princeton University

P. B. Lewis
E.I. DuPont de Nemours & Co.

F. L. McClure
Radio Corp. of America

Beatrice McConnell
U.S. Department of Labor

Ralph E. McGruther
Bendix Corp.

Kenneth MacHarg
Sperry Gyroscope Co.

Eleanor McMillen
The Fashion Group, Inc.

Carl McPeak
AFL-CIO

Charles C. McPherson
Stanley Home Products, Inc.

John W. Macy, Jr.
Commission Member
U.S. Civil Service Commission

Stella Manor
U.S. Department of Labor

Olya Margolin
National Council of Jewish Women, Inc.

R. W. Markley, Jr.
Ford Motor Co.

James E. Marquis
U.S. Department of Health, Education, and Welfare

Betty Martin
Institute on Life Insurance

Mrs. G. G. Michelson
Macy's

Minnie C. Miles
National Federation of Business and Professional Women's Clubs, Inc.

Frieda Miller
Easton, PA.

Eileen Millen
Lobsenz & Co., Inc.

William Mirengoff
U.S. Department of Labor

Mrs. C.B. Morgan
General Federation of Women's Clubs

Alice A. Morrison
U.S. Department of Labor

Corma A. Mowrey
National Education Association

Raymond Munts
AFL-CIO

Frank Pace, Jr.
Member, Commission's Committee on Private Employment
General Dynamics Corp.

David H. Pritchard
U.S. Department of Labor

Ann Roe
Harvard University

Joseph S. Schieferly
Standard Oil Company of New Jersey

William F. Schnitzler
Commission Member
AFL-CIO

Virginia L. Sanders
Lecturer, Former Coordinator of Minnesota Plan

Laura L. Spencer
U.S. Department of Labor

Mrs. Ashton Thornhill
Office of Emergency Planning

Mary E. Tobin
New York State Department of Commerce

S. W. Towle
Northrop Corp.

R. A. Whitehorne
International Business Machines Corp.

Paul F. Wold
Campbell Soup Co.

Helen Wood
U.S. Department of Labor

Philip A. Yahner
U.S. Department of Labor

Second Consultation: New Patterns in Volunteer Work

Gretchen Abbott
Washington, DC.

Miriam Albert
B'nai B'rith Women

Edna P. Amidon
Member, Commission's Committee on Education
U.S. Department of Health, Education, and Welfare

Eunice P. Baker
National Association of Colored Women's Clubs

Betty Barton
U.S. Department of Health, Education, and Welfare

A. June Bricter
American Home Economics Association

Frances Cahn
President's Committee on Juvenile Delinquency and Youth Crime

Wilda Camery
American Nurses' Association, Inc.

Madeline Codding
U.S. Department of Labor

Sarah W. Coleman
National Association of Colored Women's Clubs, Inc.

Marjorie Collins
New York

Lenora Conner
Zonta International

George Dooley
AFL-CIO

Mrs. Robert Egan
National Council of Catholic Women

Etta Engles
American Association of University Women

Mrs. A. G. Gaston
National Council of Negro Women, Inc.

Marguerite Gilmore
U.S. Department of Labor

Mrs. Arthur J. Goldberg
Washington, DC.

Mrs. Maurice Goldberg
B'nai B'rith Women

Mrs. Edward Gudeman
Washington, DC.

Margaret W. Harlan
Bethesda, Maryland

Dorothy Height
Commission Member
National Council of Negro Women, Inc.

Benjamin Henley
Urban Service Corps
District of Columbia Public Schools

Charles A. Horsky
Advisor for National Capital Affairs
The White House

Hilda Hubbell
Volunteer Service Committee Health and Welfare Council of National
    Capital Area

Viola Hymes
Commission Member
National Council of Jewish Women, Inc.

Mrs. Emerson Hynes
Member, Commission's Committee o Home and Community
Arlington, VA

T. Margaret James
School Volunteer
New York

Mrs. Paul McClellan Jones
Young Women's Christian Association of the U.S.A.

Ollie L. Koger
American Legion Auxiliary

Ruth O. Lana
American Association of Retired Persons—Nation Retired Teachers
    Association

Margaret Lipchik
Urban Service Corps
District of Columbia Public Schools

Florence W. Low
American Home Economics Association

Edith E. Lowry
National Council of Agricultural Life and Labor

Ruth T. Lucas
Cleveland City Welfare Federation

Marie McGuire
Public Housing Administration

Dianne McKaig
U.S. Department of Labor

Lillian Majally
National Federation of Business and Professional Women's Clubs, Inc.

Mrs. Abbott L. Mills
American National Red Cross

Ernestine C. Milner
Altrusa International, Inc.

Margaret M. Morris
U.S. Department of Agriculture

Mrs. Stephen J. Nicholas
General Federation of Women's Clubs

Mrs. Alexander Parr
Association of the Junior League of America, Inc.

Dorothy Pearce
U.S. Department of Health, Education, and Welfare

Dorothy Pendergast
U.S. Department of Labor

Esther Peterson
Executive Vice Chairman of the Commission
Assistant Secretary of Labor

Barbara Phinney
Girl Scouts of the United States of America

Thomas J. Prather
U.S. Department of Health, Education, and Welfare

Betty Queen
District of Columbia Department of Public Welfare

O. Leonard Quinto
Veterans' Administration

Mildred Reel
Future Homemakers of America

Mabel Ross
U.S. Department of Health, Education, and Welfare

Virginia L. Sanders
Member, Commission's Committee on Education
Lecturer, Former Coordinator of Minnesota Plan

Edith H. Sherrard
American Association of University Women

Constance Smith
Radcliffe Institute of Independent Study

Mansfield Smith
Experiment in International Living

Hilda Torrop
National Council of Women of the United States, Inc.

Betty Ward
U.S. Department of Health, Education, and Welfare

Cynthia C. Wedel
Commission Member
National Council of the Churches of Chrsit in the U.S.A.

Esther Westervelt
Member, Commission's Committee on Home and Community
Teachers College, Columbia University

Mrs. Arthur Whittemore
League of Women Voters of the United States

Mrs. Joseph Willen
National Council of Jewish Women, Inc.

Mrs. J. Skelly Wright
National Association for Mental Health

Emily Ziegler
Soroptimist Federation of the Americas, Inc.

Third Consultation: Portrayals of Women in the Mass Media

Ethel J. Alpenfels
Professor of Anthropology, New York University

Curtiss Anderson
Editor, Ladies Home Journal

Margaret Culkin Banning
Writer

Betsy Talbot Blackwell
Editor, Mademoiselle

Al Capp
Cartoonist

Louis Cowan
Communications Research Center
Brandeis University

Polly Cowan
Station WMCA: Call for Action

Henry David
Commission Member
New School for Social research

Wallace W. Elton
Senior Vice President, J. Walter Thompson, Co.

Betty Friedan
Writer

Hartford Gunn
General Manager, WGBH

Lorraine Hansberry
Playwright

George Heineman
Public Affairs, National Broadcasting Co.

Stockton Helffrich
National Association of Broadcasters

Margaret Hickey
Commission Member
Public Affairs Editor, *Ladies Home Journal*

Lisa Howard
American Broadcasting Co.

Morton Hunt
Writer

Joseph Klapper
Research Department, Columbia Broadcasting System

Bennet Korn
President, Metropolitan Broadcasting

Richard A. Lester
Vice Chairman of the Commission
Professor of Economics, Princeton University

Gerri Major
Johnson Publications

Marya Mannes
Writer

Rosalind Massow
Women's Editor, *Parade*

Arthur Mayer
Writer

Herbert R. Mayes
President, McCall Corp.

Kathleen McLaughlin
New York Times
Joy Miller
Women's Editor, Associated Press

Jane Ostrowska
Cowles Publications

Esther Peterson
Executive Vice Chairman of the Commission
Assistant Secretary of Labor

Marion K. Sanders
Harper's Magazine

Perrin Stryker
New York

Margaret Twyman
Community Relations, Motion Picture Association of America

Helen Winston
Producer, Columbia Pictures

Fourth Consultation: Problems of Negro Women

Walter Davis
Assistant Director, Civil Rights Department, AFL-CIO

Alice A. Dunnigan
Executive Committee on Equal Employment Opportunity

Katherine P. Ellickson
Executive Secretary, President's Commission on the Status of Women

Hilda Fortune
New York Urban League

Maude Gadsen
Beauty Owners Association

Dorothy Height
Commission Member
President, National Council of Negro Women, Inc.

Grace Hewell
Program Coordination Officer, U.S. Department of Health, Education, and Welfare

Cenoria D. Johnson
National Urban League

Lewis Wade Jones
Fisk University

John R. Larkins
Consultant, North Carolina State Department of Public Welfare

Inabel Lindsay
Howard University

Gerri Major
Johnson Publications

Beatrice McConnell
Women's Bureau, U.S. Department of Labor

Esther Peterson
Executive Vice Chairman of the Commission
Assistant Secretary of Labor

Nathan Pitts
UNESCO Program Officer, U.S. Department of Health, Education, and Welfare

Paul Rilling
Executive Director, District of Columbia
Council on Human Relations

Dollie Robinson
Women's Bureau, U.S. Department of Labor

Laura L. Spencer
Women's Bureau, U.S. Department of Labor

Caroline F. Ware
Commission Member, Vienna, Virginia

Ruth Whaley
Secretary, New York City Board of Estimates

Ellen Winston
Commissioner of Welfare, U.S. Department of Health, Education, and
  Welfare

Deborah Partridge Wolfe
Chief of Education, Committee on Education and Labor, U.S. House of
  Representatives

BIBLIOGRAPHY

"2 Democratic Senators Block Vote on Aid Cuts." *The Record* (Bergen County, NJ), July 1, 1995, A8.

Adams, Bob. 1992. "Women Challenging Incumbents Faced Financial Disadvantages." *St. Louis Post-Dispatch*, November 12, A20.

Alcoff, Linda. 1998. "Cultural Feminism Versus Poststructuralism: The Identity Crisis in Feminist Theory." *SIGNS* 13 (3): 405–436.

Anderson, Benedict. 1983. *Imagined Communities: Reflections on the Origins and the Rise of Nationalism.* London: Verso.

Andrews, William. 1986. *To Tell a Free Story: The First Century of Afro-American Autobiography, 1769–1865.* Chicago: University of Illinois Press.

Asante, Molefi Kete. 1992. *Afrocentricity.* Trenton, NJ: African World Press.

Ayres, B. Drummond, Jr. 1998. "Political Briefing: Big Democratic Guns Salute Illinois Senator." *The New York Times*, May 17, A1.

Bane, Mary Jo, & Ellwood, David T. 1996. *Welfare Realities: From Rhetoric to Reform.* Cambridge: Harvard University Press.

Banet Weiser, Sarah. 1999. *The Most Beautiful Girl in the World: Beauty Pageants and National Identity.* Berkeley, CA: University of California Press.

Barkley-Brown, Elsa. 1991. "Polyrhythms and Improvisations: Lessons for Women's History." *History Workshop* 31 (Spring): 85–90.

Baym, Nina. 1981. "Melodramas of Beset Manhood: How Theories of American Fictions Exclude Women Authors." *American Quarterly* 33 (2): 123–139.

Belluck, Pam. 1998a. "Beleaguered Illinois Senator Accuses a Critic of Racism." *The New York Times*, September 9. https://www.nytimes.com/1998/09/09/us/beleaguered-illinois-senator-accuses-a-critic-of-racism.html.

© The Editor(s) (if applicable) and The Author(s) 2019
D. Harris, *Black Feminist Politics from Kennedy to Trump*,
https://doi.org/10.1007/978-3-319-95456-1

Belluck, Pam. 1998b. "Democrat Loses Ground in Illinois Senate Race." *The New York Times*, October 8. https://www.nytimes.com/1998/10/08/us/democrat-loses-ground-in-illinois-senate-race.html.

Belluck, Pam. 1998c. "Moseley Braun, Trailing, Pushes Hard." *The New York Times*, November 3. https://www.nytimes.com/1998/11/03/us/the-1998-campaign-illinois-moseley-braun-trailing-pushes-hard.html.

Berke, Richard L. 1994. "In '94 'Vote for Woman' Does Not Play So Well." *The New York Times*, October 3.

Berke, Richard L. 1997. "Racial Politics Lets Flawed Candidate Find Allies." *The New York Times*, July 4. https://www.nytimes.com/1997/07/04/us/racial-politics-lets-flawed-candidate-find-allies.html.

Berry, Mary Frances. 1982. "Twentieth-Century Black Women in Education." *The Journal of Negro Education* 51 (3): 288–300.

Best, Kathleen. 1992a. "Illinois Democrats' Unity Faces Stress Test: Braun's Candidacy, Leaders' Focus Could Cause Some Friction." *St. Louis Post-Dispatch*, July 19, 4B.

Best, Kathleen. 1992b. "Braun Will Be in National Spotlight." *St. Louis Post-Dispatch*, November 8, 1B.

Black Women's Oral History Project.

Bobo, Jacqueline. 1988. "Black Women's Responses to *The Color Purple*." *Jump Cut* 33: 43–51.

Braxton, JoAnne. 1989. *Black Women Writing Autobiography: A Tradition Within a Tradition*. Philadelphia: Temple University Press.

Brent, Linda. 1973. *Incidents in the Life of a Slave Girl*. Orlando: Harcourt Brace Jovanovich.

Brewer, Rose. 1994. "Theorizing Race, Class, Gender: The New Scholarship of Black Feminist Intellectuals and Black Women's Labor." In *Theorizing Black Feminism*, edited by Stanlie M. James & Abena P. A. Busia. New York: Routledge.

Briggs, Michael. 1993. "Senator Battles Confederate Emblem." *Chicago Sun-Times*, April 8, 12.

Brooks Higginbotham, Evelyn. 1989. "Beyond the Sound of Silence: Afro-American Women in History." *Gender and History* 1 (1): 50–67.

Brooks Higginbotham, Evelyn. 1992. "African-American Women's History and the Metalanguage of Race." *SIGNS* 17 (2): 251–274.

Caraway, Nancie. 1991. *Segregated Sisterhood: Racism and the Politics of American Feminism*. Knoxville, TN: University of Tennessee Press.

Carby, Hazel. 1987. *Reconstructing Womanhood: The Emergence of the Afro-American Woman Novelist*. New York: Oxford University Press.

Chisholm, Shirley. 1970. *Unbought and Unbossed*. Boston: Houghton Mifflin.

Chmaj, Betty. 1979. "A Decade of Déjà vu." *American Quarterly* 31 (3): 358–364.

Christian, Barbara. 1988. "The Race for Theory." *Feminist Studies* 14 (1): 67–80.

Clymer, Adam. 1993. "Daughter of Slavery Hushes Senate." *The New York Times,* July 23. https://www.nytimes.com/1993/07/23/us/daughter-of-slavery-hushes-senate.html.

Cohen Henderson, Ron. 1993. "Letter to the Editor: Democracy Stood Beside Carol Moseley Braun." *The New York Times,* July 29, A22.

Collins, Patricia Hill. 1990. *Black Feminist Thought: Knowledge, Consciousness, and the Politics of Empowerment.* New York: Routledge.

Cooper, Anna Julia. 1984. "Cover Pages." In *When and Where I Enter: The Impact of Black Women on Race and Sex in America,* edited by Paula J. Giddings. New York: Morrow.

Cooper, Anna Julia. 1988. *A Voice from the South.* New York: Oxford University Press.

Cooper, Brittney C. 2017. *Beyond Respectability: The Intellectual Thought of Race Women.* Champaign, IL: University of Illinois Press.

Crenshaw, Kimberle. 1996. "Whose Story Is It, Anyway? Feminist and Antiracist Appropriations of Anita Hill." In *Applications of Feminist Legal Theory to Women's Lives: Sex, Violence, Work, and Reproduction,* edited by D. Kelly Weisberg. Philadelphia: Temple University Press.

Cudjoe, Selwyn R. 1990. "Maya Angelou: The Autobiographical Statement Updated." In *Reading Black, Reading Feminist,* edited by Henry Louis Gates, Jr. New York: Meridian Books.

Davis, Allen F. 1990. "The Politics of American Studies." *American Quarterly* 42 (3): 353–374.

Dawson, Michael C. 1994. *Behind the Mule: Race and Class in African American Politics.* Princeton, NJ: Princeton University Press.

Dill, Bonnie Thornton. 1979. "The Dialectics of Black Womanhood." *SIGNS* 4 (3): 543–555.

Dillard, Angela D. 2001. *Guess Who's Coming to Dinner Now?: Multicultural Conservativism in America.* New York: New York University Press.

Dionne, E. J. 1991. *Why Americans Hate Politics.* New York: Simon & Schuster.

DuBois, W. E. B. 1969. *The Souls of Black Folk.* New York: New American Library.

duCille, Ann. 1994. "The Occult of True Black Womanhood: Critical Demeanor and Black Feminist Studies." *SIGNS* 19 (3): 591–629.

Edsall, Mary D., & Thomas B. Edsall. 1991. *Chain Reaction: The Impact of Race, Rights, and Taxes on American Politics.* New York: W. W. Norton.

Evans, Sara. 1980. *Personal Politics: The Roots of Women's Liberation in the Civil Rights Movement and the New Left.* New York: Vintage Books.

Fenno, Richard. 1978. *Home Style: House Members in Their Districts.* Boston: Little, Brown.

Ferguson, Russell. 1990. *Out There: Marginalization and Contemporary Cultures*. Cambridge: MIT Press.

Flowers, Sandra Hollin. 1981. "Colored Girls: Textbook for the Eighties." *Black American Literature Forum* 15 (2): 51–54.

Fox-Genovese, Elizabeth. 1990. "Between Individualism and Fragmentation: American Culture and the New Literary Studies of Race and Gender." *American Quarterly* 42: 7–35.

Franke, Katherine M. 1995. "The Central Mistake of Sex Discrimination Law: The Disaggregation of Sex from Gender." *University of Pennsylvania Law Review* 144 (1): 1–99.

Freeman, Jo. 1975. *The Politics of Women's Liberation: A Case Study of an Emerging Social Movement and Its Relation to the Policy Process*. New York: Longman.

Galen, Patrick. 1992. "Braun, Williamson End Campaign with Another Barrage of Insults." *St. Louis Post-Dispatch*, November 3, 9A.

Galen, Patrick, & Novak, Tim. 1992. "Braun Victory Stuns Many." *St. Louis Post-Dispatch*, March 19, 1A.

Giddings, Paula. 1988. *In Search of Sisterhood: Delta Sigma Theta and the Challenge of the Black Sorority Movement*. New York: William Morrow and Company.

Giddings, Paula. 1992. *When and Where I Enter*. New York: Harper Collins.

Gilliam, Dorothy. 1984. "A Sad Lesson." *The Washington Post*, July 26.

Goldsby, Jackie. 1993. "Queen for 307 Days: Looking B(l)ack at Vanessa Williams and the Sex Wars." In *Sisters, Sexperts, Queers: Beyond the Lesbian Nation*, edited by Arlene Stein. New York: Plume Books.

Harrison, Cynthia. 1980a. *On Account of Sex: The Politics of Women's Issues, 1945–1968*. Berkeley, CA: University of California Press.

Harrison, Cynthia. 1980b. "A 'New Frontier' for Women: The Public Policy of the Kennedy Administration." *The Journal of American History* 67 (3): 630–646.

Height, Dorothy. 2005. *Open Wide the Freedom Gates: A Memoir*. Washington, DC: Public Affairs.

Henderson, Mae G. 2014. *Speaking in Tongues: Dialogics, Dialectics, and the Black Women Writer's Literary Tradition*. New York: Oxford University Press.

Hill, James. 1998. "Why Black Voters Flocked to the Polls." *Chicago Tribune*, November 8, 97.

Hill Collins, Patricia. 1986. "Learning from the Outsider Within: The Sociological Significance of Black Feminist Thought." *Social Problems* 33 (6): 14–32.

Hine, Darlene Clark. 1991. "Lifting the Veil, Shattering the Silence: Black Women's History in Slavery and Freedom." In *The Great Migration in Historical Perspective*, edited by Joe Trotter. Bloomington, IN: Indiana University Press.

Hooks, Bell. 1990. *Yearning: Race, Gender, and Cultural Politics.* Cambridge: South End Press.

Hull, Gloria T., Scott, Patricia Bell, & Smith, Barbara. 1982. *All the Women Are White, All the Blacks Are Men, but Some of Us Are Brave: Black Women's Studies.* New York: Feminist Press.

Hulsether, Mark. 1993. "Evolving Approaches to U.S. Culture in the American Studies Movement: Consensus, Pluralism, and the Contestation for Cultural Hegemony." *Canadian Review of American Studies* 23 (2): 1–56.

Jarrett, Vernon. 1992a. "Braun Win Is Only Bright Spot in 'Burial' of Washington Allies." *Chicago Sun-Times*, March 19, 37.

Jarrett, Vernon. 1992b. "Pols Aim to Choose Black Leaders." *Chicago Sun Times*, October 25, 49.

Jeter, Jon. 1998. "Conservative Wins GOP Primary for Senate Seat." *The Washington Post*, March 18, A02.

Jones, Jacqueline. 1985. *Labor of Love, Labor of Sorrow.* New York: Vintage Books.

Joseph, Gloria I. 1981. *Common Differences: Conflicts in Black and White Feminist Perspectives.* New York: Anchor Books.

Kelly, R. Gordon. 1974. "Literature and the Historian." *American Quarterly* 26 (2): 141–159.

Kennedy, J. F. 1961a. "Executive Order 10980—Establishing the President's Commission on the Status of Women, December 14." Online by Gerhard Peters and John T. Woolley. *The American Presidency Project.* http://www.presidency.ucsb.edu/ws/?pid=58918.

Kennedy, J. F. 1961b. "Remarks, Allentown, PA." Retrieved on May 18, 2018 from http://www.presidency.ucsb.edu/ws/index.php?pid=74265.

Kerber, Linda. 1989. "Diversity and the Transformation of American Studies." *American Quarterly* 41 (3): 415–431.

King, Deborah. 1988. "Multiple Jeopardy, Multiple Consciousness: The Context of Black Feminist Ideology." *SIGNS* 14 (2): 42–72.

Kolbert, Elizabeth. 1991. "The Thomas Nomination: Sexual Harassment at Work Is Pervasive, Survey Suggests." *The New York Times.* https://www.nytimes.com/1991/10/11/us/the-thomas-nomination-sexual-harass-ment-at-work-is-pervasive-survey-suggests.html.

Lawson, Steven. 1990. "Freedom Then, Freedom Now: The Historiography of the Civil Rights Movement." *The American Historical Review* 96 (2): 456–471.

Lee, Spike with Raymond Wiley. 1992. *By Any Means Necessary: The Trials and Tribulations of the Making of Malcolm X…Including the Screenplay.* New York: Hyperion.

Leonard, Mary. 1998. "History-Making Senator's Star Falling in Illinois." *The Boston Globe*, October 17, A1.

Lester, Neal A. 1992. "Shange's Men: For Colored Girls Revisited, and Movement Beyond." *African American Review* 26 (2): 319–328.

Long, Ray, & Brown, Mark. 1992. "Dixon, Braun Barnstorm: Hofeld Collars Commuters." *Chicago Sun-Times*, March 17, 12.

Lorde, Audre. 1984. *Sister Outsider.* Freedom, CA: The Crossing Press Feminist Series.

Lublin, David. 1997. *The Paradox of Representation: Racial Gerrymandering and Minority Interests in Congress.* Princeton, NJ: Princeton University Press.

Lugones, Maria, & Spelman, Elizabeth. 1983. "Have We Got a Theory for You!: Feminist Theory, Cultural Imperialism, and the Demand for 'The Woman's Voice.'" *Women's Studies International Forum* 6 (6): 573–581.

Malveaux, Juliane. 1979. "The Sexual Politics of Black People: Angry Black Women, Angry Black Men." *The Black Scholar* 10 (8/9): 32–35.

Mansbridge, Jane, & Tate, Katherine. 1992. "Race Trumps Gender: The Thomas Nomination in the Black Community." *Political Science and Politics* 25 (3): 488–492.

Memmi, Albert. 1965. *The Colonizer and the Colonized.* Boston: Beacon Press.

Merrion, Paul. 1993. "Braun's Own Deficit Will Be Tough to Fix." *Crain's Chicago Business*, April 5, 1.

Miller, Anita, ed. 1994. *The Complete Transcripts of the Anita Hill-Clarence Thomas Hearings.* Chicago: Academy Chicago Publishers.

Mills, Kay. 1993. *This Little Light of Mine: The Life of Fannie Lou Hammer.* New York: Dutton.

Moncrief, Gary, Thompson, Joel, & Schumann, Robert. 1991. "Gender, Race, and the State Legislature: A Research Note on the Double Disadvantage Hypothesis." *The Social Science Journal* 28 (4): 481–487.

Morrison, Toni. 1992. *Playing in the Dark: Whiteness and the Literary Imagination.* Cambridge: Harvard University Press.

Moynihan, Daniel Patrick. 1965. *The Negro Family: The Case for National Action.* Washington, DC: Office of Policy Planning and Research United States Department of Labor.

National Council of Negro Women. (n.d.). "History." Retrieved on December 20, 2007 from http://www.ncnw.org/about/index.htm.

National Organization for Women. (n.d.). "Honoring Our Founders." http://www.now.org/history/founders.html.

National Organization for Women. (n.d.). "History: Highlights." https://now.org/about/history/highlights/.

National Review. 2015. "Defeat Loretta Lynch." April. https://www.nationalreview.com/2015/04/defeat-loretta-lynch/.

Neal, Steve. 1992. "Braun Doesn't Practice What She Is Preaching." *Chicago Sun-Times*, October 2, 35.

Neal, Terry. "Three Women in Senate Targeted by GOP." *The Record* (Bergen County, NJ), December 12, A27.

The New York Times. 1993. "Ms. Moseley-Braun's Majestic Moment." http://nytimes.com/1993/07/24/opinion-ms-moseley-braun-s-majestic-moment.html.

Norton, Mary Beth, ed. 1989. *Major Problems in American Women's History.* Lexington, MA: DC. Heath and Company.

Novak, Tim. 1992. "Political Backlash Anger Boosted Braun Coalition Building Credited in Victory." *St. Louis Post-Dispatch*, March 22, 1B.

Offen, Karen. "Defining Feminism: A Comparative Historical Approach." *SIGNS* 14 (1): 119–157.

Omolade, Barbara. 1994. *The Rising Song of African American Women.* New York: Routledge.

Peters, Erskine. 1978. "Some Tragic Propensities of Ourselves: The Occasion of Ntozake Shange's 'For Colored Girls Who Have Considered Suicide/When the Rainbow Is Enuf.'" *Journal of Ethnic Studies* 6 (1): 79–85.

Pitkin, Hanna. 1967. *The Concept of Representation.* Berkeley: University of California Press.

Prestage, J. 1977. "Black Women State Legislators: A Profile." In *A Portrait of Marginality: The Political Behavior of the American Woman*, edited by Marianne Githens and Jewel Prestage. New York: David McKay.

Ragsdale, Bruce, & Treese, Joel. 1990. "Black Americans in Congress, 1870–1989." Office of the Historians, U.S. House of Representatives. U.S. Government Printing Office.

Reagan, Ronald. 1976. "Campaign Speech. Slate Voice." Retrieved on May 20, 2018 from https://soundcloud.com/slate-articles/ronald-reagan-campaign-speech.

Reising, Russell. 1986. *The Unusable Past: Theory and the Study of American Literature.* New York: Melthuen.

Ritter, Jim. 1992. "State Democratic Leaders Set to Stand Behind Dixon." *Chicago Sun Times*, March 16, 16.

Robinson, Mike. 1998. "Conservative's Victory in Illinois Primary May Hurt GOP Chances for Senate Seat." *The Buffalo News*, March 18, 9A.

Ross, Andrew. 1992. "The Private Parts of Justice." In *Race-ing Justice, En'gendering Power: Essays on Anita Hill, Clarence Thomas, and the Construction of Social Reality*, edited by Toni Morrison. New York: Pantheon Books.

Royko, Mike. 1995. "Don't Consult a Senator on Hot Dogs: One of Them Does Not Even Know That Ketchup Is a Chicago No-No." *Pittsburgh Post-Gazette*, November 22, A15.

Ruess, Michelle. 1992. "New Congress Most Diverse Women, Minorities Moved Toward Coalition." *The Plain Dealer*, November 15, 10A.

Sall, John. 1992. "Williamson-Braun Debate Heats Up on Crime Issue." *Chicago Sun-Times*, October 23, A1.

Scott, Patricia Bell. 2016. *The Firebrand and the First Lady: Portrait of a Friendship: Pauli Murray, Eleanor Roosevelt, and the Struggle for Social Justice.* New York: Vintage.

Sheftall, Beverly Guy. 2005. "Daughters of Sorrow: Historical Overview of Black Women 1880–1920." In *Black Women in America,* edited by Darlene Clark Hine. New York: Oxford University Press.

Smith, Barbara. 1997. "The Truth That Never Hurts: Black Lesbians in Fiction in the 1980s." In *Feminisms: An Anthology of Literary Theory and Criticism,* edited by Robyn R. Warhol & Diane Price Herndl. Rutgers, NJ: Rutgers University Press.

Selman, Elizabeth. 1988. *Inessential Woman: Problems of Exclusion in Feminist Thought.* Boston: Beacon.

Simien, Evelyn. 2004. "The Intersection of Race and Gender: An Examination of Black Feminist Consciousness, Race Consciousness, and Policy Attitudes." *Social Science Quarterly* 85 (3): 793–810.

Springer, Kimberly. 1999. "Our Politics Was Black Women: Black Feminist Organizations, 1968–1980." PhD Dissertation Institute for Women's Studies, Emory University.

Standley, Ann. 1993. "The Role of Black Women in the Civil Rights Movement." In *Women in the Civil Rights Movement: Trailblazers and Torchbearers: 1941–1965,* edited by Vicki L. Crawford, Jacqueline Anne Rouse, & Barbara Woods. Bloomington, IN: Indiana University Press.

Staples, Robert. 1979. "Myth of Black Macho: A Response to Angry Black Feminists." *The Black Scholar* 10 (6/7): 24–33.

S'thembile West, C. 1994. "Afrocentricity: Moving Outside of the Comfort Zone." *The Journal of Physical Education, Dance, and Recreation* 65 (5): 28–30.

Sweet, Lynn. 1992a. "GOP Pushes Braun-Savage Tie." *Chicago Sun-Times,* September 24, 6.

Sweet, Lynn. 1992b. "Mathews' Curt Manner Made Many Enemies." *Chicago Sun-Times,* December 5, 46.

Sweet, Lynn. 1992c. "Braun Still Paying Matthews; Senator-Elect Admits Romantic Tie to Aide." *Chicago Sun-Times,* December 31, 6.

Sweet, Lynn. 1993a. "Moseley-Braun, Matthews Postpones Wedding." *Chicago Sun-Times,* June 30, 20.

Sweet, Lynn. 1993b. "Moseley-Braun Lends Support to Crime Bill." *Chicago Sun-Times,* August 13, 18.

Talbott, Basil. 1992. "Braun's Back with Strong Performance." *Chicago Sun-Times,* October 23, 4.

Thelwell, Michael. 1992. "False, Fleeting, Perjured Clarence: Yale's Brightest and Blackest Go to Washington." In *Race-ing Justice, En-gendering Power:*

Essays on Anita Hill, Clarence Thomas, and the Construction of Social Reality, edited by Toni Morrison. New York: Pantheon Books.

Thirteen (PBS) American Masters. "Lorraine Hansberry: Seeing Eyes/Feeling Heart." Original Air Date: January 19, 2018.

Tinker, Irene, ed. 1983. *Women in Washington: Advocates for Public Policy*. Beverly Hills, CA: Sage.

"Vacationing With a Dictator." 1996. "Editorial." *The Boston Globe*, September 3, A10.

Wallace, Michele. 1976. *Black Macho and the Myth of the Superwoman*. New York: Verso.

Wandersee, Winifred. 1988. *On the Move: American Women in the 1970s*. Boston: Twain Publishing.

Washington, Mary Helen. 1982. "Teaching Black-Eyed Susans: An Approach to the Study of Black Women Writers." In *All the Women Are White, All the Blacks Are Men, But Some of Us Are Brave*, edited by Gloria T. Hull, Patricia Bell Scott, and Barbara Smith. New York: The Feminist Press.

Wilkerson, Isabel. 1992. "Milestone for Black Woman in Gaining U.S. Senate Seat." *The New York Times*. November 4.

Williams, Patricia. "A Rare Case Study of Muleheadedness and Men: Or How to Try an Unruly Black Witch, with Excerpts from the Heretical Testimony of Four Women, Known to Be Hysterics, Speaking in Their Own Voices, as Translated for the Publication by Brothers Hatch, Simpson, DConcini, and Specter." In *Race-ing Justice, En-gendering Power: Essays on Anita Hill, Clarence Thomas, and the Construction of Social Reality*, edited by Toni Morrison. New York: Pantheon Books.

Wise, Gene. 1979. "Paradigm Dramas in American Studies: A Cultural and Institutional History of the Movement." *American Quarterly* 31 (3):293–337.

Yamahtta Taylor, Keeanga. 2017. *How We Get Free: Black Feminism and the Combahee River Collective*. Chicago: Haymarket Books.

Zucchino, David. 1997. *Myth of the Welfare Queen: A Pulitzer Prize-Winning Journalist's Portrait of Women on the Line*. New York: Scribner.

Zuckman, Jill. 1997. "For Moseley-Braun, a Fight for Redemption." *The Boston Globe*, August 21, A1.

INTERVIEWS

President's Commission on the Status of Women
Dr. Dorothy Height June 1995
Dr. Jeanne Noble June 1995
Dr. Deborah Wolfe August 1995

National Black Feminist Organization

Jane Galvin-Lewis March 1996
Deborah Singletary March 1996
Margaret Sloan October 1995

Combahee River Collective.

Anonymous Member August 1995
Cheryl Clarke August 1995
Gloria "Akasha" Hull October 1995
Margo Okazawa-Rey October 1995
Sharon Page—Ritchie October 1995

VIDEOTAPES

Combahee River Collective.
Barbara Smith interview conducted by Susan Goodlwillie 1994.
Demita Frazier interview conducted by Susan Goodwillie 1994.

MANUSCRIPT COLLECTIONS

East, Catherine. The Catherine East Papers, American Women, 1963, 1983, 2003. Schlesinger Library.
President's Commission on the Status of Women. John F. Kennedy Library, Boston, Massachusetts.
Murray, Pauli. The Pauli Murray Papers, Schlesinger Library.

PERSONAL PAPERS

The National Black Feminist Organization Minutes. Margaret Sloan-Hunter.
The Combahee River Collective Retreat Minutes. Gloria Akasha Hull.

GOVERNMENT DOCUMENTS

U.S. President's Commission on the Status of Women. American Women: Report of the President's Commission on the Status of Women. Washington, DC: GPO, 1963.
———. Four Consultations. Washington, DC: GPO, 1963.
Report on the Committee on Civil and Political Rights. Washington, DC: GPO, 1963.

Report on the Committee on Education. Washington, DC: GPO, 1963.

Report on the Committee on Federal Employment. Washington, DC: GPO, 1963.

Report on the Committee on Home and Community. Washington, DC: GPO, 1963.

Report on the Committee on Private Employment. Washington, DC: GPO, 1963.

Report on the Committee on Protective Labor and Legislation. Washington, DC: GPO, 1963.

Report on the Committee on Social Security and Taxes. Washington, DC: GPO, 1963.

Index

Printed in the USA
CPSIA information can be obtained
at www.ICGtesting.com
LVHW022007071123
763349LV00001B/106